Learning styles and peda...

A systematic and critical review

KU-627-241

Frank Coffield
Institute of Education
University of London

David Moseley
University of Newcastle

Elaine Hall
University of Newcastle

Kathryn Ecclestone
University of Exeter

**The Learning and Skills Research Centre
is supported by the Learning and Skills Council
and the Department for Education and Skills**

The views expressed in this publication are those
of the authors and do not necessarily reflect
the views of the Learning and Skills Research Centre
or the Learning and Skills Development Agency

Published by the
Learning and Skills Research Centre
www.LSRC.ac.uk

Feedback should be sent to:

Sally Faraday
Research Manager
Learning and Skills Development Agency
Regent Arcade House
19–25 Argyll Street
London W1F 7LS

Tel 020 7297 9098
Fax 020 7297 9190
sfaraday@LSDA.org.uk

Copyedited by Helen Lund
Designed by sans+baum
Printed by Cromwell Press Ltd
Trowbridge, Wiltshire

1543/06/04/500
ISBN 1 85338 918 8

Contents

Figures

Tables

The project team would like to extend thanks to the authors of the models reviewed in this report for their comments and reactions to our work which enabled us to improve the quality of the final version.

We also wish to acknowledge the steady and sensitive support of John Vorhaus of the Learning and Skills Development Agency (LSDA) and the administrative skills of Louise Wilson of the University of Newcastle upon Tyne. Eugene Sadler-Smith read an earlier version of this report and made some useful comments for which we are also grateful.

Foreword

The theory and practice of learning styles has generated great interest and controversy over the past 20 years and more. The Learning and Skills Research Centre would like to express its appreciation to the authors of two complementary reports, for the time and effort that went into their production and for providing a valuable resource for researchers and practitioners in the learning and skills sector.

These reports serve two key purposes: first, they contribute to what we know about models of learning styles and to our knowledge of what these offer to teachers and learners. Second, the reports identify an agenda for further research: to evaluate rigorously key models in a variety of learning environments in order to better understand their merits and deficiencies. We publish these reports in the spirit of stimulating debate and enabling knowledge of learning styles to be developed for the benefit of practice and policy.

The complementary report *Should we be using learning styles?* explores what research has to say to practice. Final sections are common to both reports: these draw out the implications for pedagogy and offer recommendations and conclusions for practitioners, policy-makers and the research community.

LSDA would also like to thank the steering committee for incisive commentary and support throughout the project.

Dr John Vorhaus
Research Manager
Learning and Skills Development Agency

Steering committee members:
Professor Charles Desforges
Professor Noel Entwistle
Professor Phil Hodkinson
Dr John Vorhaus

Introduction

How can we teach students if we do not know how they learn? How can we improve the performance of our employees if we do not know how we ourselves learn or how to enhance their learning? Are the learning difficulties of so many students/employees better understood as the teaching problems of tutors/workplace training managers? How can we pretend any longer that we are serious about creating a learning society if we have no satisfactory response to the questions: what model of learning do we operate with and how do we use it to improve our practice and that of our students/staff/organisation? These are just some of the issues raised by those researchers who for the last 40–50 years have been studying the learning styles of individuals.

There is a strong intuitive appeal in the idea that teachers and course designers should pay closer attention to students' learning styles – by diagnosing them, by encouraging students to reflect on them and by designing teaching and learning interventions around them. Further evidence for the idea that we have individual learning styles appears to be offered when teachers notice that students vary enormously in the speed and manner with which they pick up new information and ideas, and the confidence with which they process and use them. Another impetus to interest in post-16 learning styles is given by a government policy that aims to develop the necessary attitudes and skills for lifelong learning, particularly in relation to 'learning to learn'. These are widely assumed by policy-makers and practitioners to be well delineated, generic and transferable.

The logic of lifelong learning suggests that students will become more motivated to learn by knowing more about their own strengths and weaknesses as learners. In turn, if teachers can respond to individuals' strengths and weaknesses, then retention and achievement rates in formal programmes are likely to rise and 'learning to learn' skills may provide a foundation for lifelong learning. Perhaps a more instrumental impetus is provided by pressures on resources in many post-16 institutions. For example, if students become more independent in their learning as a result of knowing their strengths and weaknesses, then negative effects from lower levels of contact between lecturers and students will be counterbalanced if students develop more effective learning strategies which they can use outside formal contact time.

A complex research field

Yet beneath the apparently unproblematic appeal of learning styles lies a host of conceptual and empirical problems. To begin with, the learning styles field is not unified, but instead is divided into three linked areas of activity: theoretical, pedagogical and commercial.

The first area is a growing body of theoretical and empirical research on learning styles in the UK, the US and Western Europe that began in the early years of the 20th century and is still producing ideas and an ever-proliferating number of instruments. Our review has identified 71 models of learning styles and we have categorised 13 of these as major models, using criteria outlined below. The remaining 58 (listed in Appendix 1) are not critically analysed in this report. Many consist of rather minor adaptations of one of the leading models and therefore lack influence on the field as a whole; a large number represent the outcomes of doctoral theses. Some offer new ***constructs***[1] (or new labels for existing constructs) as the basis for a claim to have developed a new model. Others have been used only on very small or homogeneous populations, and yet others have had a brief vogue but have long fallen into obscurity. It is important to note that the field of learning styles research as a whole is characterised by a very large number of small-scale applications of particular models to small samples of students in specific contexts. This has proved especially problematic for our review of evidence of the impact of learning styles on teaching and learning, since there are very few robust studies which offer, for example, reliable and valid evidence and clear implications for practice based on empirical findings.

The second area is a vast body of research into teaching and learning which draws researchers from diverse specialisms, mainly from different branches of psychology, but also from sociology, business studies, management and education. Researchers working in the field of learning styles across or within these disciplines tend to interpret evidence and theories in their own terms. Evidence about learning is guided by contrasting and disputed theories from psychology, sociology, education and policy studies, and valued in different ways from different perspectives. Education is also influenced strongly by political ideologies and social values that create preferences as to which type of theory is given greatest weight. The problem is compounded by the way in which academic researchers develop their reputations by establishing individual territories and specialisms, which are then stoutly defended against those from a different perspective. This form of intellectual trench warfare, while common throughout academia, is not a particular feature of the learning styles literature, where the leading theorists and developers of instruments tend to ignore, rather than engage with, each other. The result is fragmentation, with little cumulative knowledge and cooperative research.

1
Bold italic text indicates the first usage in the text of a term in the glossary (Appendix 3).

The third area consists of a large commercial industry promoting particular inventories and instruments. Certain models have become extremely influential and popular: in the US, for example, the Dunn, Dunn and Price Learning Styles *Inventory* (LSI) is used in a large number of elementary schools, while in the UK, both Kolb's Learning Style Inventory (LSI) and Honey and Mumford's Learning Styles Questionnaire (LSQ) are widely known and used. The commercial gains for creators of successful learning styles instruments are so large that critical engagement with the theoretical and empirical bases of their claims tends to be unwelcome.

Many teachers use the most well-known instruments with explicit acknowledgement of the source and a clear idea of why they have chosen a particular model. However, it is also common, particularly on in-service training, management or professional development courses, for participants to analyse their learning styles using an unnamed questionnaire with no accompanying explanation or rationale. In many ways, the use of different inventories of learning styles has acquired an unexamined life of its own, where the notion of learning styles itself and the various means to measure it are accepted without question. Mainstream use has too often become separated from the research field. More problematically, it has also become isolated from deeper questions about whether a particular inventory has a sufficient theoretical basis to warrant either the research industry which has grown around it, or the pedagogical uses to which it is currently put.

A final aspect of complexity is that researchers produce their models and instruments for different purposes. Some aim to contribute to theory about learning styles and do not design their instrument for use in mainstream practice. By contrast, others develop an instrument to be used widely by practitioners in diverse contexts. This difference affects the type of claims made for the instrument and the type of research studies that evaluate it.

These three areas of research and activity and their potential and pitfalls, militate against the type of integrative review that we have carried out for the Learning and Skills Research Centre (LSRC). We have found the field to be much more extensive, opaque, contradictory and controversial than we thought at the start of the research process. Evaluating different models of learning styles and their implications for *pedagogy* requires an appreciation of this complexity and controversy. It also requires some understanding of ideas about learning and measurement that have preoccupied researchers in education, psychology and neuroscience for decades.

The extensive nature of the field surprised us: we underestimated the volume of research which has been carried out on all aspects of learning styles over the last 30 years, although most of it refers to higher education and professional learning rather than work in further education (FE) colleges. Three examples illustrate this point. First, in 2000, David Kolb and his wife Alice produced a bibliography of research conducted since 1971 on his experiential learning theory and Learning Style Inventory (LSI) : it contains 1004 entries. Second, the website for the Dunn and Dunn Learning Styles Questionnaire (LSQ) has a bibliography with 1140 entries. Lastly, it has been estimated that 2000 articles have been written about the Myers-Briggs Type Indicator (MBTI) between 1985 and 1995 (see our evaluations later in this report for more detail).

The enormous size of these literatures presents very particular problems for practitioners, policy-makers and researchers who are not specialists in this field. It is extremely unlikely that any of these groups will ever read the original papers and so they are dependent on reviews like this one, which have to discard the weakest papers, to summarise the large numbers of high-quality research papers, to simplify complex statistical arguments and to impose some order on a field which is marked by debate and constructive critique as well as by disunity, dissension and conceptual confusion. The principal tasks for the reviewers are to maintain academic rigour throughout the processes of selection, condensation, simplification and interpretation, while also writing in a style accessible to a broad audience. In these respects, the field of learning styles is similar to many other areas in the social sciences where both the measurement problems and the implications for practice are complex.

Competing ideas about learning

Conflicting assumptions about learning underpin mainstream ideas about learning and the best-known models of learning styles. For example, some theories discussed in this report derive from research into brain functioning, where claims are made that specific neural activity related to learning can be identified in different areas of the brain. Other influential ideas derive from established psychological theories, such as personality *traits*, intellectual abilities and fixed traits which are said to form learning styles. From this latter perspective, it is claimed that learning styles can be defined accurately and then measured reliably and validly through psychological tests in order to predict behaviour and achievement. Claims about learning styles from the perspective of fixed traits lead to labels and descriptors of styles as the basis for strong claims about the generalisability of learning styles. These can take on unexpected predictive or controversial characteristics. For example, the belief that styles are fixed has led to propositions that marriage partners should have compatible learning styles, that people from socially disadvantaged groups tend to have a particular style or, as Gregorc (1985) believes, that styles are God-given and that to work against one's personal style will lead to ill-health (see Section 3.1 for evaluation of his Style Delineator).

Even if we dismiss these extreme examples, the notion of styles tends to imply something fixed and stable over time. However, different theorists make different claims for the degree of stability within their model of styles. Some theories represent learning styles as 'flexibly stable', arguing that previous learning experiences and other environmental factors may create preferences, approaches or strategies rather than styles, or that styles may vary from context to context or even from task to task. Nevertheless, supporters of this view still argue that it is possible to create valid and reasonably reliable measures and for these to have diagnostic and predictive use for enhancing students' learning. By contrast, other theorists eschew all notions of individual traits and argue that it is more productive to look at the context-specific and situated nature of learning and the idea of learning biographies rather than styles or approaches.

Competing ideas about learning have led to a proliferation of terms and concepts, many of which are used interchangeably in learning styles research. For example, terms used in this introduction include 'learning styles', 'learning strategies' and 'approaches to learning'. In addition, we have referred to 'models', 'instruments' and 'inventories'. Our investigation has revealed other terms in constant use: '*cognitive* styles', '*conative* styles', and 'cognitive structures'; 'thinking styles', 'teaching styles', 'motivational styles', 'learning orientations' and 'learning conditions'. Sometimes these terms are used precisely, in order to maintain distinctions between theories; at other times, they are used very loosely and interchangeably. Some theorists offer clear definitions of their key concepts at the outset, but forget to maintain the limitations they have placed on their language in later papers. Rather than attempting to offer yet another set of definitions of each concept, this report aims to define these terms as clearly as possible within particular families of ideas about learning in order to show how they are used by different learning styles theorists.

Implications for defining and measuring learning styles

It is possible to explain the main dimensions that underpin different approaches to learning styles and this report does so in later sections. Nevertheless, the competing theories and techniques of measuring them, and the effectiveness of such measures are so varied and contested that simple choices about the most suitable are difficult to substantiate. Different ideas about learning styles create distinct approaches to identifying the specific attitudes and skills that characterise styles and different measures designed to generalise between learning contexts and types of learner.

Evaluating the claims for various models requires an understanding of the *psychometric* vocabulary that underpins particular constructs and measures of *reliability* and *validity*. For example, there are various dimensions to validity: including whether the various test items appear to capture what they set out to measure (*face validity*) and whether the range of behaviours can be seen to have an impact on task performance (*predictive validity*). In addition, a number of other types of validity are important, including *ecological validity*, *catalytic validity* and *construct validity*. In addition, there is the frequently overlooked issue of *effect size*.

The notion of reliability is also important because some of the most popular models extrapolate from evidence of reliability to strong assertions of generalisability, namely that learners can transfer their styles to other contexts or that measures will produce similar results with other types of student. We provide a summary of measurement concepts in a glossary in Appendix 3.

Finally, the technical vocabulary needed to understand and interpret the various claims about learning styles also requires an appreciation that for some researchers, a reliable and valid measure of learning styles has not yet been developed; and for some, that the perfect learning style instrument is a fantasy. From the latter perspective, observation and interviews may be more likely than instruments to capture some of the broad learning strategies that learners adopt. Those who reject the idea of measurable learning styles consider it more useful to focus on learners' previous experiences and motivation.

Implications for pedagogy

A number of options for pedagogy flow from the different perspectives outlined in this introduction. For example, supporters of fixed traits and abilities argue that a valid and reliable measure is a sound basis for diagnosing individuals' learning needs and then designing specific interventions to address them, both at the level of individual self-awareness and teacher activity. This, however, might lead to labelling and the implicit belief that traits cannot be altered. It may also promote a narrow view of 'matching' teaching and learning styles that could be limiting rather than liberating.

In order to counter such problems, some theorists promote the idea that learners should develop a repertoire of styles, so that an awareness of their own preferences and abilities should not bar them from working to acquire those styles which they do not yet possess. In particular, as students move from didactic forms of instruction to settings with a mixture of lectures, seminars and problem-based learning, it may become possible for them to use a range of approaches. This can lead to a plan for teachers to develop these styles through different teaching and learning activities, or it can lead to what might be seen as a type of 'pedagogic sheep dip', where teaching strategies aim explicitly to touch upon all styles at some point in a formal programme.

Other theorists promote the idea of learning styles instruments as a diagnostic assessment tool that encourages a more self-aware reflection about strengths and weaknesses. For supporters of this idea, the notion of learning styles offers a way for teachers and students to talk more productively about learning, using a more focused vocabulary to do so. Finally, those who reject the idea of learning styles might, nevertheless, see value in creating a more precise vocabulary with which to talk about learning, motivation and the idea of *metacognition* – where better self-awareness may lead to more organised and effective approaches to teaching and learning.

A large number of injunctions and claims for pedagogy emerge from the research literature and we provide a full account of these in Section 8, together with an indication of their strengths and weaknesses. However, although many theorists draw logical conclusions about practice from their models of learning styles, there is a dearth of well-conducted experimental studies of alternative approaches derived from particular models. Moreover, most of the empirical studies have been conducted on university students in departments of psychology or business studies; and some would criticise these as studies of captive and perhaps atypical subjects presented with contrived tasks.

Aims of the project

The Learning and Skills Development Agency (LSDA) commissioned a number of research projects in post-16 learning through a new Learning and Skills Research Centre (LSRC) supported by the Learning and Skills Council (LSC) and the Department for Education and Skills (DfES). The University of Newcastle upon Tyne carried out two projects: an evaluation of models of learning style inventories and their impact on post-16 pedagogy (this report and Coffield *et al.* 2004) and an evaluation (with the University of Sunderland) of different thinking skills frameworks (Moseley *et al.* 2003). Other projects in the LSRC's programme include an evaluation by the University of Strathclyde of the impact of thinking skills on pedagogy (Livingston, Soden and Kirkwood 2003), a report by the universities of Surrey and Sheffield on the extent and impact of mixed-age learning in further education (McNair and Parry 2003) and a mapping by the University of Leeds of the conceptual terrain in relation to informal learning (Colley, Hodkinson and Malcolm 2003).

The evaluation of learning styles inventories was originally a separate project from the evaluation of the impact of learning styles on post-16 pedagogy. However, the two projects were merged in order to maximise the synergy between the theoretical research on learning styles and its practical implications for pedagogy.

The aims of the joint project were to carry out an extensive review of research on post-16 learning styles, to evaluate the main models of learning styles, and to discuss the implications of learning styles for post-16 teaching and learning. These broad aims are addressed through the following research questions and objectives.

Research questions

We addressed four main questions.

1
What models of learning styles are influential and potentially influential?

2
What empirical evidence is there to support the claims made for these models?

3
What are the broad implications for pedagogy of these models?

4
What empirical evidence is there that models of learning styles have an impact on students' learning?

Research objectives

The objectives that arose from our questions enabled us to:

- identify the range of models that are:
  - available
  - influential or potentially influential in research and practice
- locate these models within identifiable 'families' of ideas about learning styles
- evaluate the theories, claims and applications of these models, with a particular focus on evaluating the authors' claims for reliability and validity
- evaluate the claims made for the pedagogical implications of the selected models of learning styles
- identify what gaps there are in current knowledge and what future research is needed in this area
- make recommendations and draw conclusions about the research field as a whole.

In Sections 3–7, we report the results of our in-depth reviews, based on these research questions and objectives, of individual models of learning styles. In Section 8, we evaluate the implications of the main learning styles models for pedagogy; Section 9 contains our conclusions and recommendations. The report ends with lists of all the studies included in our review (in the references Section) and all the learning styles instruments identified in the course of the review (Appendix 1). We also provide a list of the search terms used in the review (Appendix 2) and a glossary of terms used in the report (Appendix 3).

The second project is presented in Coffield *et al.* (2004), which places learning styles in the educational and political context of post-16 provision in the UK. The second report discusses the appeal of learning styles as well as offering an overview of ways in which political and institutional contexts in the learning and skills sector affect the ways that learning styles might be put into practice.

The team who carried out the research have combined expertise in cognitive psychology, education, professional development of post-16 practitioners, sociology and policy studies. This combination of perspectives and interests has proved useful in understanding the research into learning styles, in providing a strong internal critique which helped to improve the quality of the written reports, and in coming to a considered and balanced judgement on the future of learning styles for a range of different audiences.

The project team also sought advice from a local advisory group whose members read our draft reports from a mainly practitioner perspective. The group comprised:

Emeritus Professor Tony Edwards
Chair
Northumberland Lifelong Learning Partnership

Lesley Gillespie
Head of the Northern Workers' Education Association

Joan Harvey
Chartered Psychologist
University of Newcastle upon Tyne

Simon James
Learning and Skills Development Agency

Jan Portillo
Director of the School of Teaching and Learning
Gateshead College

Martin Slimmings
Head of Teacher Education
Hartlepool College of Further Education

Isabel Sutcliffe
Chief Executive
NCFE
(an awarding body for qualifications and certificates in further and adult education).

We also received advice from a steering group which was set up by the LSDA. Its members were:

Professor Charles Desforges
University of Exeter

Professor Noel Entwistle
University of Edinburgh

Professor Phil Hodkinson
University of Leeds

John Vorhaus
(Steering Group Chair)
Learning and Skills Development Agency.

In addition, an important part of our evaluation of each of the 13 models was to send the authors a copy of our report on their model and to ask for comment. Apart from Robert Sternberg who has not yet replied, we have taken account of the responses of the other 12 in our report. Responses varied in terms of length, engagement with issues and constructive criticism. We are also grateful to those who sent us additional materials.

The main focus of this review is the impact of learning styles *on post-16 learning*. But the issue of the role that learning styles should play in pedagogy is of growing interest to a much broader range of constituencies. We therefore list below some of the potential audiences for this report:

■ the DfES Standards Unit

■ the National Institute of Adult and Continuing Education (NIACE)

■ post-16 Office for Standards in Education (Ofsted) and the Adult Learning Inspectorate (ALI)

■ the new Centre for Excellence in Leadership (CEL)

■ curriculum and qualification designers at the Qualifications and Curriculum Authority (QCA) and in awarding bodies

■ research managers in the local Learning and Skills Councils (LSCs)

■ staff development managers in colleges

■ staff running initial teacher education and professional development programmes for teachers and managers across the learning and skills sector

■ academics working in post-16 research

■ the Assessment Reform Group

■ the University for Industry (UfI), the Sector Skills Councils (SSCs), the Sector Skills Development Agency (SSDA)

■ the Higher Education Funding Council for England (HEFCE), the Learning and Teaching Support Network (LTSN) and the Institute for Learning and Teaching in Higher Education (ILTHE)

■ the Association of Colleges (AoC), the Association of Learning Providers (ALP)

■ the National Research and Development Centre for Adult Literacy and Numeracy

■ the Adult Basic Skills Strategy Unit (ABSSU)

■ unions: including the National Association of Teachers in Further and Higher Education (NATFHE); the Association of Teachers and Lecturers (ATL); the National Association of Head teachers (NAHT); the National Union of Teachers (NUT); the Secondary Heads Association (SHA); the Headmasters Conference (HMC); the National Association of Schoolmasters Union of Women Teachers (NASUWT)

■ employers, including the Confederation of British Industry (CBI), the Institute of Directors, the Confederation of Small Businesses

■ the House of Commons Select Committee on Education.

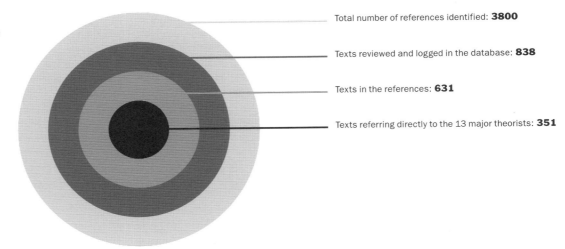

Figure 1
Selection of literature
for review

Total number of references identified: **3800**

Texts reviewed and logged in the database: **838**

Texts in the references: **631**

Texts referring directly to the 13 major theorists: **351**

Approaches to the literature review

Selecting the literature

The brief for this research was twofold: first, to assess the theoretical basis of claims made for learning styles and their importance for pedagogy; second, to map the field of learning styles and to gain an understanding of the variety of models produced, their history and pedagogical relevance. For this reason, it was not practical to follow the stringent, limiting criteria of, for example, the reviews produced by the Evidence for Policy and Practice Information and Co-ordinating Centre (EPPI-Centre), since the second aspect of the project would have been neglected. However, we adopted some of the processes of a systematic literature review, based on the research questions outlined above. These processes included: identifying literature and search terms; and locating the literature through materials already in our possession, by following up citations, interrogating databases, searching websites, and making use of personal contacts. We developed a reference management system using Endnote software and this enabled us to define and hone our criteria (see below), both for selecting literature initially and then for closer analysis.

The category 'texts in the references' covers both this report and Coffield *et al.* 2004.

In the literature review, we used a range of search terms (see Appendix 2) which revealed the titles of thousands of books, journal articles, theses, magazine articles, websites, conference papers and unpublished 'grey' literature. Our criteria have been relatively flexible compared with those used in EPPI-Centre reviews, since we have had to take into account the need to sample at least some of the large number of articles in professional magazines designed to promote particular models of learning styles, even though these articles tend not to engage critically with the instrument either theoretically or empirically.

We have accumulated a database containing over 800 references and papers relating to the field of post-16 learning styles. The majority are scholarly articles in journals or books, written by academics for other academics. We have developed the following structure to impose some order on a large, complex and confusing literature, and to evaluate all reports and papers critically. Our evaluation criteria, therefore, take account of both the scholarly quality of an article and its impact on a particular professional or academic audience.

The criteria for selecting particular theorists or research studies to examine in depth were as follows.

- The texts chosen were widely quoted and regarded as central to the field as a whole.

- The learning styles model was based on an explicit theory.

- The publications were representative of the literature and of the total range of models available (eg experiential, cognitive and brain dominance).

- The theory has proved to be productive – that is, leading to further research by others.

- The instrument/questionnaire/inventory has been widely used by practitioners – teachers, tutors or managers.

The criteria used to reject other contenders were as follows.

■ The approach was highly derivative and added little that was new; for example, the names of the individual learning styles, but little else, had been changed.

■ The research's primary focus was on an allied topic rather than on learning styles directly; for example, it was a study of creativity or of teaching styles.

■ The publication was a review of the literature rather than an original contribution to the field, such as Curry's (1983) highly influential 'onion' model which groups different approaches into three main types. Such reviews informed our general thinking, but were not selected for in-depth evaluation as models of learning style.

■ The study was a standard application of an instrument to a small sample of students, whose findings added nothing original or interesting to theory or practice.

■ The methodology of the study was flawed.

It was not necessary for all five inclusion criteria to be met for a particular theorist to be included, nor for all five rejection criteria to be fulfilled to be excluded. In fact, it did not prove very difficult or contentious to decide which models were most influential.

We outline the main models reviewed for the report, together with a rationale for their selection, in Section 2, which forms an introduction to Sections 3–7 below.

Section 2

Introduction to Sections 3–7

This report reviews the most influential and potentially influential models and instruments of learning styles and their accompanying literatures with a particular focus on validity, reliability and practical application. The main models chosen for detailed study are as follows:

- Allinson and Hayes' Cognitive Styles Index (CSI)
- Apter's Motivational Style Profile (MSP)
- Dunn and Dunn model and instruments of learning styles
- Entwistle's Approaches and Study Skills Inventory for Students (ASSIST)
- Gregorc's Mind Styles Model and Style Delineator (GSD)
- Herrmann's Brain Dominance Instrument (HBDI)
- Honey and Mumford's Learning Styles Questionnaire (LSQ)
- Jackson's Learning Styles Profiler (LSP)
- Kolb's Learning Style Inventory (LSI)
- Myers-Briggs Type Indicator (MBTI)
- Riding's Cognitive Styles Analysis (CSA)
- Sternberg's Thinking Styles Inventory (TSI)
- Vermunt's Inventory of Learning Styles (ILS).

The material we have reviewed varies enormously, both in the quality of the methodology and the scope of the investigation. In some instances, studies that might have been excluded in a typical academic review on the grounds of dubious methodology have been included here because of their impact on practitioners or on other researchers, but in all such cases, the methodological weaknesses are made explicit.

A continuum of learning styles

As we pointed out in Section 1, the research field of learning styles is both extensive and conceptually confusing. In a review of the psychometric qualities of different learning styles instruments, Curry (1987) categorised different research approaches. These were: 'instructional preferences', 'information processing style' and 'cognitive style'.

In Curry's model (1983; see Figure 2), the inner layer of cognitive personality style is both more stable (and therefore less easily modified or changed) and more significant in complex learning, while the outer layer of instructional preferences is easier to modify and influence, but less important in learning. Many researchers in the learning styles field have seen Curry's model as a useful, pragmatic way to present different models within these broad categories (eg Price and Richardson 2003). Yet, however attractive the onion metaphor may be, it is far from clear what lies at the centre. Conceptions of cognitive style relate to particular sets of theoretical assumptions, some of them psychoanalytic in origin. Ideas about stability are influenced more by theoretical concerns than by empirical evidence. There is not a single theory of cognitive or of learning style which is supported by evidence from longitudinal studies of stylistic similarities and differences in twins.

As an alternative model, Vermunt (1998; see Figure 3) aimed to integrate different learning processes, some of which are thought to be relatively stable (mental learning models and learning orientations) and some of which are contextually determined (choice between regulating and processing strategies).

Figure 2
Curry's 'onion' model of learning styles

Source: Curry (1983)

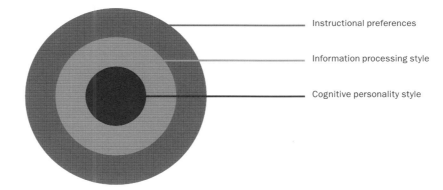

Instructional preferences

Information processing style

Cognitive personality style

Figure 3
Vermunt's model
of learning styles
(1998)

Source: Price and
Richardson (2003)

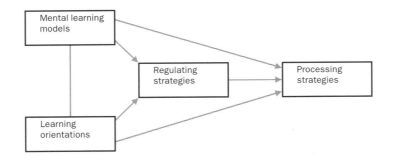

Figure 4
Families of learning
styles

Learning styles and preferences are largely **constitutionally based** including the four modalities: VAKT[2].	Learning styles reflect deep-seated features of the **cognitive structure**, including 'patterns of ability'.	Learning styles are one component of a relatively **stable personality type**.	Learning styles are **flexibly stable learning preferences**.	Move on from learning styles to **learning approaches, strategies, orientations** and **conceptions of learning**.
Dunn and Dunn[3] **Gregorc** Bartlett Betts Gordon Marks Paivio Richardson Sheehan Torrance	**Riding** Broverman Cooper Gardner *et al.* Guilford Holzman and Klein Hudson Hunt Kagan Kogan Messick Pettigrew Witkin	**Apter** **Jackson** **Myers-Briggs** Epstein and Meier Harrison-Branson Miller	**Allinson and Hayes** **Herrmann** **Honey and Mumford** **Kolb** Felder and Silverman Hermanussen, Wierstra, de Jong and Thijssen Kaufmann Kirton McCarthy	**Entwistle** **Sternberg** **Vermunt** Biggs Conti and Kolody Grasha-Riechmann Hill Marton and Säljö McKenney and Keen Pask Pintrich, Smith, Garcia and McCeachie Schmeck Weinstein, Zimmerman and Palmer Whetton and Cameron

2
VAKT = Visual, auditory, kinaesthetic, tactile

3
The theorists in bold type are those chosen for in-depth evaluation.

Some of the models we have reviewed, such as the Dunn and Dunn learning styles model, combine qualities which the authors believe to be constitutionally fixed with characteristics that are open to relatively easy environmental modification. Others, such as those by Vermunt (1998) and Entwistle (1998), combine relatively stable cognitive styles with strategies and processes that can be modified by teachers, the design of the curriculum, assessment and the ethos of the course and institution. The reason for choosing to present the models we reviewed in a continuum is because we are not aiming to create a coherent model of learning that sets out to reflect the complexity of the field. Instead, the continuum is a simple way of organising the different models according to some overarching ideas behind them. It therefore aims to capture the extent to which the authors of the model claim that styles are constitutionally based and relatively fixed, or believe that they are more flexible and open to change (see Figure 4). We have assigned particular models of learning styles to what we call 'families'. This enables us to impose some order on a field of 71 apparently separate approaches. However, like any theoretical framework, it is not perfect and some models are difficult to place because the distinction between constitutionally-based preferences or styles and those that are amenable to change is not always clear-cut. We list all 71 in the database we have created for this review (see Appendix 1).

The continuum was constructed by drawing on the classification of learning styles by Curry (1991). We also drew on advice for this project from Entwistle (2002), and analyses and overviews by key figures in the learning styles field (Claxton and Ralston 1978; De Bello 1990; Riding and Cheema 1991; Bokoros, Goldstein and Sweeney 1992; Chevrier *et al.* 2000; Sternberg and Grigorenko 2001). Although the groupings of the families are necessarily arbitrary, they attempt to reflect the views of the main theorists of learning styles, as well as our own perspective. Our continuum aims to map the learning styles field by using one kind of thematic coherence in a complex, diverse and controversial intellectual territory. Its principal aim is therefore classificatory.

We rejected or synthesised existing overviews for three reasons: some were out of date and excluded recent influential models; others were constructed in order to justify the creation of a new model of learning styles and in so doing, strained the categorisations to fit the theory; and the remainder referred to models only in use in certain sectors of education and training or in certain countries.

Since the continuum is intended to be reasonably comprehensive, it includes in the various 'families' more than 50 of the 71 learning style models we came across during this project. However, the scope of this project did not allow us to examine in depth all of these and there is therefore some risk of miscategorisation. The models that are analysed in depth are represented in Figure 4 in bold type.

Our continuum is based on the extent to which the developers of learning styles models and instruments appear to believe that learning styles are fixed. The field as a whole draws on a variety of disciplines, although cognitive psychology is dominant. In addition, influential figures such as Jean Piaget, Carl Jung and John Dewey leave traces in the work of different groups of learning styles theorists who, nevertheless, claim distinctive differences for their theoretical positions.

At the left-hand end of the continuum, we have placed those theorists with strong beliefs about the influence of genetics on fixed, inherited traits and about the interaction of personality and cognition. While some models, like Dunn and Dunn's, do acknowledge external factors, particularly immediate environment, the preferences identified in the model are rooted in ideas that styles should be worked with rather than changed. Moving along the continuum, learning styles models are based on the idea of dynamic interplay between self and experience. At the right-hand end of the continuum, theorists pay greater attention to personal factors such as motivation, and environmental factors like cooperative or individual learning; and also the effects of curriculum design, institutional and course culture and teaching and assessment tasks on how students choose or avoid particular learning strategies.

The kinds of instrument developed, the ways in which they are evaluated and the pedagogical implications for students and teachers all flow from these underlying beliefs about traits. Translating specific ideas about learning styles into teaching and learning strategies is critically dependent on the extent to which these learning styles have been reliably and validly measured, rigorously tested in authentic situations, given accurate labels and integrated into everyday practices of information gathering, understanding, and reflective thinking.

We devised this classificatory system to impose some order on a particularly confusing and endlessly expanding field, but as a descriptive device, it has certain limitations. For example, it may overemphasise the differences between the families and cannot reflect the complexity of the influences on all 13 models. Some authors claim to follow certain theoretical traditions and would appear, from their own description, to belong in one family, while the application (or indeed, the marketing) of their learning styles model might locate them elsewhere. For example, Rita Dunn (Dunn and Griggs 1998) believes that style is (in the main) biologically imposed, with the implication that styles are relatively fixed and that teaching methods should be altered to accommodate them. However, in a UK website created by Hankinson (Hankinson 2003), it is claimed that significant gains in student performance can be achieved 'By just understanding the concept of student learning styles and having a personal learning style profile constructed'. Where such complexity exists, we have taken decisions as a team in order to place theorists along the continuum.

Families of learning styles

For the purposes of the continuum, we identify five families and these form the basis for our detailed analyses of different models:

- constitutionally-based learning styles and preferences
- cognitive structure
- stable personality type
- 'flexibly stable' learning preferences
- learning approaches and strategies.

Within each family, we review the broad themes and beliefs about learning, and the key concepts and definitions which link the leading influential thinkers in the group. We also evaluate in detail the 13 most influential and potentially influential models, looking both at studies where researchers have evaluated the underlying theory of a model in order to refine it, and at empirical studies of reliability, validity and pedagogical impact. To ensure comparability, each of these analyses, where appropriate, uses the following headings:

- origins and influence
- definition, description and scope of the learning style instrument
- measurement by authors
- description of instrument
- reliability and validity
- external evaluation
- reliability and validity
- general
- implications for pedagogy
- empirical evidence for pedagogical impact.

Section 3

Genetic and other constitutionally based factors

Introduction

Widespread beliefs that people are born with various element-based temperaments, astrologically determined characteristics, or personal qualities associated with right- or left-handedness have for centuries been common in many cultures. Not dissimilar beliefs are held by those theorists of cognitive and/or learning style who claim or assume that styles are fixed, or at least are very difficult to change. To defend these beliefs, theorists refer to genetically influenced personality traits, or to the dominance of particular sensory or perceptual channels, or to the dominance of certain functions linked with the left or right halves of the brain. For example, Rita Dunn argues that learning style is a 'biologically and developmentally imposed set of characteristics that make the same teaching method wonderful for some and terrible for others' (Dunn and Griggs 1998, 3). The emphasis she places on 'matching' as an instructional technique derives from her belief that the possibility of changing each individual's ability is limited. According to Rita Dunn, 'three-fifths of style is biologically imposed' (1990b, 15). She differentiates between environmental and physical elements as more fixed, and the emotional and 'sociological' factors as more open to change (Dunn 2001a, 16).

Genetics

All arguments for the genetic determination of learning styles are necessarily based on analogy, since no studies of learning styles in identical and non-identical twins have been carried out, and there are no DNA studies in which learning style genes have been identified. This contrasts with the strong evidence for genetic influences on aspects of cognitive ability and personality.

It is generally accepted that genetic influences on personality traits are somewhat weaker than on cognitive abilities (Loehlin 1992), although this is less clear when the effects of shared environment are taken into account (Pederson and Lichtenstein 1997). Pederson, Plomin and McClearn (1994) found substantial and broadly similar genetic influences on verbal abilities, spatial abilities and perceptual speed, concluding that genetic factors influence the development of specific cognitive abilities as well as, and independently of, general cognitive ability (g). However, twin-study researchers have always looked at ability factors separately, rather than in combination, in terms of relative strength and weakness. They have not, for example, addressed the possible genetic basis of visual-verbal differences in ability or visual-auditory differences in imagery which some theorists see as the constitutional basis of cognitive styles.

According to Loehlin (1992), the proportion of non-inherited variation in the personality traits of agreeableness, conscientiousness, **extraversion**, **neuroticism** and openness to experience is estimated to range from 54% for 'openness' to 72% for 'conscientiousness'. Extraversion lies somewhere near the middle of this range, but the estimate for the trait of impulsivity is high, at 79%. To contrast with this, we have the finding of Rushton et al. (1986) that positive social behaviour in adults is subject to strong genetic influences, with only 30% of the variation in empathy being unaccounted for. This finding appears to contradict Rita Dunn's belief that emotional and social aspects of behaviour are more open to change than many others.

The implications of the above findings are as follows.

- Learning environments have a considerable influence on the development of cognitive skills and abilities.

- Statements about the biological basis of learning styles have no direct empirical support.

- There are no cognitive characteristics or personal qualities which are so strongly determined by the genes that they could explain the supposedly fixed nature of any cognitive styles dependent on them.

- As impulsivity is highly modifiable, it is unwise to use it as a general stylistic label.

- 'People-oriented' learning style and motivational style preferences may be relatively hard to modify.

Modality-specific processing

There is substantial evidence for the existence of modality-specific strengths and weaknesses (for example in visual, auditory or kinaesthetic processing) in people with various types of learning difficulty (Rourke et al. 2002). However, it has not been established that matching instruction to individual sensory or perceptual strengths and weaknesses is more effective than designing instruction to include, for all learners, content-appropriate forms of presentation and response, which may or may not be multi-sensory. Indeed, Constantinidou and Baker (2002) found that pictorial presentation was advantageous for all adults tested in a simple item-recall task, irrespective of a high or low learning-style preference for imagery, and was especially advantageous for those with a strong preference for verbal processing.

The popular appeal of the notion that since many people find it hard to concentrate on a spoken presentation for more than a few minutes, the presenters should use other forms of input to convey complex concepts does not mean that it is possible to use bodily movements and the sense of touch to convey the same material. Certainly there is value in combining text and graphics and in using video clips in many kinds of teaching and learning, but decisions about the forms in which meaning is represented are probably best made with all learners and the nature of the subject in mind, rather than trying to devise methods to suit vaguely expressed individual preferences. The modality-preference component of the Dunn and Dunn model (among others) begs many questions, not least whether the important part of underlining or taking notes is that movement of the fingers is involved; or whether the important part of dramatising historical events lies in the gross motor coordination required when standing rather than sitting. Similarly, reading is not just a visual process, especially when the imagination is engaged in exploring and expanding new meanings.

More research attention has been given to possible fixed differences between verbal and visual processing than to the intelligent use of both kinds of processing. This very often involves flexible and fluent switching between thoughts expressed in language and those expressed in various forms of imagery, while searching for meaning or for a solution or decision. Similarly, little attention has been given to finding ways of developing such fluency and flexibility in specific contexts. Nevertheless, there is a substantial body of research which points to the instructional value of using multiple representations and specific devices such as graphic organisers and 'manipulatives' (things that can be handled). For example, Marzano (1998) found mean effect sizes of 1.24 for the graphic representation of knowledge (based on 43 studies) and 0.89 for the use of manipulatives (based on 236 studies). If such impressive learning gains are obtainable from the general (ie not personally tailored) use of such methods, it is unlikely that basing individualised instruction on modality-specific learning styles will add further value.

Cerebral hemispheres

It has been known for a very long time that one cerebral hemisphere (usually, but not always, the left) is more specialised than the other for speech and language and that various non-verbal functions (including face recognition) are impaired when the opposite hemisphere is damaged. Many attempts have been made to establish the multifaceted nature of hemispheric differences, but we still know little about how the two halves of the brain function differently, yet work together. New imaging and recording techniques produce prettier pictures than the **electroencephalographic (EEG)** recordings of 50 years ago, but understanding has advanced more slowly. To a detached observer, a great deal of neuroscience resembles trying to understand a computer by mapping the location of its components. However, there is an emerging consensus that both hemispheres are usually involved even in simple activities, not to mention complex behaviour like communication.

Theories of cognitive style which make reference to 'hemisphericity' usually do so at a very general level and fail to ask fundamental questions about the possible origins and functions of stylistic differences. Although some authors refer to Geschwind and Galaburda's (1987) testosterone-exposure hypothesis or to Springer and Deutsch's (1989) interpretation of **split-brain research**, we have not been able to find any developmental or longitudinal studies of cognitive or learning styles with a biological or neuropsychological focus, nor a single study of the **heritability** of 'hemisphere-based' cognitive styles.

Yet a number of interesting findings and theories have been published in recent years which may influence our conceptions of how cognitive style is linked to brain function. For example, Gevins and Smith (2000) report that different areas and sides of the brain become active during a specific task, depending on ability level and on individual differences in relative verbal and non-verbal intelligence. Burnand (2002) goes much further, summarising the evidence for his far-reaching 'problem theory', which links infant strategies to hemispheric specialisation in adults. Burnand cites Wittling (1996) for neurophysiological evidence of pathways that mainly serve different hemispheres. According to Burnand, the left hemisphere is most concerned with producing effects which may lead to rewards, enhancing a sense of freedom and self-efficacy. The neural circuitry mediating this is the dopamine-driven Behaviour Activation System (BAS) (Gray 1973). The right hemisphere is most concerned with responding to novel stimuli by reducing uncertainty about the environment and thereby inducing a feeling of security. In this case, the neurotransmitters are serotonin and non-adrenalin and the system is Gray's Behavioural Inhibition System (BIS). These two systems (BAS and BIS) feature in Jackson's model of learning styles (2002), underlying the *initiator* and *reasoner* styles respectively.

However plausible Burnand's theory may seem, there is a tension, if not an incompatibility, between his view of right hemisphere function and the well-known ideas of Springer and Deutsch (1989) – namely that the left hemisphere is responsible for verbal, linear, **analytic** thinking, while the right hemisphere is more visuospatial, **holistic** and emotive. It is difficult to reconcile Burnand's idea that the right hemisphere specialises in assessing the reliability of people and events and turning attention away from facts that lower the hope of certainty, with the kind of visually imaginative, exploratory thinking that has come to be associated with 'right brain' processing. There is a similar tension between Burnand's theory and Herrmann's conception of brain dominance (see the review of his 'whole brain' model in Section 6.3).

New theories are constantly emerging in neurobiology, whether it be for spatial working memory or extraversion, and it is certainly premature to accept any one of them as providing powerful support for a particular model of cognitive style. Not only is the human brain enormously complex, it is also highly adaptable. Neurobiological theories tend not to address adaptability and have yet to accommodate the switching and unpredictability highlighted in Apter's reversal theory (Apter 2001; see also Section 5.2). It is not, for example, difficult to imagine reversal processes between behavioural activation and behavioural inhibition, but we are at a loss as to how to explain them.

We can summarise this sub-section as follows.

■ We have no satisfactory explanation for individual differences in the personal characteristics associated with right- and left-brain functioning.

■ There does not seem to be any neuroscientific evidence about the stability of hemisphere-based individual differences.

■ A number of theories emphasise functional differences between left and right hemispheres, but few seek to explain the interaction and integration of those functions.

■ Theorists sometimes provide conflicting accounts of brain-based differences.

Comments on specific models, both inside and outside this 'family'

Gregorc believes in fixed learning styles, but makes no appeal to behavioural genetics, neuroscience or biochemistry to support his idiosyncratically worded claim that 'like individual DNA and fingerprints, one's mind quality formula and point arrangements remain throughout life.' He argues that the brain simply 'serves as a vessel for concentrating much of the mind substances' and 'permits the software of our spiritual forces to work through it and become operative in the world' (Gregorc 2002). Setting aside this **metaphysical** speculation, his distinction between *sequential* and *random* ordering abilities is close to popular psychology conceptions of left- and right-'brainedness', as well as to the neuropsychological concepts of simultaneous and successive processing put forward by Luria (1966).

Torrance *et al.* (1977) produced an inventory in which each item was supposed to distinguish between left, right and integrated hemisphere functions. They assumed that left hemisphere processing is sequential and logical, while right hemisphere processing is simultaneous and creative. Fitzgerald and Hattie (1983) severely criticised this inventory for its weak theoretical base, anomalous and faulty items, low reliabilities and lack of **concurrent validity**. They found no evidence to support the supposed location of creativity in the right hemisphere, nor the hypothesised relationship between the inventory ratings and a measure of laterality based on hand, eye and foot preference. It is worth noting at this point that Zenhausern's (1979) questionnaire measure of **cerebral dominance** (which is recommended by Rita Dunn) was supposedly 'validated' against Torrance's seriously flawed inventory.

One of the components in the Dunn and Dunn model of learning styles which probably has some biological basis is time-of-day preference. Indeed, recent research points to a genetic influence, or 'clock gene', which is linked to peak alert time (Archer *et al.* 2003). However, the idea that 'night owls' may be just as efficient at learning new and difficult material as 'early birds' seems rather simplistic. Not only are there reportedly 10 clock genes interacting to exert an influence, but according to Biggers (1980), morning-alert students generally tend to outperform their peers. We will not speculate here about the possible genetic and environmental influences which keep some people up late when there is no imperative for them to get up in the morning, but we do not see why organisations should feel obliged to adapt to their preferences.

A number of theorists who provide relatively flexible accounts of learning styles nevertheless refer to genetic and constitutional factors. For example, Kolb (1999) claims that *concrete experience* and *abstract conceptualisation* reflect right- and left-brain thinking respectively. Entwistle (1998) says the same about (holist) *comprehension* learning and (**serialist**) *operation* learning, as do Allinson and Hayes (1996) about their *intuition-analysis* dimension. On the other hand, Riding (1998) thinks of his **global**-*analytic* dimension (which is, according to his definition, very close to *intuition-analysis*) as being completely unrelated to hemisphere preference (unlike his *visual-verbal* dimension). This illustrates the confusion that can result from linking style labels with 'brainedness' in the absence of empirical evidence. The absence of hard evidence does not, however, prevent McCarthy from making 'a commonsense decision to alternate right- and left-mode techniques' (1990, 33) in each of the four quadrants of her learning cycle (see Section 8 and Figure 13; also Coffield *et al.* 2004, Section 4 for more details).

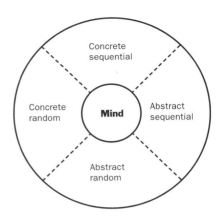

Figure 5
Gregorc's four-channel learning-style model

Although we have placed Herrmann's 'whole brain' model in the 'flexibly stable' family of learning styles, we mention it briefly here because it was first developed as a model of brain dominance. It is important to note that not all theorists who claim a biochemical or other constitutional basis for their models of cognitive or learning style take the view that styles are fixed for life. Two notable examples are Herrmann (1989) and Jackson (2002), both of whom stress the importance of modifying and strengthening styles so as not to rely on only one or two approaches. As indicated earlier in this section, belief in the importance of genetic and other constitutional influences on learning and behaviour does not mean that social, educational and other environmental influences count for nothing. Even for the Dunns, about 40% of the factors influencing learning styles are not biological. The contrast between Rita Dunn and Ned Herrmann is in the stance they take towards personal and social growth.

3.1
Gregorc's Mind Styles Model and Style Delineator

Introduction

Anthony Gregorc is a researcher, lecturer, consultant, author and president of Gregorc Associates Inc. In his early career, he was a teacher of mathematics and biology, an educational administrator and associate professor at two universities. He developed a metaphysical system of thought called *Organon* and after interviewing more than 400 people, an instrument for tapping the unconscious which he called the Transaction Ability Inventory. This instrument, which he marketed as the Gregorc Style Delineator (GSD), was designed for use by adults. On his website, Gregorc (2002) gives technical, ethical and philosophical reasons why he has not produced an instrument for use by children or students. Gregorc Associates provides services in self-development, moral leadership, relationships and team development, and 'core-level school reform'. Its clients include US government agencies, school systems, universities and several major companies.

Origins and description

Although Gregorc aligns himself in important respects with Jung's thinking, he does not attribute his dimensions to others, only acknowledging the influence of such tools for exploring meaning as word association and the semantic differential technique. His two dimensions (as defined by Gregorc 1982b, 5) are '***perception***' ('the means by which you grasp information') and 'ordering' ('the ways in which you authoritatively arrange, systematize, reference and dispose of information'). 'Perception' may be 'concrete' or 'abstract' and 'ordering' may be 'sequential' or 'random'. These dimensions bear a strong resemblance to the Piagetian concepts of '***accommodation***' and '***assimilation***', which Kolb also adopted and called 'prehension' and 'transformation'. The distinction between 'concrete' and 'abstract' has an ancestry virtually as long as recorded thought and features strongly in the writings of Piaget and Bruner. There is also a strong family resemblance between Gregorc's 'sequential processing' and Guilford's (1967) '***convergent thinking***', and between Gregorc's 'random processing' and Guilford's '***divergent thinking***'.

Gregorc's Style Delineator was first published with its present title in 1982, although the model underlying it was conceived earlier. In 1979, Gregorc defined learning style as consisting of 'distinctive behaviors which serve as indicators of how a person learns from and adapts to his environment' (1979, 234). His Mind Styles™ Model is a metaphysical one in which minds interact with their environments through 'channels', the four most important of which are supposedly measured by the Gregorc Style Delineator™ (GSD). These four channels are said to mediate ways of receiving and expressing information and have the following descriptors: concrete sequential (CS), abstract sequential (AS), abstract random (AR), and concrete random (CR). This conception is illustrated in Figure 5, using channels as well as two axes to represent concrete versus abstract perception and sequential versus random ordering abilities.

Gregorc's four styles can be summarised as follows (using descriptors provided by Gregorc 1982a).

- The **concrete sequential** (CS) learner is ordered, perfection-oriented, practical and thorough.

- The **abstract sequential** (AS) learner is logical, analytical, rational and evaluative.

- The **abstract random** (AR) learner is sensitive, colourful, emotional and spontaneous.

- The **concrete random learner** (CR) is intuitive, independent, impulsive and original.

Everyone can make use of all four channels, but according to Gregorc (2002) there are inborn (God-given) inclinations towards one or two of them. He also denies that it is possible to change point arrangements during one's life. To try to act against stylistic inclinations puts one at risk of becoming false or inauthentic. Each orientation towards the world has potentially positive and negative attributes (Gregorc 1982b). Gregorc (2002) states that his mission is to prompt self-knowledge, promote depth-awareness of others, foster harmonious relationships, reduce negative harm and encourage rightful actions.

Measurement by the author

Description of measure

The GSD (Gregorc 1982a) is a 10-item self-report questionnaire in which (as in the Kolb inventory) a respondent rank orders four words in each item, from the most to the least descriptive of his or her self. An example is: perfectionist (CS), research (AS), colourful (AR), and risk-taker (CR). Some of the words are unclear or may be unfamiliar (eg 'attuned' and 'referential'). No normative data is reported, and detailed, but unvalidated, descriptions of the style characteristics of each channel (when dominant) are provided in the GSD booklet under 15 headings (Gregorc 1982a).

Reliability and validity

When 110 adults completed the GSD twice at intervals ranging in time from 6 hours to 8 weeks, Gregorc obtained reliability *(alpha) coefficients* of between 0.89 and 0.93 and test–retest *correlations* of between 0.85 and 0.88 for the four sub-scales (1982b).

Gregorc presents no empirical evidence for construct validity other than the fact that the 40 words were chosen by 60 adults as being expressive of the four styles. Criterion-related validity was addressed by having 110 adults also respond to another 40 words supposedly characteristic of each style. Only moderate correlations are reported.

External evaluation

Reliability and validity

We have not found any independent studies of *test–retest reliability*, but independent studies of *internal consistency* and *factorial validity* raise serious doubts about the psychometric properties of the GSD. The alpha coefficients found by Joniak and Isaksen (1988) range from 0.23 to 0.66 while O'Brien (1990) reports 0.64 for CS, 0.51 for AS, 0.61 for AR, and 0.63 for CR. These figures contrast with those reported by Gregorc and are well below acceptable levels. Joniak and Isaksen's findings appear trustworthy, because virtually identical results were found for each channel measure in two separate studies. The AS scale was the least reliable, with alpha values of only 0.23 and 0.25.

It is important to note that the *ipsative* nature of the GSD scale, and the fact that the order in which the style indicators are presented is the same for each item, increase the chance of the hypothesised dimensions appearing. Nevertheless, using correlational and factor analytic methods, Joniak and Isaksen were unable to support Gregorc's theoretical model, especially in relation to the concrete-abstract dimension. Harasym *et al.* (1995b) also performed a *factor analysis* which cast doubt on the concrete-abstract dimension. In his 1990 study, O'Brien used confirmatory factor analysis with a large sample (n=263) and found that 11 of the items were unsatisfactory and that the random/sequential construct was problematic.

Despite the serious problems they found with single scales, Joniak and Isaksen formed two composite measures which they correlated with the Kirton Adaption-Innovation Inventory (Kirton 1976). It was expected that sequential processors (CS+AS) would tend to be adapters (who use conventional procedures to solve problems) and random processors would tend to be innovators (who approach problems from novel perspectives). This prediction was strongly supported.

Bokoros, Goldstein and Sweeney (1992) carried out an interesting study in which they sought to show that five different measures of cognitive style (including the GSD) tap three underlying dimensions which have their origins in Jungian theory. A sample of 165 university students and staff members was used, with an average age of 32. Three factors were indeed found, the first being convergent and objective at one pole (AS) and divergent and subjective at the other (AR). The second factor was said to represent a data-processing orientation: immediate, accurate and applicable at one pole (CS) and concerned with patterns and possibilities at the other (CR). The third factor was related to *introversion* and extraversion and had much lower *loadings* from the Gregorc measures. It is important to note that in this study also, composite measures were used, formed by subtracting one raw score from another (AS minus AR and CS minus CR). For two studies of predictive validity, see the section on pedagogical impact below.

From the evidence available, we conclude that the GSD is flawed in construction. Even though those flaws might have been expected to spuriously inflate measures of reliability and validity, the GSD does not have adequate psychometric properties for use in individual assessment, selection or prediction. However, the reliability of composite GSD measures has not been formally assessed and it is possible that these may prove to be more acceptable statistically.

General

Writing in 1979, Gregorc lists other aspects of style, including preferences for deduction or induction, for individual or group activity and for various environmental conditions. These he sees as more subject to developmental and environmental influences than the four channels which he describes as 'properties of the self, or soul' (1979, 224). However, no evidence for this metaphysical claim is provided. We are not told how Gregorc developed the special abilities to determine the underlying causes (*noumena*) of behaviour (*pheno*) and the nature of the learner (*logos*) by means of his 'phenomenological' method.

The concept of sequential, as opposed to simultaneous or holistic, processing is one that is long established in philosophy and psychology, and is analogous to sequential and parallel processing in computing. Here, Gregorc's use of the term 'random' is value-laden and perhaps inappropriate, since it does not properly capture the power of intuition, imagination, divergent thinking and creativity. Although the cognitive and emotional mental activity and linkages behind intuitive, empathetic, 'big picture' or 'out of the box' thinking are often not fully explicit, they are by no means random.

It is probable that the 'ordering' dimension in which Gregorc is interested does not apply uniformly across all aspects of experience, especially when emotions come into play or there are time or social constraints to cope with. Moreover, opposing 'sequential' to 'random' can create a false dichotomy, since there are many situations in which thinking in terms of part-whole relationships requires a simultaneous focus on parts and wholes, steps and patterns. To seek to capture these dynamic complexities with personal reactions to between 10 and 20 words is clearly a vain ambition.

Similar arguments apply to the perceptual dimension concrete-abstract. It is far from clear that these terms and the clusters of meaning which Gregorc associates with them represent a unitary dimension, or indeed much more than a personal set of word associations in the mind of their originator. Lack of clarity is apparent in Gregorc's description of the 'concrete random' channel as mediating the 'concrete world of reality and abstract world of intuition' (1982b, 39). He also describes the world of feeling and emotions as 'abstract' and categorises thinking that is 'inventive and futuristic' and where the focus of attention is 'processes and ideals' as 'concrete'.

Implications for pedagogy

Gregorc's model differs from Kolb's (1999) in that it does not represent a learning cycle derived from a theory of experiential learning. However, Gregorc was at one time a teacher and teacher-educator and argues that knowledge of learning styles is especially important for teachers. As the following quotation (1984, 54) illustrates, he contends that strong correlations exist between the individual's **disposition**, the media, and teaching strategies.

Individuals with clear-cut dispositions toward concrete and sequential reality chose approaches such as ditto sheets, workbooks, computer-assisted instruction, and kits. Individuals with strong abstract and random dispositions opted for television, movies, and group discussion. Individuals with dominant abstract and sequential leanings preferred lectures, audio tapes, and extensive reading assignments. Those with concrete and random dispositions were drawn to independent study, games, and simulations. Individuals who demonstrated strength in multiple dispositions selected multiple forms of media and classroom approaches. It must be noted, however, that despite strong preferences, most individuals in the sample indicated a desire for a variety of approaches in order to avoid boredom.

Gregorc believes that students suffer if there is a lack of alignment between their adaptive abilities (styles) and the demands placed on them by teaching methods and styles. Teachers who understand their own styles and those of their learners can reduce the harm they may otherwise do and 'develop a repertoire of authentic skills' (Gregorc 2002). Gregorc argues against attempts to force teachers and learners to change their natural styles, believing that this does more harm than good and can alienate people or make them ill.

Empirical evidence for pedagogical impact

We have found no published evidence addressing Gregorc's claims about the benefits of self-knowledge of learning styles or about the alignment of Gregorc-type learning and teaching styles. However, there are some interesting studies on instructional preference and on using style information to predict learning outcomes. Three of these come from the University of Calgary, where there has been large-scale use of the GSD.

Lundstrom and Martin (1986) found no evidence to support their predictions that CS students would respond better to self-study materials and AR students to discussion. However, Seidel and England (1999) obtained results in a liberal arts college which supported some of Gregorc's claims. Among the subsample of 64 out of 100 students showing a clear preference for a single cognitive style, a sequential processing preference (CS and AS) was significantly associated with a preference for structured learning, structured assessment activities and independent laboratory work. Random processing (CR and AR) students preferred group discussion and projects and assessments based on performance and presentation. There was a clear tendency for science majors to be sequential processors (19/22) and for humanities majors to be random processors (17/20), while social science majors were more evenly balanced (11/22).

Harasym *et al.* (1995b) found that sequential processors (CS and AS) did not perform significantly better than random processors (CR and AR) in first-year nursing anatomy and physiology examinations at the University of Calgary. The nursing courses involved both lectures and practical work and included team teaching. It is probably unfair to attribute this negative result to the unreliability and poor validity of the instrument. It may be more reasonable to assume either that the examinations did not place great demands on sequential thinking or that the range of experiences offered provided adequately for diverse learning styles.

Drysdale, Ross and Schulz (2001) reported on a 4-year study with more than 800 University of Calgary students in which the ability of the GSD to predict success in university computer courses was evaluated. As predicted (since working with computers requires sequential thinking), it was found that the dominant sequential processing groups (CS and AS) did best and the AR group did worst. The differences were substantial in an introductory computer science course, with an effect size of 0.85 between the highest- and lowest-performing groups (equivalent to a mean advantage of 29 *percentile* points). Similar results, though not as striking, were found in a computer applications in education course for pre-service teachers.

Drysdale, Ross and Schulz (2001) presented data collected for 4546 students over the same 4-year period at the University of Calgary. The GSD was used to predict first-year student performance in 19 subject areas. Statistically significant stylistic differences in grade point average were found in 11 subject areas, with the largest effects appearing in art (the only subject where CR students did well), kinesiology, statistics, computer science, engineering and mathematics. In seven subjects (all of them scientific, technological or mathematical), the best academic scores were obtained by CS learners, with medical science and kinesiology being the only two subjects where AS learners had a clear advantage. Overall, the sequential processors had a very clear advantage over random processors in coping with the demands of certain academic courses, not only in terms of examination grades but also retention rates. Courses in which no significant differences were found were those in the liberal arts and in nursing.

It seems clear from these empirical studies as well as from the factor analyses reported earlier that the sequential-random dimension stands up rather better than the concrete-abstract dimension. Seidel and England's study (1999) suggests that some people who enjoy and are good at sequential thinking seek out courses requiring this type of thinking, whereas others avoid them or try to find courses where such thinking is valued rather less than other qualities. The results from the University of Calgary demonstrate that people who choose terms such as 'analytical', 'logical', 'objective', 'ordered', 'persistent', 'product-oriented' and 'rational' to describe themselves tend to do well in mathematics, science and technology (but not in art).

Conclusion

The construct of 'sequential', as contrasted with 'random', processing has received some research support and some substantial group differences have been reported in the literature. However, in view of the serious doubts which exist concerning the reliability and validity of the Gregorc Style Delineator and the unsubstantiated claims made about what it reveals for individuals, its use cannot be recommended.

Table 1

Gregorc's Mind Styles
Model and Style
Delineator (GSD)

	Strengths	Weaknesses
General	The GSD taps into the unconscious 'mediation abilities' of '*perception*' and 'ordering'.	Styles are natural abilities and not amenable to change.
Design of the model	■ There are two dimensions: concrete-abstract and sequential-random. ■ Individuals tend to be strong in one or two of the four categories: concrete sequential, concrete random, abstract sequential and abstract random.	■ Some of the words used in the instrument are unclear or may be unfamiliar. ■ No normative data is reported, and detailed descriptions of the style characteristics are unvalidated.
Reliability	The author reports high levels of internal consistency and test–retest reliability.	Independent studies of reliability raise serious doubts about the GSD's psychometric properties.
Validity	Moderate *correlations* are reported for criterion-related validity.	■ There is no empirical evidence for construct validity other than the fact that the 40 words were chosen by 60 adults as being expressive of the four styles. ■ The sequential/random dimension stands up rather better to empirical investigation than the concrete/abstract dimension.
Implications for pedagogy	Although Gregorc contends that clear-cut Mind Style dispositions are linked with preferences for certain instructional media and teaching strategies, he acknowledges that most people prefer instructional variety.	Gregorc makes the unsubstantiated claim that learners who ignore or work against their style may harm themselves.
Evidence of pedagogical impact	Results on study preference are mixed, though there is evidence that choice of subject is aligned with Mind Style and that success in science, engineering and mathematics is correlated with sequential style.	We have not found any published evidence addressing the benefits of self-knowledge of learning styles or the alignment of Gregorc-type learning and teaching styles.
Overall assessment	Theoretically and psychometrically flawed. Not suitable for the assessment of individuals.	
Key source	Gregorc 1985	

3.2
The Dunn and Dunn model and instruments of learning styles

Introduction

Rita Dunn is the director of the Centre for the Study of Learning Styles and professor in the division of administrative and instructional leadership at St John's University, New York; Kenneth Dunn is professor and chair in the department of educational and community programs, Queens College, City University of New York. Rita and Kenneth Dunn began their work on learning styles in the 1960s in response to the New York State Education Department's concern for poorly achieving students. Rita Dunn's teaching experience with children in the early years at school and with students with learning difficulties or disabilities created an interest in individual children's responses to different stimuli and conditions. She believed that students' preferences and learning outcomes were related to factors other than intelligence, such as environment, opportunities to move around the classroom, working at different times of the day and taking part in different types of activity. For Dunn, such factors can affect learning, often negatively.

For over 35 years, the Dunns have developed an extensive research programme designed to improve the instruments that derive from their model of learning style preferences. The model has become increasingly influential in elementary schooling and teacher training courses in states across the US. It is also used by individual practitioners in other countries including Australia, Bermuda, Brunei, Denmark, Finland, Malaysia, New Zealand, Norway, the Philippines, Singapore and Sweden (Dunn 2003a). The Centre for the Study of Learning Styles at St John's University, New York has a website, publishes the outcomes of hundreds of empirical studies, trains teachers and produces resource materials for teachers, together with many articles in professional journals and magazines.

A number of instruments have evolved from an extensive programme of empirical research. These are designed for different age groups, including adults. Proponents of the Dunn and Dunn model are convinced that using a scientific model to identify and then 'match' students' individual learning style preferences with appropriate instructions, resources and homework will transform education. Supporters of the model encourage the public to become vigilant consumers of education. For example:

You can determine a lot about your own child's learning style, share the information with teachers, challenge any facile diagnosis ... or any remedial work that isn't working ... You can be instrumental in making educators realise that children of different needs need to be taught differently.
(Ball 1982, quoted by Dunn 2001b, 10)

The popularity of the model with practitioners in the US has resulted in substantial government support for developing 'learning styles school districts' there (Reese 2002). There is also emerging interest in whether the model could be used in the UK. In 1998, the QCA commissioned a literature review of Dunn and Dunn's model (Klein 1998). More recently, the DfES sponsored a project undertaken by the London Language and Literacy Unit and South Bank University. The authors recommended further research to explore whether the Dunn and Dunn model should be used in FE colleges to improve achievement and student retention (Klein *et al.* 2003a, 2003b).

An extensive range of publications on the Dunn and Dunn model is listed on a website (www.learningstyles.net) offering a research bibliography containing 879 items. This includes 28 books, 10 of which are written by the model's authors; 20% of the material (177 items) comprises articles in scholarly, peer-reviewed journals. Around one-third of the bibliography (306 items) consists of articles in professional journals and magazines and 37 articles published in the *Learning Styles Network Newsletter*, which is the journal of the Dunns' Centre for the Study of Learning Styles. A further third (292 items) consists of doctoral and master's dissertations and the remaining references are to unpublished conference papers, documents on the ERIC database and multimedia resources. A recent publication itemises many studies that support the model and its various instruments (Dunn and Griggs 2003).

Rita Dunn often quotes certain external evaluations that are positive, but appears to regard empirical studies by those trained and certified to use her model to be the most legitimate sources for evaluation. External criticisms, whether they are of the model and its underlying theories or of the instruments, are deemed 'secondary' or 'biased' (Dunn 2003a). However, as with other reviews of learning style models in this report, we include internal and external evaluations of underlying theory and of instruments derived from the model. We selected and reviewed a representative range of all the types of literature that were available.

Description and definition of the model

According to the Dunn and Dunn model, 'learning style is divided into 5 major strands called *stimuli*. The stimulus strands are: a) environmental, b) emotional, c) sociological, d) psychological, and e) physiological elements that significantly influence how many individuals learn' (Dunn 2003b, 2).

From these strands, four variables affect students' preferences, each of which includes different factors. These are measured in the model and summarised in Table 2.

	Variable	Factors			
Table 2	**Variable**	**Factors**			
Variables and factors in the Dunn and Dunn learning-styles model	Environmental	Sound	Temperature	Light	Seating, layout of room, etc
	Emotional	Motivation	Degree of responsibility	Persistence	Need for structure
	Physical	Modality preferences – ie for visual, auditory, kinaesthetic or tactile learning (VAKT)	Intake (food and drink)	Time of day	Mobility
	Sociological	Learning groups	Help/support from authority figures	Working alone or with peers	Motivation from parent/teacher

The *environmental* strand incorporates individuals' preferences for the elements of sound, light, temperature, and furniture or seating design. The *emotional* strand focuses on students' levels of motivation, persistence, responsibility, and need for structure. The *sociological* strand addresses students' preference for learning alone, in pairs, with peers, as part of a team, with either authoritative or collegial instructors, or in varied approaches (as opposed to in patterns). The *physiological* strand examines perceptual strengths (visual, auditory, kinaesthetic or tactile), time-of-day energy levels, and the need for intake (food and drink) and mobility while learning. Finally, the *psychological* strand incorporates the information-processing elements of global versus analytic and impulsive versus reflective behaviours, but it is not measured in earlier versions of the model (see below for discussion). Each preference factor in Table 3 (indicated in bold type) represents an independent continuum and is not necessarily related to those on the right or left side of other factors.

'Sociological' in the model does not refer to broader social conditions affecting learning, but simply to whether students prefer to work alone or with peers, and whether they are motivated by authority figures. 'Responsibility' is also defined in a particular way: the responsible individual is one who can conform to instruction, albeit while exercising choice about his or her preferences for methods of instruction, rather than someone who takes responsibility for his or her own learning. Responsibility can be constrained by teachers; for example:

When permitting students to sit comfortably while studying, it may be important to the teacher to add the requirement that students sit like a lady or a gentleman

When permitting intake while concentrating, teachers may wish to limit the kind of intake to raw vegetables. Teachers who need quiet may wish to impose the additional mandate of cooking vegetables for at least two minutes

(Dunn 2003c, 190–191; original emphasis)

The model places a strong emphasis on biological and developmentally imposed characteristics. Dunn and Dunn (1992) define style as 'the way in which individuals begin to concentrate on, process, internalise and retain new and difficult academic information.'

Students identify their own preferences in using one of the instruments (see below for discussion of the measures), and teachers receive a formal diagnostic profile of their students from a processing centre at the University of Kansas or directly online if using the Building Excellence Survey (BES). Feedback from the BES also includes advice on how to use strengths when studying or working with difficult materials (see below for discussion of the instruments). This assessment identifies *strong preferences*, *preferences*, *non-preferences*, *opposite preferences* and *strong opposite preferences*. Each person's unique combination of preferences comprises his or her learning style.

Teachers are advised to use the diagnosis to adapt instruction and environmental conditions by allowing learners to work with their strong preferences and to avoid, as far as possible, activities for which learners report having very low preferences. People who have no high or low preferences do not need 'matching' and can therefore adapt more easily to different teaching styles and activities. According to Rita Dunn (2003d), the inability of schools and teachers to take account of preferences produces endemic low achievement and poor motivation and must be challenged by parents, professionals and researchers who understand the research base of the model.

The Dunn and Dunn model measures preferences rather than strengths. A positive feature of the model is that it affirms preferences rather than aiming to remedy weaknesses. It does not stigmatise different types of preference. Supporters argue that anyone can improve their achievement and motivation if teachers match preferences with individualised instruction and changes to environment, food and drink intake, time-of-day activities and opportunities to work alone or with others.

Table 3
Elements of learning
style from the
Dunn and Dunn model

Source: Jonassen and
Grabowski (1993)

Environmental

Noise level	Prefers quiet	Prefers sound
Lighting	Prefers low light	Prefers bright light
Temperature	Prefers cool temperature	Prefers warm temperature
Design	Prefers formal design	Prefers informal design
	Prefers wooden, steel, or plastic chairs	Prefers lounge chair, bed, floor, pillow, or carpeting
	Prefers conventional classroom or library	Prefers unconventional classroom, kitchen, living room

Sociological

Learning groups	Learn alone	Peer-oriented
	Covert thinking	Discussion and interactions
Presence of authority figures	No one of authority	Recognised authority
Learning in several ways	Routine	Variety of social groups
Motivation from adults (for the Learning Styles Inventory only; not included in Productivity Environmental Preference Survey)	Need to please parents or parent figures Need to please teachers	No need for parental approval No need to please teachers

Emotional

Motivation	Motivated	Unmotivated
	Needs to achieve academically	No need to achieve academically
Responsibility	Responsible	Irresponsible
	Conforming	Non-conforming
	Does what he or she thinks ought to be done	Does what he or she wants
	Follows through on what is asked	Doesn't like to do something because someone asks
Persistence	Persistent	Non-persistent
	Inclination to complete tasks	Need for intermittent breaks
Needs for structure	Wants structure	Does not want structure
	Prefers specific directions	Prefers to do it his or her way

Physical modality preferences

Auditory	**Visual**	**Tactile**	**Kinaesthetic**
Listening	Reading	Use their hands	Whole body movement
Lecture	Print	Underline	Real-life experiences/ visiting
Discussion	Diagrams	Take notes	Total involvement
Recording	Close eyes to recall		Acting/drama/puppetry
			Building/designing
			Interviewing
			Playing

Intake	Eat, drink, chew, or bite while concentrating	No intake while studying
Time of day	Morning energy	Evening energy
	Late morning energy	Afternoon energy
Mobility	Needs to move	Able to sit still

The measures

Over 25 years, Dunn and Dunn have produced the following self-report instruments:

- the Dunn and Dunn Learning Styles Questionnaire (LSQ) (1979)
- the Dunn, Dunn and Price Learning Styles Inventory (LSI) (1992, 1996)
- the Dunn, Dunn and Price Productivity Environmental Preference Survey (PEPS) (1996)
- the Building Excellence Survey (BES) (2002)
- Our Wonderful Learning Styles (OWLS) 2002.

The instruments are supported by the following resources and material for teaching and homework:

- Contract Activity Packages (CAPs)
- Programmed Learning Sequences (PLSs)
- Multi-Sensory Instructional Packages (MIPs).

The CAPs are packages for teachers containing objectives, alternative resources and activities, small-group techniques and assessment tasks related to the objectives. According to Rita Dunn, they are most effective with independent and motivated students, as well as with non-conformists who prefer to meet the objectives in their own way. A PLS is an instructional strategy that enables teachers and students to programme activities and materials visually, tactilely or on tape. An MIP is a box of resources, including CAPs and PLSs, that enables teachers and students to individualise learning according to preferences across different academic achievement levels (Dunn 2003d).

The LSI was refined from the first Learning Styles Questionnaire (LSQ) through factor analysis of individual items. The PEPS is an adult version of the LSI that omits items in relation to motivation based on the need for parental or teacher approval. The BES adds items for analytic/global and impulsive/reflective processing and items that differentiate between verbal kinaesthetic and tactile kinaesthetic preferences, visual text and picture preferences. The LSI is designed for school students in US grades 3–12 (ages 9–18). It comprises 104 self-report items, with a 3-point *Likert scale* (true, uncertain, false) for students in grades 3–4 and a 5-point scale (strongly disagree, disagree, uncertain, agree, strongly agree) for students in grades 5–12. The PEPS has a Flesch-Kincaid readability level of 9–9.5 years and a 5-point Likert scale identical to that in the LSI. Both inventories are available on computer, tape or as a paper-based questionnaire, and each takes 30–40 minutes to complete. Typical items are as follows.

- I study best when the lights are dim.
- When I do well at school, grown-ups in my family are proud of me.
- I like to listen to music while I'm studying.

Scores can range from a low of 20 to a high of 80. A score of 60 or above denotes a high preference for a particular element; 39 or below is a low preference. A score of 40–49 shows neither a high nor low preference which means that students will not benefit from being matched to instructional style or environmental factors. It is important to note that the scoring system for the model as a whole ensures that most people come out with one or more strong preferences.

Origins

Sources and theories for individual elements in the model are diverse and draw on research literatures from many different fields, including brain development, physiological studies of performance and the enormous field of *modality preference*. This diversity means that literature in support of the model tends to present theoretical explanations of individual elements of preference in rather general terms. It is not within the scope of this review to engage with aspects of neuropsychology and sociobiology in depth. Instead, we review literature that discusses specific elements of the model and literature that discusses the underlying theories.

An important principle in the Dunn and Dunn model is the idea that students' potential and achievement are heavily influenced by relatively fixed traits and characteristics (Dunn and Griggs 1988, 3). This raises a fundamental educational question – namely, how far individuals can remedy their low preferences or change their preferences altogether. The most recent overview of the model contains the claim that 'the learning styles of students changed substantially as they matured from adolescence into adulthood' (Gremli 2003, 112). It seems, then, that some change in learning styles takes place over time.

Environmental factors: lighting, temperature, sound and design

The LSI manual (Price and Dunn 1997) suggests that as students get older, preferences for sound, light and informal design become stronger. It is not clear how far this development is an intensification of already existing preferences, since Rita Dunn (eg 2001a) also characterises environmental preferences as relatively fixed. In addition, details of the evidence on which this claim is based are not given, at least in this source.[4]

The LSI manual cites the work of Nganwa-Bagumah and Mwamenda (1991) to support the importance of informal or formal design preferences. However, there are some methodological and statistical flaws in that study, including the reporting of non-significant results as significant.

4
The number of supporting studies is so vast that the problem we raise here may have been addressed in studies that we were not able to review for this report. We therefore advise readers interested in evaluating claims made in these studies to refer to the website www.learningstyles.net

Emotional factors: motivation, responsibility, persistence and need for structure

Rita Dunn (2001a) claims that emotional factors are relatively unstable, or perhaps the most responsive to experience. Nevertheless, matching these kinds of preference to instruction is said to result in learning gains with a mean effect size[5] of d=0.54 according to the **meta-analysis** by Dunn et al. (1995) of doctoral studies supporting the LSI.

Physical factors: modality preference, intake, time of day and mobility

A person's preference as to whether tasks or activities are presented to appeal to auditory, visual, tactile or kinaesthetic senses (modality preference) is an important dimension in the model. Carbo (1983), on the Dunns' behalf, questioned earlier research into modality preference, suggesting that 'although only 2 of the 19 studies … achieved significant interactions between reading method and modality strengths', methodological weaknesses in the majority of studies have obscured the connection between reading instruction and modality preference. This led Carbo to assert that there is, after all, a connection.

Many other researchers on modality preference (not using the Dunns' model) have reported a lack of evidence for modality preference as a guide to teaching strategy. For example, in a review of 22 studies, Kampwirth and Bates (1980, 603) reported that 20 'failed to indicate a significant interaction', while Tarver and Dawson (1978) found that only two out of 14 studies showed an interaction between modality preference and teaching method. Similarly, Deverensky (1978) argued that research had not shown a causal relationship between modality and reading performance, but he suggested that this might be because of the difficulty of finding sensitive measures of preference.

Recent research into modalities suggests that different modality effects are associated with reading performance, in particular with the problems that poor readers have with echoic (sound-based) memory (Penney and Godsell 1999). This implies that auditory instruction may benefit good readers more than poor readers. Westman and Stuve (2001) suggest that modality preferences exist and that self-report questions based around enjoyment are one way to elicit them. Yet, as the introduction to this section shows, there is disagreement as to whether modality preferences are important. There is also evidence to suggest that learning styles are more likely to be influenced by students' understanding of the demands of a particular task than by modality preference (Westman, Alliston and Thierault 1997).

In other research on modality preference, Kavale and Forness (1987) confronted the widespread belief among teachers working with learners with learning difficulties and/or disabilities that targeting modality preferences is an effective instructional strategy, arguing that the 'question of the efficacy of the modality model remains controversial' (1987, 229). After performing a meta-analysis of 39 empirical studies of the effects of matching modality strengths to special instruction in reading, they concluded that the diagnosis of modality preference was, in itself, problematic. In terms of the effects of modality-based instruction, they reported that the effect size of 0.14 'translates into only a 6 percentile rank improvement' (1987, 233). They argued that 'Although the presumption of matching instructional strategies to individual modality preferences to enhance learning efficiency has great intuitive appeal, little empirical support … was found … Neither modality testing nor modality teaching were shown to be efficacious.' (1987, 237).

Kavale and Forness excluded many studies in support of the LSI because these did not fit their meta-analysis criteria – namely, that studies should assess modality preference formally, design instructional materials and techniques to capitalise specifically on the assessed preference, and assess results of that instruction with a standardised outcome measure. This external research into one of the most important underlying claims of the Dunn and Dunn model provoked a response from Rita Dunn (1990a) and a riposte from Kavale and Forness (1990). These have been referred to as a 'blistering exchange' over 'allegations and counter-charges of shoddy scholarship and vested interests [that] have clouded the issue and made it all the more difficult for practitioners to decide what's worth pursuing' (O'Neil 1990).

Rita Dunn rejected the findings of Kavale and Forness because they excluded studies produced in support of the LSI and asserted that high achievers 'may strongly prefer one modality more than another, but often they have two or more preferences and can learn easily through one or the other. In contrast, underachievers may have either no preference or only one – usually tactual or kinesthetic' (Dunn 1990a, 354). In response, Kavale and Forness re-asserted the criteria for including studies in their meta-analysis and added (1990, 358): 'When even a cursory examination revealed a study to be so inadequate that its data were essentially meaningless, it was eliminated from consideration. This is the reason that only two of Dunn's studies were included in our analysis.'

5
Throughout this section, we have converted effect sizes into d values, using the formula provided by Cohen (1988, 23).

Table 4
Percentages of respondents preferring a specific time of day for study (students with no preference not recorded)

Study	Measure	Cohort	Morning		Afternoon	Evening
			Early morning	**Late morning**		
Callan 1999	LSI	Grade 9 (n=245)	9%	10%	18%	21%
Biggers 1980	LSI	Grades 7–12 (n=641)	22.8%		42.4%	34.8%
Carey, Stanley and Biggers 1988	Peak alert 4-item survey	College freshmen (n=242)	16%		27%	57%

Instead of modality-based teaching, Kavale and Forness recommended that specific instructional strategies could benefit all students. This idea is supported by the Dunn's own research (Miller *et al.* 2000/01), which found that a teaching strategy based on a 'programmed learning sequence' and designed to favour visually- and tactilely-oriented students increased attainment for all students in the experimental group. Jaspers (1994) rejected the utility of identifying dominant modality preferences as a basis for designing targeted instructional materials, arguing that there is both a lack of theoretical support and doubts about the practical efficiency of such an approach. Targeted instructional materials were not supported by Moreno and Mayer (1999, 366) who found that mixed modality presentations (visual/auditory) produce better results, 'consistent with Paivio's theory that when learners can concurrently hold words in auditory working memory and pictures in visual working memory, they are better able to devote attentional resources to building connections between them.'

Time-of-day preference is another important dimension in the Dunn and Dunn model; it is divided into early morning, late morning, afternoon and evening. A number of studies dealing with variations in reported time-of-day preference are shown above in Table 4. A meta-analysis of studies by Dunn *et al.* (1995) indicates that the group termed 'physiological' by the authors has the largest effect size.

However, it is important to note that many of the studies cited by Dunn *et al.* (1995) are concerned with test performance, rather than with learning in different conditions. Another methodological drawback is that the studies are also affected by the human need to present consistently in self-report instruments and either prior or subsequent performance.

In addition, some of the studies (eg Biggers 1980; Carey, Stanley and Biggers 1988) have only three categories (morning, afternoon and evening) and use different measures to assess preference. There does not appear to be a clear distribution of populations across the preferences that predict the percentage of students who may have strong preferences for a particular time of day. Further caution about the importance of time-of-day preference emerges from research into the 'clock gene', discussed in the introduction to this section, which suggests that inferring an uncomplicated relationship between preference, peak alert and performance is highly questionable. Even if a relationship does exist, it is important not to confuse correlation with causation.

Sociological influences: learning groups, authority figures, working alone and motivation from adults

The absence of the element 'motivation' from the PEPS is perhaps surprising in the light of evidence that the desire to please parents persists well into adulthood (eg Luster and McAdoo 1996). Moreover, although adult learners continue to be influenced by authority figures, the PEPS does not deal with the impact of more experienced adults on learning cultures in the workplace – for example, in formal and informal mentoring relationships (see eg Allinson, Armstrong and Hayes 2001).

A study of learning style preferences among males and females in different countries (Hlawaty and Honigsfeld 2002) claims statistically significant differences, with girls showing stronger preferences in motivation, responsibility and working with others than boys, and boys showing stronger preferences for kinaesthetic learning.

Dominant hemispheres

The LSI and PEPS do not contain a measure for hemispheric dominance, although brain hemispheres are cited as an important factor by Rita Dunn (eg Dunn *et al.* 1990; Dunn 2003b). Dunn *et al.* recommended the use of an instrument devised by Rita Dunn's colleague Robert Zenhausern (1979), which comprises a questionnaire of psychometric properties to investigate the impact of hemispheric dominance on maze learning (Zenhausern and Nickel 1979), and recall and recognition (Zenhausern and Gebhardt 1979).

Dunn *et al.* (1990) also reported that students who are strong 'right activators' differed significantly from strong 'left activators' in being unmotivated, preferring to learn with one peer, liking to move around and having tactile preferences. However, an examination of Zenhausern's instrument reveals that it involves self-rating of verbal and visual cognitive abilities, so the differences found may simply be a function of cognitive ability or of lack of self-knowledge, rather than modality preference. No means and standard deviations are provided by Dunn *et al.* (1990), making it impossible to determine effect sizes. It is also unsurprising that learners of low verbal ability describe themselves as unmotivated, in need of peer support, and as preferring practical activities.

Despite the importance given to 'left' and 'right' brain influence, its distribution among different populations is unclear. One study of 353 biology students in high school grades 9–12 found that 39% of male students identified themselves as 'left-brain activated', compared to only 28% of female students, but that the majority of both sexes identified themselves as 'right-brain activated'. Right-brain activated people are deemed to be disadvantaged 'in our left hemisphere-oriented educational system' (Zenhausern *et al.* 1981, 37). The explanation given for this 'right-brain' majority in high school is *either* that the maturational process produces a tendency in some individuals to become more 'left brain' in college *or* that 'right brain' individuals are more likely to be unsuited to the traditional learning environment. However, there is no unequivocal evidence from independent, external research to support either hypothesis.

The work of Thies, a neuropsychologist at Yale University, is used by Dunn and Griggs (2003) to highlight the implications of neuroscience for the Dunn and Dunn model. Yet Thies admitted (2003, 52) that 'the relationship between the elements of learning style and any brain activation is still hypothetical'. Moreover, the brain scanning that he has carried out by means of 'functional resonance imaging' has so far been concerned only with the learning of simple tasks and has yet to tackle the complex learning found in classrooms. In addition, the definition of 'learning' is crucial, since Thies defined it as 'the acquisition of skills and knowledge' (2003, 50). However, this is only one aspect of learning, and recent research into 'situated learning' suggests that it may not be the most important.

Further doubt about the prominence that the Dunns give to brain dominance in their model arises from other research and interpretations of neuropsychology which indicate that left/right divisions are perhaps more meaningful as metaphors than as concrete representations of brain activity (see eg Herrmann 1989). The idea that a preference for using one hemisphere is set in early childhood is also challenged; for example, 'The significant, new finding is that neuronal plasticity persists in the mature nervous system, not that there are critical periods early in development' (Bruer 1998, 481).

Analytic/global and reflective/impulsive processing

According to Rita Dunn (2003b, 2; original emphasis):

the majority of students at all academic levels are global *rather than analytic, they respond better to information taught globally than they do to information taught analytically. … Integrated processors can internalise new and difficult data either globally or analytically but retain it only when they are interested in what they are learning.*

Drawing on Coleman and Zenhausern (1979), Dunn *et al.* (1990) assert that it is possible to identify *'lefts/analytics/****inductives****/successive processors'* and *'rights/globals/****deductives****/simultaneous processors'* as distinct 'types' of learner. In addition, these types have significant relationships with learning style preferences as defined by the LSI categories. For example:

Analytics learn more easily when information is presented step by step in a cumulative sequential pattern that builds towards a conceptual understanding … many analytics tend to prefer learning in a quiet, well-illuminated, informal setting: they often have a strong emotional need to complete the task they are working on, and they rarely eat, drink, smoke or chew, or bite on objects while learning. (Dunn *et al.* 1990, 226)

Burke (2003) also argued that analytic processing clashes with quiet and formal design and/or with bright light, intake and persistence, while global processing clashes with sound, dim lights, intake, informal design and low persistence.

Descriptions and prescriptions such as these tend to present differences as polar extremes, yet most cognitive psychologists and neuropsychologists agree that learners use both sides of the brain for communication and for the most sophisticated learning challenges.

The BES instrument has elements for learners to self-assess 'analytic' versus 'global', and 'reflective' versus 'impulsive' processing. In a survey of 73 trainee teachers using the BES, 71.3% identified themselves as strong to moderately analytic while 49.4% identified themselves as strong to moderately reflective. These findings were used to support the claim that trainee teachers who are themselves more likely to be analytic need to be prepared to teach 'a relatively high number of global processors amongst youngsters' (Honigsfeld and Schiering 2003, 292).

Evaluation by authors

Rita Dunn makes strong claims for reliability, validity and impact; for example (1990b, 223):

Research on the Dunn and Dunn model of the learning style is more extensive and far more thorough than the research on any other educational movement, bar none. As of 1989, it had been conducted at more than 60 institutions of higher education, at multiple grade levels … and with every level of academic proficiency, including gifted, average, underachieving, at risk, drop-out, special education and vocational/industrial arts populations. Furthermore, the experimental research in learning styles conducted at St John's University, Jamaica [in] New York has received one regional, twelve national, and two international awards and citations for its quality. No similar claim can be made for any other body of educational knowledge.

By 2003, the number of research studies had increased, being conducted in over 120 higher education institutions (Lovelace 2003).

Reliability

The LSI manual (Price and Dunn 1997) reported research which indicated that the test–retest reliabilities for 21 of the 22 factors were greater than 0.60 (n=817, using the 1996 revised instrument), with only 'late morning' preferences failing to achieve this level (0.56). It is important to reiterate here that the number of elements varies between the different inventories because the PEPS omits elements for motivation in the case of adults. For the PEPS, Price (1996) reported that 90% of elements had a test–retest reliability of greater than 0.60 (n=504), the 'rogue element' in this case being the 'tactile modality' preference (0.33). It is important to note that the 0.60 criterion for acceptable reliability is a lax one, since at that level, misclassification is actually more likely than accuracy. The PEPS was tested with 975 females and 419 males aged 18 to 65 years. Test–retest reliabilities for the 20 sub-scales ranged from 0.39 to 0.87 with 40% of the scales being over 0.8 (Nelson et al. 1993).

Although at the time of writing, there are no academic articles or book chapters dealing with the reliability and validity of the Building Excellence Survey (BES), in 1999, one of Rita Dunn's doctoral students made a detailed statistical comparison of the PEPS and the BES (Lewthwaite 1999). Lewthwaite used a paper-based version of the BES which contained 150 items and resembled the current electronic version in 'look and feel'. Both the PEPS and the BES were completed by an opportunity sample of 318 adults, with the PEPS being done first, followed by part of the BES, the rest being completed by most participants at home. Lewthwaite felt the need to preface the questionnaire with a 20–30 minute lecture about the Dunn and Dunn learning styles model and an explanation about how to self-score the BES. There was therefore ample opportunity for participants to revise their choices in response to section-by-section feedback, since they had a fortnight before bringing their completed booklets to a follow-up session. This was hardly an ideal way to study the statistical properties of the BES, since both the lecture and the way in which the BES presents one strand at a time for self-scoring encouraged participants to respond in a consistent manner.

What is of particular interest about Lewthwaite's study is the almost total lack of agreement between corresponding components of the PEPS and the BES. Rita Dunn was closely involved in the design of both instruments, which are based on the same model and have similarly worded questions. Yet the correlations for 19 shared components range from –0.14 (for learning in several ways) and 0.45 (for preference for formal or informal design and for temperature), with an average of only 0.19. In other words, the PEPS and the BES measure the same things only to a level of 4%, while 96% of what they measure is inconsistent between one instrument and the other. The only conclusion to be drawn is that these instruments have virtually no concurrent validity even when administered in circumstances designed to maximise such validity.

The literature supporting the model presents extensive citations of studies that have tested the model in diverse contexts (see Dunn et al. 1995; Dunn and Griggs 2003). The authors claim that age, gender, socio-economic status, academic achievement, race, religion, culture and nationality are important variables in learning preferences, showing multiple patterns of learning styles *between* and *within* diverse groups of students (eg Ewing and Yong 1992; Dunn et al. 1995). The existence of differences both between and within groups means that the evidence does not support a clear or simple 'learning styles prescription' which differentiates between these groups.

Features of studies that Dunn and Dunn cite as demonstrating reliability include:

- controls on data collection through tight administration of the model, using authorised centres and certified learning styles trainers

- random selection of students

- sample sizes that generate statistically reliable scores.

Nevertheless, the random selection of students in studies reviewed for this report does not apply universally: some studies select an experimental sub-group of people with strong preferences, others use whole classes or year groups and some do not explain their selection criteria. Where such information is provided, we have included sample sizes in our evaluations.

Validity

Proponents of the model claim high face, construct and predictive validity for elements within the model and for the model as a whole. For example, the lack of a correlation between LSI type and measures of intelligence is cited as 'support for its [the LSI's] construct validity' (Sinatra, Primavera and Waked 1986, 1243). Further support is offered by De Bello, who cited a 2-year study of different learning style instruments at Ohio State University and reported that the Dunn, Dunn and Price LSI had 'impressive reliability, face and construct validity' (Kirby 1979, cited by De Bello 1990, 206). From 'award-winning, experimental and correlational research with the LSI conducted at more than 50 universities', De Bello (1990, 206) went on to claim 'extremely high predictive validity'. De Bello's paper, however, does not contain any statistics relating to reliability and validity and is simply a description of different learning styles instruments. In a similar vein, Hlawaty and Honigsfeld (2002) cited De Bello (1990), Curry (1987) and Tendy and Geiser (1998/9) to support their claim that the LSI has 'good or better validity and reliability than nine other instruments'.

In a study of 1087 full-time first-year undergraduates, Nelson et al. (1993) tested the impact of the PEPS on achievement and retention. They claimed that working with preferences identified through the PEPS showed significant percentage differences of achievement and retention between control and experimental groups, with academic achievement improving the longer that students studied according to their preferences.

External evaluation

General comments

Apart from the many studies that the Dunns cite as showing validity and reliability, there appears to be little independent evaluation of their model. A further difficulty is created by Rita Dunn's rejection of any evaluations that are 'third party' and therefore carried out by people 'uncertified and untrained in the model' (Dunn 2003c, 37).

Confirmation of the model's validity was offered by Curry (1987) who evaluated the LSI and PEPS against nine other instruments within a 'family of models measuring instructional preferences'. However, Curry did not give details of the studies from which she drew her data or her criteria for selecting particular studies as offering 'good' support for validity. In addition, her report made clear that, despite judging reliability and validity to be good (see below), Curry regarded instructional preferences as less important in improving learning than other factors such as strategies or cognitive styles. In addition, data presented by Curry as evidence of good validity only confirmed predictive validity and not construct or face validity. When we examined the Curry paper, we found that being better than nine very poor instruments is not the same as being sufficiently reliable and valid for the purpose of making individual assessments. In her evaluation, Curry appeared to rely more on quantity, namely that there should be at least 20 supporting studies, rather than quality.

There has been criticism about the choice of individual elements in the LSI. For example: 'there is little information regarding the reasons for the choice of the 18 elements, nor is there any explanation given of possible interactions of the elements. The greatest problem … is its lack of attention to the learning process' (Grigorenko and Sternberg 1995, 219). Hyman and Roscoff (1984, 38) argue that:

The Learning Styles Based Education paradigm calls for the teacher to focus on the student's learning style when deciding how to teach. This call is misleading … Teaching is not a dyadic relationship between teacher and student … [but] a triadic relationship made up of three critical and constant elements: teacher, student and subject matter.

Some reviewers dispute both validity and reliability in the model. For example, reviews by Knapp (1994) and Shwery (1994) for the *1994 Mental Measurements Yearbook* incorporated conclusions from two other reviews (Hughes 1992 and Westman 1992). Knapp (1994, 461) argued that: the LSI has no redeeming values', and that 'the inventory had a number of weaknesses'. He concluded that: 'I am no expert on learning styles, but I agree with Hughes [one of the reviewers] that this instrument is a psychometric disaster.'

Shwery (1994) also questioned aspects of the LSI: 'The instrument is still plagued by issues related to its construct validity and the lack of an *a priori* theoretical paradigm for its development.'

Reliability

Curry (1987) judged the internal reliability of the LSI and PEPS to be good, with an average of 0.63 for the LSI and 0.66 for the PEPS. Yet she did not indicate what she regarded as 'good' coefficients and these are normally accepted to be 0.7 or above for a sub-scale. LaMothe *et al.* (1991) carried out an independent study of the internal consistency reliability of the PEPS with 470 nursing students. They found that only 11 of the 20 scales had alpha coefficients above 0.70, with the environmental variables being the most reliable and the sociological variables the least reliable.

Knapp (1994)[6] expressed concerns both about the approach to reliability in the design of the LSI and the reporting of reliability data: in particular, he criticised repeating questions in the LSI to improve its reliability. He added:

No items are, in fact, repeated word for word. They are simply reworded ... Such items contribute to a consistency check, and are not really concerned with reliability at all ... Included in the directions on the separate answer sheet ... is the incredible sentence 'Some of the questions are repeated to help make the inventory more reliable'. If that is the only way the authors could think of to improve the reliability of the inventory, they are in real trouble!

There are also concerns about the Dunns' claims for internal consistency. For example, Shwery (1994) says:

Scant evidence of reliability for scores from the LSI is provided in the manual. The authors report [that] *'research in 1988 indicated that 95 percent' (p.30) of the 22 areas ... provided internal consistency estimates of 0.60 or greater. The actual range is 0.55–0.88. Internal consistency of a number of areas ... was low. As such, the link between the areas and justifiably making decisions about instruction in these areas is questionable.*

Murray-Harvey (1994) reported that the reliability of 'the majority' of the PEPS elements was acceptable. However, she considered 'tactile modality' and 'learning in several ways' to 'show poor internal consistency' (1994, 378). In order to obtain retest measures, she administered the PEPS to 251 students in 1991 and again in 1992. Environmental preferences were found to be the most stable, with coefficients of between 0.48 ('design') and 0.64 ('temperature'), while sociological and emotional preferences were less so (0.30 for 'persistence' and 0.59 for 'responsibility'), as might be expected from Rita Dunn's (2001a) characterisation of these areas as more open to change. However, the physiological traits, which are supposed to be relatively stable, ranged from 0.31 for a specific 'late morning' preference to 0.60 for a general 'time of day' preference (Price and Dunn 1997). Overall, 13 out of 20 variables exhibited poor test–retest reliability scores of below 0.51.

Two separate reviews of the PEPS by Kaiser (1998) and Thaddeus (1998) for the *Mental Measurements Yearbook* highlighted concerns about the Dunns' interpretations of reliability. Both reviews noted the reliability coefficients of less than 0.60 for 'motivation', 'authority-oriented learning', 'learning in several ways', 'tactile learning' and 'kinaesthetic learning'. Thaddeus also noted that some data was missing, such as the characteristics of the norm group to whom the test was administered.

Validity

Criticism was directed at a section entitled 'reliability and validity' in the LSI manual (Price and Dunn 1997, 10). Knapp (1994) argued that 'there is actually no mention of validity, much less any validity data' and Shwery (1994) noted that 'the reader is referred to other studies to substantiate this claim'. These are the dissertation studies which supporters cite to 'provide evidence of predictive validity' (De Bello 1990, 206) and which underpin the meta-analyses (Dunn *et al.* 1995). There were also problems in obtaining any information about validity in the PEPS (Kaiser 1998; Thaddeus 1998) and a problem with extensive lists of studies provided by the Dunns, namely that: 'the authors expect that the validity information for the instrument can be gleaned through a specific examination of these studies.' (Kaiser[7] 1998). Kaiser also makes the point that 'just listing the studies in which the PEPS was used does not add to its psychometric properties'.

Page numbers are not available for online Buros reports from the *Mental Measurements Yearbooks*. The same applies to Shwery (1994).

Page numbers are not available for online Buros reports from the *Mental Measurements Yearbooks*. The same applies to Thaddeus (1998).

Table 5	Preference	Measure of ability	Source
Studies of the learning-style preferences of able students	Morning	Higher performance	Callan 1999
	Learning alone Self-motivated Tactile modality	Gifted	Pyryt, Sandals and Begorya 1998
	Learning alone Persistent	Gifted	Griggs 1984
	Authority figure present Parent/teacher-motivated Mobility	Gifted	Hlwaty 2002

Reviews of the PEPS also raised problems about missing data and the quality of Dunn et al.'s citations, referencing and interpretations of statistics. Thaddeus (1998) concluded that, once the underlying theory was developed, the PEPS would be a more valuable instrument and provide a direction for future research to establish its reliability and validity. Likewise, Kaiser (1998) concluded that 'the PEPS is not recommended for use until more evidence about its validity and reliability is obtained'.

Implications for pedagogy

The model and its instruments are intended to be a diagnostic alternative to what supporters of the Dunns' model call 'soft evaluation' by teachers (presumably informal observation, although this is not made clear), which they argue is often inaccurate. When used in conjunction with teachers' own insight and experience, the model is claimed to be a reliable and valid measure for matching instruction and environmental conditions to high preferences shown by the inventory, especially when students have to learn new and difficult material. Rita Dunn (2003c, 181) claimed that:

students whose learning styles were being accommodated could be expected to achieve 75% of a standard deviation higher than students who had not had their learning styles accommodated. Thus, matching students' learning style preferences was beneficial to their academic achievement.

The main purpose of the model is to improve students' attainment through matching instruction, environment and resources to students' high preferences. Nelson et al. (1993) argued that a 'matching' approach based on preferences is more effective than conventional study skills and support programmes which are remedial. Supporters of the model claim a substantial body of evidence for academic success resulting from changing teaching approaches. We summarise the key claims here.

- Most people have learning style preferences.

- Individuals' learning style preferences differ significantly from each other.

- Individual instructional preferences exist and the impact of accommodating these preferences can be measured reliably and validly.

- The stronger the preference, the more important it is to provide compatible instructional strategies.

- Accommodating individual learning style preferences (through complementary instructional and counselling interventions, environmental design and resources) results in increased academic achievement and improved student attitudes toward learning.

- Students whose strong preferences are matched attain statistically higher scores in attainment and attitude than students with mismatched treatments.

- Most teachers can learn to use a diagnosis of learning style preferences as the cornerstone of their instruction.

- Most students can learn to capitalise on their learning style strengths when concentrating on new or difficult academic material.

- The less academically successful the individual, the more important it is to accommodate learning style preferences.

- There are characteristic patterns of preference in special groups, particularly the 'gifted' and 'low achievers'.

Claims made for patterns of preference and abilities in gifted students are summarised in Table 5 above, together with references to studies that claim these patterns.

However, the notion of 'gifted' varies between the three reports that use it to measure ability, as do the outcomes that emerge from the preferences. Pyryt, Sandals and Begorya (1998, 76) advised caution about these patterns since, although differences were found between gifted students, average ones and students with learning difficulties or disabilities, 'the magnitude of group differences is small'. Burns, Johnson and Gable (1998) found that while statistically significant differences were found between gifted and average students, the elements of the LSI associated with giftedness were different in each study. They concluded (1998, 280) that 'it is difficult to accept the idea that the population of academically able students share common learning styles preferences'.

We have attempted to draw from the literature any instances in which the preferences tend to 'cluster', but the reporting of data has not enabled us to ascertain the strength of preferences that might interact with each other. Where scores are reported, their interpretation appears rather loose. For example, Gadt-Johnson and Price (2000) reported that tactile learners in their large sample of over 25,000 children in grades 5–12 have associated preferences for the 'kinaesthetic', 'auditory', 'intake', 'learn in several ways', 'less conforming', 'teacher motivated' and 'parent motivated' elements. It is only later in the reporting of this research that it becomes clear that none of these 'associated preferences' was represented by a score of more than 60 or less than 40; that is, they were not high or low preferences as defined by the model.

Supporters of the model offer detailed prescriptions for teaching various types of student: for example, they report that 'globals' appear to need more encouragement; short, varied tasks (because of their lower motivation); and when faced with new and difficult information, it should be interesting, related to their lives and allow them to become actively involved. Advice covers individuals and groups, classroom management, lesson pace, activity, kinaesthetics and sequencing of material. Advice is related directly to different types of learner; for example, the idea that underachievers, 'at risk' and dropout students are almost exclusively tactual/kinaesthetic learners (see eg Dunn 1990c). Supporters also offer advice for other preferences. For example, students who learn better with sound should have music without lyrics as opposed to melodies with words, while baroque appears to cause better responsiveness than rock, and students who prefer light should have soft, not bright, light. The empirical basis for a distinction between the effects of different musical genres and quality of lighting is not given.

There is also detailed advice for developing flexible and attractive environmental conditions; for example:

Redesign conventional classrooms with cardboard boxes, bookshelves, and other useable items placed perpendicular to the walls to make quiet, well-lit areas and, simultaneously, sections for controlled interaction and soft lighting. Permit students to work in chairs, on carpeting, on beanbag chairs, or on cushions, or seated against the wall, as long as they pay attention and perform better than they have previously. Turn the lights off and read in natural day light with underachievers or whenever the class becomes restless.
(Dunn 1990b, 229)

Such advice derives from empirical evidence from studies cited by Dunn as supporting her model (see Dunn and Griggs 2003).

Several books offer advice through examples of how particular schools have transformed seating, decor, classroom planning and timetabling in order to respond to students' preferences as expressed through the LSI (see eg Dunn and Griggs 1988). These offer detailed 'before and after' vignettes of schools, their students, local communities and learning environments as well as 'The How-to Steps'. In addition, the Dunn, Klavas and Ingham (1990) *Homework prescription* software package is offered to provide 'a series of directions for studying and doing homework based on each individual's … scores' (Dunn and Stevenson 1997, 336) which, it is claimed, increases student achievement and reduces anxiety (Nelson *et al.* 1993; Lenehan *et al.* 1994). These studies, however, are open to the criticism that the observed benefits reflect a '*level* of intervention' effect rather than a '*nature* of intervention' effect, since all groups received 'traditional instruction' and the most successful group had 'homework prescriptions' as an *additional* element. This suggests that success may be attributed to the greatest *quantity* of input; the methodological problems of catalytic validity and the 'Hawthorne Effect' are also likely to play an important part.

Empirical evidence of pedagogical impact

Reporting on a meta-analysis of 36 experimental studies based on the LSI and PEPS with different groups of students, Dunn *et al.* (1995) claimed a mean effect size equivalent to a mean difference of 0.75 – described as 'in the medium to large range'. Of the 36 studies, only six examined the effect sizes of the Dunn and Dunn model as a whole, while the remaining 30 focused on one of the four sub-areas of the inventory (environmental, emotional, sociological, physiological). For example, of the two studies in the emotional sub-area, Napolitano (1986) focused exclusively on the 'need for structure' element, while White (1981) looked more broadly at 'selected elements of emotional learning style'.

The largest mean effect size found relates to the 14 studies in the physiological sub-area (n=1656). Five studies which relate specifically to modality preference yield a mean effect size of about 1.4 and four studies on time-of-day preference average out to 0.9.

In terms of analytic and global processing, a significant difference in test scores was found for students described as 'simultaneous processors' when they were matched with two kinds of 'global' instructional materials (Dunn *et al.* 1990).

A more recent and extensive meta-analysis was carried out at St John's University, New York, by Lovelace (2003). This included many of the earlier studies (from 1980 onwards) and the overall results were similar to those reported above. The mean weighted effect sizes for matching students' learning style preferences with complementary instruction were 0.87 for achievement (131 effect sizes) and 0.85 for attitude (37 effect sizes).

We certainly cannot dismiss all of the experimental studies which met the inclusion criteria used in these meta-analyses. However, we detect a general problem with the design of many of the empirical studies supporting the Dunn and Dunn learning styles model. According to the model, the extent to which particular elements should be tackled depends upon the scores of students within a particular learning group. However, many of the dissertations that are the basis of the supporting research focus on individual elements in the model, and appear to have chosen that element in advance of testing the preferences of the experimental population and sometimes only include students with strong preferences. In addition, the studies often test one preference and then combine results from single studies to claim overall validity.

The only study we have found that applies the Dunn and Dunn model in the UK was carried out by Klein *et al.* (2003a, 2003b); the intervention took place in two FE colleges, with another two acting as a control group. Teachers were trained to use the PEPS with 120 first-year and 139 second-year students taking an intermediate level General National Vocational Qualification (GNVQ). The researchers claimed a positive impact on achievement and motivation, but withdrawal rates did not show a statistically significant difference between the intervention and the comparison group, at 52% and 49% respectively. In relation to the final GNVQ grade, just over 40% gained a 'pass' and 8% a 'merit' in the intervention group, while 60% gained a 'pass' and 8% a 'merit' in the comparison group. In initial and final basic skills tests, the intervention group's performance improved, but the comparison group's improvement was statistically significant. However, attendance in the intervention group was significantly higher than in the comparison group, as were students' positive perceptions of the quality of their work. The report used data from observations and interviews with staff and students to show increased enjoyment, class control and motivation.

Our evaluation of this research raises questions about research design and conclusions. For example, the study did not control for a 'Hawthorne Effect' and so it is unclear whether positive responses were due to novelty, the variety of aids and new teaching methods and a more empathetic and flexible approach from teachers. Any intervention that offers an enthusiastic new approach and attention from researchers in a context where there is little management interest and few resources for staff development might have similar effects. Variables such as college culture, staffing and degree of management support were not controlled for, yet such factors are likely to affect the performance of the two groups.

Caution is also needed in commending students' positive evaluations of their own work when their final grades remained poor. Our review suggests that research should take into account the impact of the model and consider the very different cultures of colleges and the fact that teachers in further education deal with diverse classes, have very little control over important factors (such as time of day and environment), are frequently part-time and have been subjected to repeated changes in curricula, organisation and funding (see Coffield *et al.* 2004, Section 2). Finally, as Klein *et al.* (2003a, 2003b) confirmed, the intervention did not raise achievement and retention rates. Indeed, the performance of the intervention group was poorer than that of the comparison group, suggesting the possibility that an intervention that focuses too much on process as opposed to subject knowledge and skills could militate against higher achievement. Withdrawal, attendance and achievement rates on many vocational courses in FE colleges are poor. Perhaps the focus of attention should be on these more fundamental problems in further education, since they are highly unlikely to be ameliorated by the administration of a learning styles instrument.

Conclusions

A number of strengths in the Dunn and Dunn model emerge from this review. First, it offers a positive, inclusive affirmation of the learning potential of all students, based on a belief that anyone can benefit from education if their preferences are catered for. This view of learning, and particularly of individuals who have not succeeded in the education system, encourages teachers to ask themselves an insightful and critical question, namely: how can we teach our students if we do not know how they learn?

Second, the model encourages teachers to respect difference, instead of regarding students who fail to learn as 'stupid' or 'difficult'. In contrast to an educational culture in the UK that labels learners as either of 'low' or 'high' ability, the model encourages teachers to reject negative judgements about learners and to see them as able to learn in different ways, providing that the methods of teaching change. The approach encourages learners and teachers to believe that it does not matter *how* people learn as long as they *do* learn.

Third, the model has support among practitioners and encourages a range of teaching and assessment techniques, as well as flexibility and imagination in designing resources and in changing environmental conditions. It suggests to teachers that many of their teaching problems will diminish if they change their focus and begin to respond more sensitively to the different learning preferences of their students. The model pressurises teachers to re-examine their own learning and teaching styles and to consider the possibility that they are appropriate for a minority of students, but seriously inappropriate for a majority.

Fourth, the model encourages teachers and students to talk about learning and gives them a language (eg kinaesthetic) which may legitimise behaviour, such as moving about the room, that was previously stigmatised as disruptive.

Despite these strengths, our evaluation highlights serious concerns about the model, its application and the quality of the answers it purports to offer about how to improve learning. First, the model is based on the idea that preferences are relatively fixed and, in the case of some elements, constitutionally based. Our continuum of learning styles (see Figure 4) shows that other models are not based on fixed traits, but instead on approaches and strategies that are context-specific, fluid and amenable to change. Moreover, references to brain research, time-of-day and modality preferences in the Dunn and Dunn model are often at the level of popular assertion and not supported by scientific evidence.

Second, a view that preferences are fixed or typical of certain groups may lead to labelling and generalising in the literature that supports the model (eg Dunn 2003c). In addition, a belief that people should work with their strong preferences and avoid their weak ones suggests that learners work with a comforting profile of existing preferences matched to instruction. This is likely to lead to self-limiting behaviour and beliefs rather than openness to new styles and preferences. Although the model offers a language about learning, it is a restricted one.

Furthermore, despite claims for the benefits of 'matching', it is not clear whether matching is desirable in subjects where learners need to develop new or complex preferences or different types of learning style altogether. Supporters of the model make the general claim that working with preferences is necessary at the beginning of something new or difficult, but this is unlikely to be true of all subjects or levels. Nor does this assertion take account of a need to develop new preferences once one is familiar with a subject. A preoccupation with matching learning and teaching styles could also divert teachers from developing their own and students' subject skills. The amount of contact time between teachers and students is increasingly limited and the curricula of many post-16 qualifications in the UK system are becoming more prescriptive. Time and energy spent organising teaching and learning around preferences is likely to take time away from developing students' knowledge of different subjects.

The individualisation of matching in the model could also detract from what learners have in common or discourage teachers from challenging learners to work differently and to remedy weaknesses. Although the model fits well with growing interest in individualisation in the UK system as 'good practice', our review of this issue in Coffield *et al.* (2004, Section 4), suggests that ideas about matching individual learning needs and styles tend to be treated simplistically by policy-makers, inspectors and practitioners.

Third, supporters claim that a self-report measure is 'objective'. We have to ask how far objective measurement is possible when many learners have limited self-awareness of their behaviour and attitudes in learning situations. This fact may help to explain why it is so difficult to devise reliable self-report instruments.

A further difficulty is that a large number of the studies examined for this review evaluated only one preference in a test or short intervention. For this reason, there is a need for longitudinal evaluation (lasting for months rather than days or weeks) of the reliability and validity of students' preferences, both within and outside learning style interventions. Since supporters claim reliability and validity to promote its widespread use as a *scientifically robust* model, evaluation should be carried out by external, independent researchers who have no interest in promoting it.

There are also particular difficulties for non-specialists in evaluating this model. Until a number of studies have been read in the original, the nature of the sources which are repeatedly cited in long lists by the model's authors and supporters does not become apparent. Academic conventions of referencing mask this problem. For example, Collinson (2000) quotes at length one study by Shaughnessy (1998) to support claims for the LSI, but the original source is a rather glowing interview with Rita Dunn in a teachers' magazine. It is therefore important to evaluate critically the evidence used to make sweeping claims about transforming education.

Fourth, claims made for the model are excessive. In sum, the Dunn and Dunn model has the appearance and status of a total belief system, with the following claims being made.

- It is relevant to, and successful with, all age groups from children in kindergarten through middle school, secondary school, university or college and on to mature, professional adults.

- It is successful with students who have strong, moderate and mixed degrees of environmental preference.

- Using teaching strategies that are congruent with students' learning styles leads to statistically significant higher scores in academic attainment, attitudes to learning and behaviour.

- Higher scores in attainment, attitudes and behaviour have been achieved with students at all academic levels from those with learning difficulties or disabilities through low-achieving, to average and gifted students.

- It has been successfully implemented in urban, suburban and rural schools; in public, private and combined schools.

- It is effective with all subject areas from those taught in school to those taught in higher education; for example, allied health professions, anatomy, bacteriology, biology, business studies, education, engineering, health information management, law, legal writing, marketing, mathematics, music, nursing, physics, sonography and study skills.

- In higher education, 'most students will retain more knowledge ... for a longer period of time ... enjoy learning more ... and college retention rates will increase' (Mangino and Griggs 2003,185).

- It is supported by 'approximately 800 studies conducted by a) researchers at more than 120 institutions of higher education ... b) practitioners throughout the United States ... and c) The United States government' (Dunn 2003d, 269).

Fifth, the main author of the model and her supporters generalise about the learning of whole groups without supporting evidence. For example, Rita Dunn has argued recently that 'it is not the *content* that determines whether students master the curriculum; rather, it is *how that content is taught*' (2003d, 270; original emphasis). There are, however, numerous, interacting reasons why students fail to learn and process is only one of them. Similarly, one of Dunn's successful higher-degree students claimed that '*Auditory* learners remember three quarters of the information they hear by listening to a teacher, a tape or recording, or other students. *Visual* learners retain three quarters of the information they see' (Roberts 2003, 93; original emphasis). Such overblown claims only serve to give the research field of learning styles a bad name. It may, however, be argued that such assertions can and should be dismissed, but those who have become champions of the Dunn and Dunn model speak the language of conviction and certainty; for example, 'it is mandatory that educators provide global ... and tactual and kinaesthetic resources' (Burke 2003,102).

Sixth, supporters do not appear to consider the problem of *catalytic validity*, where the impact of an intervention is affected significantly by the enthusiasm of its implementers.

In the light of these problems, independent evaluation is crucial in a UK context, where the DfES is showing an interest in the model as a way to improve teaching and learning. In the face of poor motivation and achievement in further education, there is no evidence that the model is either a desirable basis for learning or the best use of investment, teacher time, initial teacher education and professional development.

Finally, the model is promoted by its chief protagonist, Rita Dunn, as though it were incapable of being falsified. For example, she and her co-authors write: 'It is immoral and it should be illegal for certified teachers to negatively classify children who learn differently, instead of teaching them the way they learn' (Dunn *et al.* 1991). It is apparently '*inconceivable* ... that communities, parents and the judiciary would permit schools to function conventionally and continue to damage global, tactual, kinaesthetic children who need Mobility (sic) and informal classroom environments to function effectively' (Dunn 2003d, 269; original emphasis). It is exactly this inability of Rita Dunn to conceive that other professionals have the right to think and act differently from the injunctions of the model that constitutes its most serious weakness. This anti-intellectual flaw makes the Dunn and Dunn model unlike any other evaluated in this review.

Table 6
Dunn and Dunn's
model and instruments
of learning styles

	Strengths	Weaknesses
General	A user-friendly model that includes motivational factors, social interaction, physiological and environmental elements.	The model makes simplistic connections between physiological and psychological preferences and brain activity.
Design of the model	■ High or low preferences for 22 different factors are identified by learners. ■ Strong preferences form the basis for teachers to adopt specific techniques or make environmental changes to areas such as light, sound, design, time of day or mobility.	■ It is a model of instructional preferences, not learning. ■ It is unsophisticated in its adoption of ideas from other fields, eg modality preference, circadian rhythm, hemispheric dominance. ■ Training courses and manuals simply list large numbers of studies where preferences are either prioritised or connected to others. Practitioners therefore have to take the theoretical support on trust.
Reliability	Supporters make strong claims for reliability.	Critics highlight major problems with the design and reliability of key instruments.
Validity	Supporters make strong claims for validity	There have been external criticisms of evidence of validity.
Implications for pedagogy	It is claimed that: ■ individual differences in preference can be discerned ■ it is possible to adapt environments and pedagogy to meet these preferences ■ the stronger the preference, the more effect an intervention will have ■ the impact will be even greater if low-achieving learners' strong preferences are catered for.	■ The implications for pedagogy are so forcefully expressed that no other options are considered. ■ Labelling and generalising about types of student may lead to simplistic injunctions about 'best practice'.
Evidence of pedagogical impact	■ The model has generated an extensive programme of international research. ■ Isolation of individual elements in empirical studies allows for evaluation of the effects of those elements.	■ Effect sizes of individual elements are conflated. ■ There is a serious lack of independent evaluation of the LSI.
Overall assessment	Despite a large and evolving research programme, forceful claims made for impact are questionable because of limitations in many of the supporting studies and the lack of independent research on the model. Concerns raised in our review need to be addressed before further use is made of the model in the UK.	
Key source	Dunn and Griggs 2003	

Section 4

The cognitive structure family

Introduction

The group of theorists summarised in this section have been clustered because we consider that they have a shared view (implicitly or explicitly expressed) of learning styles as 'structural properties of the cognitive system itself' (Messick 1984, 60). They also, as Riding and Rayner (1998) note, concentrate on the interactions of cognitive controls and cognitive processes.

For this group, styles are not merely habits, with the changeability that this implies; rather, 'styles are more like generalised habits of thought, not simply the tendency towards specific acts ... but rather the enduring structural basis for such behaviour.' (Messick 1984, 61) and as such, are not particularly susceptible to training. For this reason, many of these styles are very similar to measures of ability. For the theorists in this family, styles are linked to particular personality features, with the implication that cognitive styles are deeply embedded in personality structure.

Descriptions, origins and scope of the instruments

The theorists from this family who are mentioned in this overview are listed in Table 7 below. The learning styles in this family tend to be expressed as bipolar constructs. For many in the cognitive structure family, there is a strong intellectual influence from psychotherapy; for example, Kagan and Kogan (1970, 1276) paraphrase Klein (1958):

cognitive structures intervene between drives and environmental demands. It is because cognitive structures are conceived to have a steering and modulating function in respect to both drives and situational requirements that Klein has given them the designation of 'cognitive control principles'.

The importance of drives – Freud's pleasure/reality principle and Anna Freud's ***defence mechanisms*** – are particularly evident in the learning styles models developed by Holzman and Klein (1954), Hunt *et al.* (1978) and Gardner and Long (1962). The descriptors – 'constricted/flexible', 'need for structure' and 'tolerant/intolerant' – reveal the authors' engagement with issues of learning security and intellectual 'comfort zones'.

Table 7

Learning-styles instruments in the cognitive structure family

Author (date)	Instrument	Principal descriptors
Witkin (1962)	Rod and Frame Test	***field dependence-independence***
Witkin (1971)	Group Embedded Figures Test (GEFT)	
Kagan (1963, 1966)	Conceptual Style Test (CST)	analytic-descriptive/relational/ inferential-categorical
Kagan (1967)	Matching Familiar Figures Test	impulsivity/reflexivity
		focus/scan (focus: facts and examples; scan: principles and concepts)
Guilford (1967)		cognitive attitudes
Gardner *et al.* (1953, 1962)	Free Sorting Test	equivalence range
		tolerance for unrealistic experiences
Pettigrew (1958)	Category Width Scale	broad/narrow
Holzman and Klein (1954)	Schematising Test	leveller/sharpener (constricted/flexible control)
Hunt (1978)	Paragraph Completion Method	need for structure: conforming/dependent
Hudson (1966)		convergent-divergent thinking
Broverman (1960)	Stroop Word Colour Inference Test	limits of learning, automisation

The most influential member of the cognitive structure group is Witkin, whose bipolar dimensions of field dependence/field independence have had considerable influence on the learning styles discipline, both in terms of the exploration of his own constructs and the reactions against it which have led to the development of other learning styles descriptors and instruments. The educational implications of field dependence/independence (FDI) have been explored mainly in the curriculum areas of second-language acquisition, mathematics, natural and social sciences (see Tinajero and Paramo 1998a for a review of this evidence), although its vogue as a purely learning styles instrument has arguably passed. However, FDI remains an important concept in the understanding of individual differences in motor skills performance (Brady 1995) and musical discrimination (Ellis 1996).

Three tests are used to study FD and FI: the Rod and Frame Test, the Body Adjustment Test and the Group Embedded Figures Test. The Rod and Frame Test involves sitting the participant in a dark room. The participant can see a luminous rod in a luminous frame. The frame is tilted and the participant is asked to make the rod vertical. Some participants move the rod so that it is in alignment with the tilted frame; others succeed in making the rod vertical. The former participants take their cues from the environment (the surrounding field) and are described as 'field dependent'; the latter are uninfluenced by the surrounding field (the frame) and are described as 'field independent'.

The Body Adjustment Test is similar to the Rod and Frame Test in that it also involves space orientation. The participant is seated in a tilted room and asked to sit upright. Again, field-dependent participants sit in alignment with the room, while field-independent participants sit upright, independent of the angle of the room. The Group Embedded Figures Test is a paper and pencil test. The participant is shown a geometric shape and is then shown a complex shape which contains the original shape 'hidden' somewhere. The field-independent person can quickly find the original shape because they are not influenced by the surrounding shapes; the opposite is true of the field-dependent person. The authors claim that results from the three tests are highly correlated with each other (Witkin and Goodenough 1981).

Davies (1993, 223) summarises the claims made by the authors for field dependence/independence: 'According to Witkin and Goodenough (1981), field independents are better than field dependents at tasks requiring the breaking up of an organised stimulus context into individual elements and/or the re-arranging of the individual elements to form a different organisation.'

Measurement of the instruments

Overall, there are two key issues in relation to the cognitive structure learning styles: the conflation of style with ability and the validity of the bipolar structure of many of the measures.

Style and ability

While he reports that measures of cognitive style appear to have test–retest reliability, Messick (1984, 59) considers that there is an 'unresolved question … the extent to which the empirical consistencies attributed to cognitive styles are instead a function of intellective abilities', since cognitive styles are assessed with what he calls 'ability-like measures'. In particular, he argues (1984, 63) that measurements of field independence and field dependence are too dependent on ability: 'by linking global style to low analytical performance, field dependence is essentially measured by default.'

That this weakness of the cognitive structure family appears to be particularly true of Witkin is borne out by empirical studies: 'the embarrassing truth of the matter is that various investigators have found significant relations between the Witkin indexes, on the one hand, and measures of verbal, mathematical and spatial skills, on the other.' (Kogan 1973, 166). Indeed, Federico and Landis, in their analysis of field dependence, category width and 22 other measures of cognitive characteristics, found (1984, 152) that 'all cognitive styles except reflection-impulsivity are significantly related to ability and/or aptitudes. Field independence has more (ie 10) significant correlations [ranging from 0.15 to 0.34] with abilities and aptitudes than any other style'. Huang and Chao (2000) found that in a small study (n=60, mean age 17), students with learning disabilities were more likely to be field dependent than a matched group of 'average' students. Indeed, the construction of field dependence as a disability in itself is highlighted by Tinajero et al. (1993) who report on studies from the field of neuropsychology which attempt to link field dependence with cerebral injury, though the question as to which hemisphere is injured is an unresolved one. The theorists in the cognitive structure family take great pains to differentiate between ability and style – 'Abilities concern level of skill – the more and less of performance – whereas cognitive styles give greater weight to the *manner* and *form* of cognition' (Kogan 1973, 244; original emphasis) – but we are forced to conclude that if the measures used to assess style are too closely linked to ability tasks, then we may have what Henry Fielding in *Tom Jones* memorably describes as 'a distinction without a difference'.

Table 8 Kogan's classification of learning styles Source: Kogan (1973)	**Type 1**	Maximal performance measures	These instruments measure style overtly or implicitly in terms of accuracy of performance (eg Witkin's field dependence/independence and Gardner's restricted/flexible control).
	Type 2	Value-directional measures	These measures, while not dependent on accuracy of performance for their scoring, nevertheless have a distinct preference for one dimension over another (eg Kagan's analytic-non-analytic dimensions, Guilford's ideational fluency [creativity measure]).
	Type 3	Value-differentiated measures	This third group of measures is designed to be 'most purely stylistic' by describing a range of behaviours which are not deemed to be intrinsically more or less advantageous (eg Pettigrew's broad/narrow categorisation).

In an attempt to engage with this problem, Kogan (1973, 161) presented a view of styles in terms of a 'threefold classification … in terms of their respective distance from the construct of ability' as shown in Table 8 above.

However, Kogan points out (1973, 162) that while the third style may be 'value neutral' in conception, 'As construct validation proceeds and extrinsic correlates are examined, it is entirely feasible that an initially value-free cognitive style will assimilate value properties which will render it formally indistinguishable from the second type of style'. Indeed, the pursuit of 'value-free' measures of learning leaves the theorist vulnerable to omitting both the social structures within learning environments and the socially desirable factors associated with the 'ideal learner' which are created within these environments.

To give one example from the research literature, Schuller (1998) uses Pettigrew's (1958) instrument, described by Kogan as at least potentially value differentiated. However, Schuller's description (1998, 250) of the measure does show evidence of values:

The extreme – the broad categoriser – attains better results in tasks where he/she can better use integrated holistic strategies. The narrow categoriser is superior in tasks which require detail or analytical information processing. In general, the narrow categoriser has a tendency to be careful, is rigid and has high certainty in cognitive decision making; narrow categorisation reflects intellectual passivity. The broad categoriser manifests greater independence and the need for 'freedom' and variety of experiences.

The perceived inferiority of field dependence is highlighted by Hergovitch (2003, 207) who, reporting on a relationship between FD, superstition and suggestibility, concludes that 'Field independents, who can organise and structure the world by themselves, don't need external references … Field dependents function less autonomously'.

While Kogan's distinction between styles (see Table 8) is helpful in some respects, it has problems of its own in terms of hierarchy. Guilford (1980) points out that Kogan's Type 2 'half-way house', which contains Guilford's fluency measure, collapses back into Type 1, since fluency is merely another form of performance to be measured; this criticism could also apply to Kagan's Matching Familiar Figures Test (1966). It is clear that, in his desire to differentiate between ability and style, Kogan disfavours those styles which can be more readily confused with ability measures, regardless of the intent of the authors. For example, he categorises Gardner and Holzman and Klein as Type 1 styles, since the effect of experience and increased expertise tends to improve the ability to generate distinctions and categories, while Sternberg and Grigorenko (2001) make a distinction between equivalence range as a measure of preference and as a measure of cognitive complexity.

The true bipolarity of these instruments is particularly important in terms of differentiating style and ability: Guilford (1980, 716) makes the point that 'Abilities are unipolar traits while styles are bipolar. Abilities are narrower in scope. Abilities are measured in terms of *level* of performance, where styles are measured by degree of some *manner* of performance.'

Here too, however, there is some disagreement. Messick (1984) considers that the use of a relatively independent measure for both converging and diverging makes Hudson's (1966) model genuinely bipolar. Meanwhile, Meredith (1985) finds that focus-scan is in fact not wholly bipolar: that the scan strategy has greater predictive power than the focus strategy, and that both are more predictive of educational outcomes and course satisfaction than teacher style.

Table 9
Studies of the interaction of field independence and attainment with learners aged 14+ years

Source: Tinajero and Paramo (1998a)

Achievement in:	FI subjects perform better (number of studies)	Non-significant results (number of studies)
Second-language acquisition	8	0
Mathematics	6	1
Natural sciences	11	3
Social sciences	3	0

Implications for pedagogy

There is an underlying assumption from the theorists in this family that cognitive styles are not particularly amenable to change, since the idea of cognitive structure implies deep-seated and relatively fixed traits. The obvious implications for pedagogy, therefore, concern issues of diagnosis and 'matching', or compensation for the disadvantages of, typically, field dependence. However, Saracho (1998b, 288) warns of the dangers of matching FD students with 'socially oriented learning tasks' and FI students with 'abstract and less social assignments'. She argues (1998b, 289) that: 'students could be denied the opportunity to learn the broad range of intellectual skills they need to function in society. Discrepancies among students would be amplified and students could be restricted by stereotyped expectations of what they can achieve.'

In order to give teachers meaningful information about students, cognitive structure learning styles should be demonstrably different from measures of ability. As shown in Table 9, Tinajero and Paramo (1998a) demonstrate that field independence is a good predictor of performance.

'With the exception of Witkin *et al.* (1977), all studies of the relationship between FDI and overall achievement. have indicated that field independent subjects perform better' (Tinajero and Paramo 1998a, 237).

Tinajero and Paramo (1997, 1998b) are typical of later FDI advocates in that they willingly accept the interaction of field independence and achievement and focus their attention, in terms of implications for pedagogy, on ways of exploring field-dependent students' strategies in order to improve their performance.

Gender differences in the relationship between field independence and self-esteem are reported by Bosacki, Innerd and Towson (1997). They posit (1997, 692) that '[field independent] Attributes such as autonomy and analytic thinking may be more valued by society and, because they are traditionally masculine, may be more reinforced in males than females'. Thus, in this study, while there were no overall differences in self-esteem by gender, FI girls were more likely to have lower self-esteem, but FI boys more likely to have higher self-esteem. The authors urge caution in the use of descriptors or idealised behaviours which are limiting rather than empowering for pupils.

Field-dependent individuals are described as more reliant on external referents and, as we have seen, this is generally interpreted negatively by researchers investigating achievement and cognitive function. However, the social abilities of field-dependent subjects may be advantageous in some aspects of learning. In a small study, Johnson, Prior and Artuso (2000) make the link between second-language acquisition and field dependence, although their measure of attainment (greater communicative production) is not the same as that employed in other studies of attainment in second-language acquisition (which tend to use test scores).

Glicksohn and Bozna (2000), although studying an esoteric sample of bomb-disposal experts and anti-terrorist operatives, make explicit the link between prosocial FD preferences and autonomous FI preferences in governing career choice, when other predisposing factors – in this instance, thrill-seeking behaviours – are taken into account.

Davies' (1993) findings that FD subjects are more vulnerable to 'hindsight bias' – that is, the inability to imagine alternative outcomes once a result is known – are attributed to a 'rigidity in information processing' which reduces FD subjects' ability to 'engage in cognitive restructuring' (1993, 233). This suggests that FD learners might need additional support in tasks requiring imaginative flexibility.

Empirical evidence of pedagogical impact

There is little strong evidence for improved outcomes for any of the styles in this family.

Meredith is unable to find links between focus/scan (Kagan and Krathwohl 1967) and student appraisal of instructional effectiveness which were strong enough to support predictions, and concludes (1981, 620) that: 'Though research on learning styles and orientations are [sic] intriguing, there is scant evidence that these "cognitive styles" are strongly linked to instructor/course evaluations.'

Peer matching and mismatching research on 64 dyads by Frank and Davis (1982) implies that FI individuals can lift the performance of an FD partner, while Saracho and Dayton (1980) infer from their results that the impact of an FI teacher on both FI and FD students can be significantly greater than the impact of an FD teacher. However, this study was conducted with younger children and should be placed in the context that individuals tend to be more FD as children and to become more FI as they get older. Moreover, Saracho (1998a) found that FI teachers had a more positive view of their matched FI students than did FD teachers of FD students, thus giving rise to a possible confusion between positive effects due to FDI matching, and positive effects due to positive affect.

However, Garlinger and Frank (1986), in a meta-analysis of 'matching' studies relating to field dependence/independence, find that matching FD students with FD teachers does not increase attainment, although matching FI students with FI teachers does, but effect sizes for the post-16 samples are very small (0.21 for 386 community college students; 0.12 for 192 14–17 year olds).

Conclusions

It is a common criticism of the learning styles field that 'style research is peppered with unstable and inconsistent findings, while style theory seems either vague in glossing over inconsistencies or confused in stressing differential features selectively' (Messick 1984, 59).

Kagan and Kogan (1970, 1273) draw a favourable distinction between the battery of tests used by Cattell in the 1890s, measuring temporal awareness, sensory acuity and motor skills, and those used by their own contemporaries: 'The contemporary battery evaluates richness of language, reasoning, classification and perceptual synthesis and decision process.' But while they attribute the tests used by Victorians to 'the intellectual prejudices of the nineteenth century', they do not explicitly recognise that late 20th century definitions of cognition are equally influenced by social and economic *mores*.

They are keen to link their conceptions of cognitive functioning, at least analogously, with the language of genetics – citing environment-specific behaviour as similar to pleiotropy (one gene, many effects) and multi-determined behaviours/polygeny (many genes, single development). In doing this, they want (1970, 1275) to link thematically with the 'hard sciences':

The laws of biology, chemistry and physics consist, in the starkest sense, of collections of functional statements about entities. In biology the cell and the gene are basic units. In chemistry the molecule and the atom ... In physics, particles and planets are units ... Psychology's units may turn out to be cognitive structures, and laws about cognitive process will describe how these units function.

Many members of this group express a desire for a meta-**taxonomy**.

Messick (1984, 66) argues that a comprehensive view of cognitive style:

*would include broad versus narrow categorising; complexity versus simplicity and the closely related constructs of conceptual level and integrative complexity; field independence versus field dependence (or field sensitivity); **levelling** versus **sharpening**; scanning versus focussing; converging versus diverging; automatization versus restructuring; reflection versus impulsivity and possibly risk taking versus cautiousness.*

However, some theorists have moved on from cognitive styles and structures into new theories of intelligence, albeit shaped by ideas of style; for example, Guilford's Structure of Intellect model (1967, 1977) and Gardner's Multiple Intelligences theory (1983, 1993). Kogan's complaint (1973, 177) that 'The real-world referents of cognitive styles outside the context of formal schooling have simply not been spelled out in any systematic fashion' has not been addressed by empirical work stemming directly from this family of learning styles.

Researchers have drawn on the work of the cognitive structure family before moving away to focus more specifically on approaches and strategies for learning. Given the increasing focus on the strategies which are peculiar to FI and FD students and which may, therefore, underpin good or poor performance (Tinajero and Paramo 1998b), it may be logical to suggest that the intellectual heirs of the cognitive structure family may be Entwistle (see Section 7.1) and Vermunt (see Section 7.2).

4.1
Riding's model of cognitive style and his Cognitive Styles Analysis (CSA)

Richard Riding is director of the Assessment Research Unit at the University of Birmingham's School of Education. He has extensively researched cognitive style, learning design and personality and is joint editor of the journal *Educational Psychology*. He markets the Cognitive Styles Analysis (CSA) privately through Learning and Training Technology.

Definitions, description and scope

Riding and Rayner (1998, 7–8) define cognitive style as 'the way the individual person thinks' and as 'an individual's preferred and habitual approach to organising and representing information'. They define learning strategy as 'those processes which are used by the learner to respond to the demands of a learning activity'. To distinguish between cognitive style and learning strategy, Riding and Cheema (1991, 195–196) claim that: 'Strategies may vary from time to time, and may be learned and developed. Styles, by contrast are static and are relatively in-built features of the individual.'

Riding and Rayner (1998) do not define learning style, but group models of learning style in terms of their emphasis on:

- experiential learning
- orientation to study
- instructional preference
- the development of cognitive skills and learning strategies.

They state that their own model is directed primarily at how cognitive skills develop, and claim that it has implications for orientation to study, instructional preference and experiential learning, as well as for social behaviour and managerial performance.

The structure of Riding's model and of his computerised assessment tool, the CSA, is two-dimensional. The model has two independent (uncorrelated) dimensions, one relating to cognitive organisation (holist-analytic) and one relating to mental representation (verbal-imagery) (see Figure 6, based on Riding and Rayner 1998). It is important to note that the verbaliser-imager dimension is intended to measure a natural tendency to process information quickly in verbal or in visual form, not to indicate the relative strength of verbal and visual cognitive abilities as measured by intelligence tests. With both dimensions, the concern is with speed of reaction and processing rather than with accuracy.

Riding and Cheema (1991) claim that previous models of cognitive/learning style can be accommodated within their two-dimensional framework and that the differences between models are largely matters of labelling. For example, they claim that their holist-analytic dimension is essentially the same as Entwistle's surface-deep dimension and Hudson's diverger-converger dimension. These claims rest almost completely on conceptual 'analysis', but have some empirical support in the form of a factor analysis carried out by Riding and Dyer (1983) on data collected from 150 12 year olds.

Figure 6
The two dimensions of the CSA

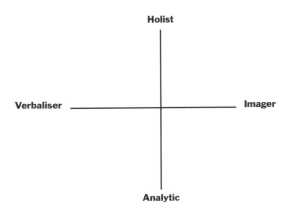

Origins

The theoretical basis for Riding's work is diverse, as he seeks to encompass many other models. Riding and Buckle (1990) state that the holist-analytic dimension derives from the work of Witkin (1962) on field dependence and field independence. The verbal-imagery dimension is related to Paivio's dual coding theory (1971) and aligned by Glass and Riding (1999) with the neuropsychological evidence that language is predominantly a left-brain function, while visual thinking tends to be accompanied by more right-brain activity. On the basis of two early studies, Riding thought that the verbal-imagery dimension was also related to introversion-extraversion, with introverts tending to be imagers and extraverts to be verbalisers, but he later found no relationship between these qualities in a large sample of FE students (Riding and Wigley 1997).

The Cognitive Styles Analysis (CSA)

Description of the measure

Riding (1991a, 1991b, 1998a, 1998b) has developed a computerised assessment method called the Cognitive Styles Analysis (CSA). This is not a self-report measure, but presents cognitive tasks in such a way that it is not evident to the participant exactly what is being measured. The test items in the CSA for the holist-analytic dimension are all visual, and the scoring is based on a comparison of speed of response (not accuracy) on a matching task (holist preference) and on an embedded figures task (analytic preference). The items for the verbal-imagery dimension are all verbal and are based on relative speed of response to categorising items as being similar by virtue of their conceptual similarity (verbal preference) or colour (visual preference). The literacy demand of the verbal test is not high, as only single words are involved, but this has not been formally assessed. The instrument is suitable for use by adults and has been used in research studies with pupils as young as 9 years.

Reliability and validity

No information about the reliability of the CSA has been published by Riding. Using a sample of 50 undergraduates, Peterson, Deary and Austin (2003a) report that the short-term test–retest reliability of the CSA verbal-imager dimension is very low and statistically not significant (r=0.27), while that of the holist-analytic dimension is also unsatisfactory in psychometric terms (r=0.53, p<0.001). With 38 students who were retested on the CSA after 12 days, Redmond, Mullally and Parkinson (2002) reported a negative test–retest correlation for the verbal-imager dimension (r=–0.21) and a result of r=0.56 for the holist-analytic dimension. These studies provide the only evidence of reliability to date, despite more than a decade of research with the instrument. Riding's criticisms (2003a) of Peterson, Deary and Austin's study have been more than adequately answered by that study's authors (2003b).

As adequate test reliability has not been established, it is impossible to evaluate properly the many published studies in which construct, concurrent or predictive validity have been addressed. Riding (2003b) takes issue with this point, claiming that a test can be valid without being reliable. Yet he offers no reasons for suggesting that the CSA is valid when first administered, but not on later occasions. He claims that the CSA asks people to do simple cognitive tasks in a relaxed manner, so ensuring that they use their natural or 'default' styles. A counter-argument might be that people are often less relaxed in a new test situation, when they do not know how difficult the tasks will be.

The unreliability of the CSA may be one of the reasons why correlations of the holist-analytic and verbal-imagery ratios with other measures have often been close to zero. Examples of this include Riding and Wigley's (1997) study of the relationship between cognitive style and personality in FE students; the study by Sadler-Smith, Allinson and Hayes (2000) of the relationship between the holist-analytic dimension of the CSA and the intuition-analysis dimension of Allinson and Hayes' Cognitive Style Index (CSI), and Sadler-Smith and Riding's (1999) use of cognitive style to predict learning outcomes on a university business studies course.

Evaluation

Despite the appeal of simplicity, there are unresolved conceptual issues with Riding's model and serious problems with its accompanying test, the CSA.

Riding and Cheema (1991) argue that their holist-analytic dimension can be identified under different descriptors in many other typologies. However, being relatively quick at recognising a rectangle hidden in a set of superimposed outlines is not necessarily linked with valuing conceptual or verbal accuracy and detail, being a deep learner or having preference for convergent or stepwise reasoning. Analysis can mean different things at perceptual and conceptual levels and in different domains, such as cognitive and affective. In his taxonomy of educational objectives, Bloom (1956) views analysis as a simpler process than synthesis (which bears some resemblance to holistic thinking). Riding takes a rather different view, seeing holists as field-dependent and impulsive, unwilling to engage in complex analytical tasks. Another point of difference is that where Riding places analysis and synthesis as polar opposites, Bloom sees them as interdependent processes. We simply do not know enough about the interaction and interdependence of analytic and holistic thinking in different contexts to claim that they are opposites.

There are also conceptual problems with the verbaliser-imager dimension. Few tasks in everyday life make exclusive demands on either verbal or non-verbal processing, which are more often interdependent or integrated aspects of thinking. While there is convincing evidence from factor-analytic studies of cognitive ability for individual differences in broad and specific verbal and spatial abilities (eg Carroll 1993), this does not prove that people who are very competent verbally (or spatially) tend consistently to avoid other forms of thinking.

Further problems arise over the extent to which styles are fixed. Riding's definition of cognitive styles refers to both preferred and habitual processes, but he sees 'default' cognitive styles as incapable of modification. Here he differs from other researchers such as Vermunt (1996) and Antonietti (1999), both of whom emphasise the role of metacognition and of metacognitive training in modifying learning styles. For Riding, metacognition includes an awareness of cognitive styles and facilitates the development of a repertoire of learning *strategies* (not styles).

Riding seems to consider the 'default' position as being constant, rather than variable. He has not designed studies to look at the extent to which learners are capable of moving up and down cognitive style dimensions in accordance with task demands and motivation. Although he cautions against the dangers of labelling learners, he does not avoid this in his own writing.

Turning now to the CSA instrument, there are problems with basing the assessment of cognitive style on only one or two tasks and in using an exclusively verbal or non-verbal form of presentation for each dimension. The onus must be on the test constructor to show that consistent results are obtainable with different types of task and with both verbal and non-verbal presentation. There are also serious problems in basing the assessment on a ratio measure, as two sources of unreliability are present instead of one.

It is possible that the conceptual issues raised above can be resolved, and that the construct validity of Riding's model of cognitive styles may eventually prove more robust than the reliability of the CSA would suggest. As Riding and Cheema (1991) argue, similar dimensions or categories do appear in many other typologies. However, as things stand, our impression is that Riding has cast his net too wide and has not succeeded in arriving at a classification of learning styles that is consistent across tasks, consistent across levels of task difficulty and complexity, and independent of motivational and situational factors.

Implications for pedagogy

Riding (2002) claims that his model has important implications for many aspects of human behaviour. He believes that for less able learners, it is important to achieve a match between cognitive style, the way in which resources are structured and the teaching approach. At the same time, he acknowledges that many variables (especially working memory) interact with style to determine performance. He and his students and colleagues have carried out a large number of correlational and predictive studies focusing on learning outcomes, but it would be unwise to accept unreplicated findings in view of the problems of reliability indicated above. An instrument which is so inadequate in terms of test–retest reliability cannot be said to provide robust evidence for adopting particular strategies in post-16 learning and teaching. This point certainly holds for the CSA's highly unreliable verbal-imager measure, but it is possible that meaningful group differences may exist in relation to the holist-analytic measure, even though its reliability is at best modest.

Perhaps the most convincing study of the pedagogical implications of CSA scores in the post-16 sector is the one carried out by Sadler-Smith and Riding (1999) with 240 business studies students. Here it was found that holists favoured collaborative learning and the use of non-print materials such as overhead transparencies (OHTs), slides and videos. However, it is a step too far to move from this finding to the recommendation that students should be given what they prefer. Indeed, in a study of 112 GCSE Design and Technology students in eight schools, Atkinson (1998) found that holistic students who were taught by teachers using a collaborative approach obtained poorer grades than any other group.

A small-scale study of some interest is that by Littlemore (2001), who found a significant difference between 28 holistic and 20 analytic language students. The holists tended to make greater use of analogy when unable to find the correct word when naming pictures in a second language, whereas the analysts more often used analytic strategies, such as naming parts, uses or the functions of the objects. However, the differences were not large, and as all students made use of both types of strategy, there do not seem to be any instructional implications.

Riding *et al.* (2003, 167) acknowledge that in the past, 'studies of style effects have often not shown clear results or have shown relatively little effect'. They suggest that this may be because interactions between individual difference variables have not been widely studied. They report on interactions between cognitive style and working memory in 206 13 year olds, finding four significant effects out of 11 in the case of the holist-analytic dimension. Teacher ratings of learning behaviour and subject performance tended to be low for analytics who were below average on a working memory test, but high for analytics with above-average working memory scores. For holists, working memory was less clearly related to teacher ratings, except in mathematics.

There was no convincing evidence of a similar interaction effect for the verbaliser-visualiser dimension, with only one significant result out of 11 ANOVA (analysis of variance) analyses. This study needs replication, preferably with more reliable measures of cognitive style and using a test of working memory of known reliability and validity.

Positive evidence supporting the 'matching' hypothesis as applied to the global-analytic dimension in a computer-based learning environment comes from two small-scale studies by Ford (1995) and Ford and Chen (2001). These made use of two very carefully designed ways of teaching a classification task and HTML programming, each believed to suit different ways of learning. In the second experiment, it was found that, as predicted, global learners did significantly better with 'breadth first' and analytic learners did best with 'depth first' instruction. The effect sizes in these two experiments were large, and together, the findings should be taken seriously, despite the relatively small sample sizes (34 and 57 respectively).

With the exception of this last finding by independent researchers, there is a dearth of well-grounded empirical evidence to support the extensive range of pedagogical recommendations made by Riding (2002). The same is true of the set of profiles for each cognitive style which Riding (1994) has offered. These are set out in terms of:

- social attitude
- response to people
- decision making
- consistency and reliability
- managing and being managed
- learning and communication
- team roles
- response to difficulties.

The research basis for these profiles is not explained, but some relevant correlational studies are summarised by Riding and Rayner (1998). However, in the case of team roles, the evidence is very slight, being based on an unpublished study involving only 10 managers.

Despite these empirical drawbacks, it is possible to argue that Riding's model, rather than the CSA, may have important implications for teaching. Although not proven by research, it is plausible that teaching which is biased towards any one of the extreme poles of the model would disadvantage some learners. If this is so, the implication is that teachers should deal both with generalities and particulars; structure material so that part-whole relationships are clear; make demands on both deductive and inductive reasoning; and make use of both visual and verbal forms of expression.

Table 10
Riding's Cognitive Styles
Analysis (CSA)

	Strengths	Weaknesses
General	Learning strategies may be learned and improved.	'Default' learning styles are assumed to be fixed.
Design of the model	Two dimensions which are independent of intelligence: holist-analytic (ways of organising information) and verbaliser-imager (ways of representing information).	■ Two very specific tasks bear the weight of broad and loosely defined constructs. ■ Deals with cognitive, not affective or conative aspects of thinking and learning.
Reliability		■ No evidence provided by the author. ■ Others have shown that internal consistency and test–retest reliability is very poor, especially for the verbaliser-imager ratio score.
Validity	■ Both dimensions have reasonable face validity. ■ The holist-analytic measure may be useful for assessing group rather than individual differences.	■ Performance is sampled over a very limited range of task difficulty. ■ As the reliability of the CSA is so poor, studies of validity should not be accepted unless they have been replicated.
Implications for pedagogy	■ There is evidence of links between cognitive styles and instructional preferences. ■ There is evidence that in computerised instruction, 'holist' learners do better with 'breadth first' and 'analytic' learners with 'depth first'. ■ Riding claims that teachers need to take account of individual differences in working memory as well as style.	■ Most teachers use a variety of instructional approaches anyway (eg verbal and visual). ■ A large number of recommendations are made without adequate empirical evidence.
Evidence of pedagogical impact		Inconclusive.
Overall assessment	The simplicity and potential value of Riding's model are not well served by an unreliable instrument, the CSA.	
Key source	Riding and Rayner 1998	

Empirical evidence of pedagogical impact

Although there are many published studies in which
significant differences in learning outcomes have
been found between groups with different CSA scores,
we do not consider that these studies provide more
than interesting suggestions for pedagogical practice.
We are not aware of any lasting changes in instructional
practice which have been brought about as a result
of using the CSA on a regular basis.

Section 5

Stable personality type

Introduction

The instruments and models grouped in this family have a common focus upon learning style as one part of the observable expression of a relatively stable personality type, a theory primarily influenced by the work of Jung (1968). The most prominent theorists who operate 'at the interface of intelligence and personality' (Grigorenko and Sternberg 1995) are Myers-Briggs (Myers and McCaulley 1985) and Jackson (2002), although they share certain key characteristics with measures developed by Bates and Keirsey (1978), Harrison and Bramson, (1982, 1988) and Miller (1991).

While debates continue within psychology about the appropriate descriptors for personality traits and, indeed, how many factors underpin individual differences (see eg Furnham 1995; Jackson *et al.* 2000), the theorists in this family are concerned with constructing instruments which embed learning styles within an understanding of the personality traits that shape all aspects of an individual's interaction with the world.

The descriptors of personality are, in taxonomic terms, *polythetic* – that is, grouping together observed phenomena with shared features, but not excluding from groups phenomena which share some, but not all, of the relevant features (Eysenck 1997). This approach is both a strength, since it allows for reasonable variation, and a weakness, since 'numerical solutions are essentially indeterminate in the absence of causal relations' (Eysenck 1997, 23). Eysenck makes the argument for a distinction between the reliability of personality factors, such as those in the 'big five' (see Section 5.1 below), which is relatively consistent and their validity, which is dependent upon a theoretical construction which allows for the causal nature of personality factors to be experimentally tested.

An alternative approach – to explore genetic markers for specific, observable personality traits – has proved, as yet, elusive (Stevenson 1997) and it is therefore more difficult to trace the heritability of personality compared, for example, to measures of IQ, though there are some indications that strong traits towards extraversion overcome environmental effects in adoption and twin studies (Loehlin 1992).

5.1
The Myers-Briggs Type Indicator (MBTI)®[8]

Introduction

The Myers-Briggs Type Indicator (MBTI) was designed by Katherine Cook Briggs and her daughter Isabel Briggs Myers. They began to develop their instrument in the early 1940s with the avowed aim of making Jung's theory of human personality understandable and useful in everyday life: 'Jung saw his theory as an aid to self-understanding, but the application of the theory (like the theory itself) extends beyond the point where Jung was content to stop.' (Myers, quoted by Mosley 2001, 8). This resulted in the publication of the first MBTI manual in 1962, the subsequent versions of which (Myers and McCaulley 1985, 1998) are most frequently referred to in studies drawn on for this review.

The MBTI focuses more upon the description of normally observed types, rather than idealised theoretical types which, as Jung himself argued, would rarely be met in everyday life (Jung, quoted by Mosley 2001, 3). In terms of academic heritage, the MBTI has often been strongly linked to personality instruments using the 'big five' personality factors (extraversion, openness, agreeableness, conscientiousness and neuroticism – the last of which is not included in the MBTI), exemplified by the most popular instrument in personality testing in the UK and the US, the NEO-Personality Inventory (McCrae and Costa 1987). However, the MBTI differs strongly from the NEO-PI and other instruments in that it is, according to Quenck (2003):

a theory-based instrument grounded in Jung's typology rather than an empirically derived trait instrument … neuroticism is not part of the MBTI because Jung did not include such a dimension in his typology, which was meant to reflect normal, non-pathological personality differences. It is for that reason that the opposite poles of each of the dichotomies are conceptualized as qualitatively distinct and opposite to each other, with each pole defined as legitimate in its own right. One pole is never described as indicating a 'deficit' in the opposite pole, or [as being] *more valued than the other pole, as is the case in the NEO-PI and other trait conceptions of personality.*

8
Myers-Briggs Type Indicator and MBTI are registered trademarks of CPP Inc, Palo Alto, California.

Figure 7
The four bipolar
discontinuous scales
of the MBTI

Extraversion (E)	⟷	Introversion (I)
Sensing (S)	⟷	Intuition (N)
Thinking (T)	⟷	Feeling (F)
Judging (J)	⟷	Perceiving (P)

Table 11
The 16 MBTI
personality types

ISTJ	ISFJ	ISTP	INTP
INTJ	INFJ	ISFP	INFP
ESTJ	ESFJ	ESTP	ENTP
ENTJ	ENFJ	ESFP	ENFP

Table 12
Summary of the
10 most common
MBTI types

Source: Thorne
and Gough (1999)

Type	Positive traits	Negative traits
INFP	Artistic, reflective, sensitive	Careless, lazy
INFJ	Sincere, sympathetic, unassuming	Submissive, weak
INTP	Candid, ingenious, shrewd	Complicated, rebellious
INTJ	Discreet, industrious, logical	Deliberate, methodical
ISTJ	Calm, stable, steady	Cautious, conventional
ENFP	Enthusiastic, outgoing, spontaneous	Changeable, impulsive
ENFJ	Active, pleasant, sociable	Demanding, impatient
ENTP	Enterprising, friendly, resourceful	Headstrong, self-centred
ENTJ	Ambitious, forceful, optimistic	Aggressive, egotistical
ESTJ	Contented, energetic, practical	Prejudiced, self-satisfied

Table 13
Authors' report
of test–retest
reliability of the
MBTI Form G

Dimension	Male respondents	Female respondents
E-I	0.82	0.83
S-N	0.83	0.85
T-F	0.82	0.80
J-P	0.87	0.86

The MBTI has been included in this review because
it has had a considerable academic impact: an
estimated 2000 articles were written about the
instrument between 1985 and 1995 (Hammer 1996;
Thorne and Gough 1999), while the bibliographic
service at the Center for the Application of Psychological
Type currently holds 240 references to the MBTI
and learning styles. Moreover, the MBTI is 'the most
popularly used measure in the consultancy and training
world' (Furnham 1996a, 307) and is widely used
in medicine (Thompson and Bing-You 1998; Stilwell
et al. 1998; Houghton 2000), as well as in business,
management and religious communities, both as
a career development and managerial tool. Pittenger
(1993) reports that over 2m copies of the MBTI are
sold annually.

Definition, description and scope.

The instrument has a series of forced-choice questions
relating to four bipolar discontinuous scales, as shown
in Figure 7.

The standard version of the MBTI is the 93-item Form M
(1998), which has a US 7th Grade reading level. The
126-item Form G is also sometimes referred to (1985)
and there is, in addition, an abbreviated (50-item)
version. Some of the improvements of Form M include:
the structure of the instrument, in that all items have
only two response options; the introduction of Item
Response Theory (IRT) scoring; and standardisation
based on a large group of adults (n=3009). In all
cases, scores are assigned to produce one of 16
combinations of preferences (see Table 11), which
are regarded as distinctive from one another in terms
of cognitive, behavioural, affective and perceptual
style (see Table 12 for a summary). The complexity
of the MBTI needs to be emphasised:

On the surface, the theory behind the MBTI appears to be fairly simple. However, it is actually very complex and casual users may have problems fully understanding its implications. According to Myers and Briggs, each four letter type represents a complex set of relationships among the functions (S, N,T and F), attitudes (E and I) and attitudes toward the outer world (J and P). These various interactions are known as type dynamics. (Fleenor 2001[9])

Some commentators in the learning styles field prefer to exclude the MBTI on the grounds that its scope as a personality measure goes beyond cognitive controls and behaviour specifically related to learning. However, the scope of the MBTI includes learning, and it was the authors' intention that it should be a tool to aid learners (Myers, cited by Di Tiberio 1996). The MBTI was specifically designed as a tool to categorise an individual's personality type in general, and their approaches to relationships with others. For this reason, the MBTI differs in tone from other influential personality trait theories, by being more positive or neutral in its descriptors. This aspect may account for its influence in the learning styles field, where theorists who have drawn upon it have tended to emphasise descriptors of normal behaviour and reactions, rather than the identification of pathological traits or tendencies.

Miller (1991, 217) argues for the relevance of the MBTI in the learning styles field, since 'many well-established conceptions of "learning styles", such as Pask's ... reflect [a] cognitive emphasis ... at the expense of affective and conative' aspects. Others have tried to circumvent this problem by selecting the particular sections of the MBTI that they consider most relevant to learning. For example, Claxton and McIntyre (1994; Claxton *et al.* 1996) focus on 'sensing-intuition and thinking-feeling ... the combination of an individual's preferred information-intake mode with the preferred mode of decision making' (1994, 752), although there may be some methodological reservations about this 'pick and mix' approach. If the instrument has been designed to provide a holistic view of the individual, selecting and omitting scales may prejudice the validity of its research.

Evaluation: reliability and validity

The face validity of the MBTI is generally accepted as fairly sound by researchers from personality theory backgrounds, with the caveat (not accepted by MBTI researchers, see quote from Quenck 2003 above) that the omission of neuroticism is a theoretical weakness (Eysenck and Eysenck 1985).

There has, however, been considerable debate about the construct validity of the MBTI, particularly in relation to the bimodality of the four dimensional scales. Researchers generally agree that bimodality has not been demonstrated in any of the dimensions (Hicks 1984; McCrae and Costa 1989); indeed, some argue that the bipolarity of all four scales is unsubstantiated. Girelli and Stake (1993) confirm that introversion-extraversion, sensing-intuition and thinking-feeling are not incontrovertibly bipolar, when tested in Lickert format on 165 undergraduate and postgraduate students, since more than a quarter of the subjects in their study scored highly on both pairs of a dimension. They argue (1993, 299) that as a result of these findings, 'not only the format of the MBTI but the theoretical premise of bipolarity and type differentiation has *(sic)* been brought into question'. Bess and Harvey, in their analysis of 48,638 MBTI questionnaires completed by managers, found (2002, 185) that previous reports of bimodality on all four scales had been 'artifacts caused by the particular number (and location) of the quadrature points used by default in BILOG' – in effect, processing errors. They conclude that 'the absence of empirical bimodality ... does indeed remove a potentially powerful line of evidence that was previously available to 'type' advocates to cite in defence of their position'.

One of the most telling criticisms is that the forced-choice format is inappropriate: 'the ipsative scores that derive from forced-choice measures tend to yield negative intercorrelations that are difficult to interpret' (Girelli and Stake 1993, 291). Moreover, if the dimensions are *genuinely* bipolar, then this will be evident even when subjects are not forced to choose (Loomis and Singer 1980). Furthermore, the MBTI has no lie scale, nor any measures designed to tap into respondents' inclination to make socially acceptable responses (Boyle 1995), although the latter is dealt with statistically by the IRT selection and scoring method used for Form M (Quenck 2003).

9
Page numbers are not available for online Buros reports from the *Mental Measurements Yearbooks.*

Myers and McCaulley (1985) report a test–retest reliability meta-analysis on a sample of 102,174 respondents (Table 13) which appears to be robust. Boyle's review (1995) notes that the best results (for Form F) are reported stability coefficients of between 0.69 (T-F) and 0.78 (E-I), which, though lower than those in Table 13, are still acceptable. Advocates who have interpreted MBTI retest scores positively (eg Carlson 1980, De Vito 1985, Murray 1990) have, according to Pittenger (1993), used trait judgement criteria, implying a continuum, rather than type criteria, reflecting the (allegedly) **dichotomous** nature of the scales. This criticism is repeated in reviews of Form M where it is accepted that MBTI scales show 'very high levels of internal consistency (mostly >0.90) and acceptable [actually very high] levels of test–retest reliability (0.83–0.97 for a 4-week interval). However, the authors clearly state that the MBTI is meant to identify a person's whole type (eg ENTP)' (Fleenor 2001; see also Mastrangelo 2001). The evidence of whole-type stability from the manual (Myers and McCaulley 1985) appears to be a little less impressive, with 65% of respondents maintaining their type and most of the remaining 35% showing consistency in three out of four scales (n=424).

The stability of the MBTI type allocations are open to question in part because the middle scores are prone to misinterpretation, since they are forced one way or the other, despite small numerical differences. For example, Howes and Carskadon (1979) found that for scores within 15 points of neutral, between 25% and 32% of respondents had changed on the second test. A meta-analysis of reliability across 210 recent studies (Capraro and Capraro 2002) notes that most authors of studies using the MBTI do not engage with issues of reliability at all; however, when reliability data was available, 'the MBTI tended to yield acceptable score reliabilities' (2002, 596) of around 0.81 (standard deviation 0.08). In addition, Capraro and Capraro (2002, 599) emphasise that the reliability of an instrument is context-specific: 'dependent on sample characteristics and testing conditions.' Indeed, while Salter, Evans and Forney (1997, 595) report 'some stability (ranging from 0.69 to 0.77)' over 20 months, they warn that the impact of environmental factors on changes to individuals' MBTI scores is under-researched.

A lot of work has been done comparing the MBTI to other scales, which can be summarised as follows.

■ McCrae and Costa's (1989) study indicates that there are correlations between the NEO-PI scales and the MBTI, despite the omission of neuroticism from the MBTI; while Furnham (1996a, 306) detects 'clear overlap', despite promoting the psychometric superiority of the NEO-PI.

■ Drummond and Stoddard (1992, 103) note connections between the MBTI and the Gregorc Style Delineator, concluding that 'the Gregorc measures some of the same dimensions as the Myers-Briggs but uses different labels'.

■ Spirrison and Gordy (1994) find the Constructive Thinking Indicator predictive of scores on the MBTI.

■ Lim (1994) found moderate relationships between introversion on the MBTI and abstract and reflective tendencies on Kolb's LSI.

■ Higgs (2001) was able to find only partial correlations between MBTI type and emotional intelligence.

While there are many attempts to link and correlate the MBTI with other measures of learning style, some of these (eg Nordvik 1996; or see Di Tiberio 1996 for an overview) seem to be predicated on the belief that if there are some modest correlations between, say, three disparate measures, they all somehow validate one another. Indeed, it could be argued that the theoretical descriptions of dimensions in the MBTI differ substantially from dimensions with similar names in other typologies, since the MBTI is the only one of these that remains firmly connected to Jung's theoretical constructs. This suggests that the connections with other tests are not of themselves a good measure of the MBTI's validity or relevance to the field of learning styles, since the field of learning styles is beset with problems in terms of establishing shared definitions of key terms.

The huge body of work which exists on the MBTI must be examined with the critical awareness that a considerable proportion (estimated to be between a third and a half of the published material) has been produced for conferences organised by the Center for the Application of Psychological Type or as papers for the *Journal of Psychological Type*, both of which are organised and edited by Myers-Briggs advocates. Pittenger (1993, 478) asserts that 'the research on the MBTI was designed to confirm not refute the MBTI theory'. A good example of this is the study by Saggino, Cooper and Kline (2001), which starts from a position which assumes the validity of the MBTI and tests new versions of it against itself. As Mastrangelo (2001) argues, the 'research [on the MBTI] need[s] to be presented in journals besides the *Journal of Psychological Type* ... The most widely used psychological measure should demand scientific scrutiny to improve service to the public.'[10]

10
Page numbers are not available for online Buros reports from the *Mental Measurements Yearbooks*.

Implications for pedagogy

Some supporters of the MBTI stress the versatility of individuals to move beyond their 'dominant function' to exploit or develop 'auxiliary preferences' (Bayne 1994); however, both Jung and Myers subscribed to a view of personality type as at least dominant by adulthood, suggesting that this versatility would be limited by the individual's strong and habituated preferences. Moreover, the complex interaction of type dynamics tends to be obscured when the debate moves to 'testing' and 'matching' in educational contexts. Here, as elsewhere, the evidence is inconclusive: Hartman, Hylton and Sanders (1997) argue that their study of 323 undergraduates lends weight to the idea that some elements of MBTI type are linked to the dominance of a particular brain hemisphere (specifically, intuition-perceiving/right-brained and sensing-judging/left-brained), which implies that a change in style is less likely. The MBTI's claim to classify individuals into taxonomic categories has been described (Bouchard and Hur 1998, 147) as 'a controversial claim ... virtually no mainstream personality researchers adopt this view ... [and if] the latent traits underlying the MBTI are truly categorical rather than continuous, it is still likely to be the case that the influences underlying the categories are strongly genetic in origin.' This calls into question the idea that MBTI results can or should be used for enhancing students' repertoires of styles.

Some MBTI advocates appear to accept the stability of types and suggest that the utility of the instrument lies in using test results to provide 'matching' pedagogical experiences for students in a bid to improve retention (Van 1992) – in particular, taking account of the apparent correlation between high academic achievement and intuitive-judging types (NJ). Gordon and Yocke's extremely small study (1999) of 22 new entrants to the teaching profession appears to support the link between sensing types and lower levels of performance. Sears, Kennedy and Kaye (1997) have mapped in detail the links between MBTI types and specialism choices among student teachers, and among other results, report the finding that sensing types are dominant among teachers in elementary (primary) education. Extra support for sensing types, including the provision of more practical and multimedia instructional opportunities is suggested, although the utility of this approach has been questioned by Spence and Tsai (1997). Their study was unable to find any significant relationship between MBTI type and method of information processing, finding instead that subjects used a range of methods which were task-specific. In addition, Di Tiberio (1996), reflecting on 10 years of research on the MBTI, concludes that there is no satisfactory evidence to suggest that matching instructor and learner style has any impact on student satisfaction or achievement.

The use of the MBTI for 'best fit' career advice, while widespread, particularly in medicine (Stilwell et al. 1998) and business (McIntyre and Meloche 1995), is flawed because testing people already within a profession does not include the effects of environment and communities of practice on observable personality traits. In addition, there are gender differences in different professions; for example, correlations between type and career choice are much higher for female teachers than for male teachers. Moreover, the tendency to use the results from a group of vocational students as evidence of the range of career orientations within the population as a whole, or within a profession (see eg Jarlstrom 2000) is disturbing, since the obvious social, cultural and racial limitations of undergraduate samples are ignored.

The MBTI, while it focuses on the personality type of the individual, has a well-established role in locating and understanding interpersonal and community dynamics. The findings of Edwards, Lanning and Hooker (2002, 445) that intuitive-judging types are 'better able to rationally integrate situational factors in making judgements of personality', may have some application to teacher–student relationships, particularly in relation to assessment. The MBTI has been adapted for many different countries and some advocates of the instrument feel that it has utility in describing national or cultural differences, for although Jung believed that type is universal, there may be differences in distribution and cultural influences which mitigate the expression of type (Quenck 2003). Abramson et al. (1993) argue, for example, that an awareness of the fact that Japanese MBA students have a more feeling-based cognitive style than Canadian MBA students, combined with a greater self-awareness on the part of managers about their own cognitive style, could improve business negotiations more effectively than simple 'cultural awareness' training.

Empirical evidence for pedagogical impact

As yet, evidence of use for the MBTI in terms of specific learning outcomes is sparse, although Woolhouse and Bayne (2000) claim that individual differences in the use of intuition are correlated with the sensing-intuitive dimension. Thorne and Gough (1999), in their analysis of 10 years of MBTI results, are able to identify only moderate links between high verbal and vocabulary scores and extrovert males and sensing females. Similarly, Harasym et al. (1995a, 1996) find that type does not predict achievement for nursing students, while Oswick and Barber (1998) find no correlation between MBTI type and achievement in their sample of undergraduates.

Van's review (1992) of evidence to predict academic achievement by MBTI type is able to cite two examples of successful intervention studies: one used focused strategies for 2100 students identified as being at high risk of dropping out of university; the second used a 'reading style' measure with school children experiencing reading difficulties. Both were intervention studies without controls and so the risk of a 'halo' effect is not excluded. Cooper and Miller (1991) found that while a degree of 'match' between students' learning styles and lecturers' teaching styles did improve evaluations of teacher performance, student outcomes were not improved. It appears, from this evidence, that there are few, if any, studies which are able to show correlations between specific MBTI types and improved attainment.

Conclusions

Despite the enormous commercial success of the MBTI, the research evidence to support it – both as a valid measurement of style and as an aid to pedagogy – is inconclusive, at best. The extent to which the MBTI has been accepted as part of the normal arsenal of measurements has had the unfortunate result that some of the analytical and empirical work done with it is uncritical and unreflective. Also, critically, an instrument which was designed for use by an individual to extend his or her understanding of reactions and preferences is increasingly used by institutions to assess suitability, strengths and weaknesses. This is not the fault of the authors, though it is perhaps an inevitable concomitant of commercial pressures. Moreover, since there is no clear evidence of how stable the types are over an individual's lifetime, nor a clear understanding of how type dynamics impact on education, the question of the practical application of MBTI types in pedagogy – whether to aim for 'match' or 'repertoire enhancement' – has, as yet, no clear answer.

Table 14
Myers-Briggs Type
Indicator (MBTI)

	Strengths	Weaknesses
General	Provides a view of the whole personality, including learning.	Not specifically about learning.
Design of the model	Based on Jung's theory on four bipolar scales, producing a possible 16 personality 'types'.	The relationships between elements and scales – 'type dynamics' – are extremely complex.
Reliability	Reliability co-efficients are high for individual pairs of scores relating to each of the scales.	The stability of the 16 types is less impressive.
Validity	The face validity of the MBTI is generally accepted.	Construct validity is controversial because of the debate about whether the constructs are best represented by opposing pairs.
Implications for pedagogy	■ The apparent correlation between achievement and intuitive-judging types has led to calls for extra support for sensing types. ■ The use of type in career counselling is widespread and has been used to steer students into 'appropriate' areas of study.	■ Links between type and methods of information processing have not been proved. ■ There is no evidence to suggest that matching teacher and learner types has any positive effects on achievement.
Evidence of pedagogical impact	There is limited evidence to suggest that matching teacher and learner types may increase student affect.	■ Type does not appear to predict performance. ■ The proportion of critical literature, both reviews of the instrument and the resolution of the debate about personality measures in learning styles, has been seen as too low.
Overall assessment	It is still not clear which elements of the 16 personality types in the MBTI are most relevant for education.	
Key source	Myers and McCaulley 1985	

5.2
Apter's reversal theory of motivational styles, the Motivational Style Profile (MSP) and related assessment tools

The nature and purpose of reversal theory

Reversal theory is a theory of personality, not of learning style. It is evaluated here because learning cannot be understood in isolation from motivation, and because the concept of reversal is both relevant and challenging when applied to learning styles.

Apter's theory provides a structure for understanding human behaviour and experience, not in terms of fixed personality 'types', but by outlining the dynamic interplay between 'reversing' motivational states. Mental life is seen in terms of changes within and between four domains: means-ends, rules, transactions and relationships. According to Apter (2001, 317), 'Everything stems from and returns to this fundamental series of binary oppositions between seriousness and play, acquiescence and resistance, power and love, self and other.' Apter believes that 'within domain' reversals (eg switching from serious, goal-directed work to playful recreation) ensure 'that the individual has the possibility of every type of psychological satisfaction' (2001, 13). He claims that genetic, unconscious and situational factors influence the frequency and extent of such reversals and that individuals differ in the time they spend in various motivational states and in their perceived importance. As illustrated in Figure 8, each motivational state is driven by a core psychological need and is characterised by a particular style of interacting with the world.

A range of physically experienced and transactional emotions is associated with each motivational style, depending on style combinations and other factors such as felt arousal and anticipated outcome. Reversals between emotions (eg between excitement and anxiety, or between gratitude and guilt) are said to result from 'underlying' reversals in one or more of the four experiential domains. These underlying reversals are said to be involuntary, although they can be triggered by perceived environmental changes and can come under indirect voluntary control to the extent that people can control relevant environmental factors. Two of the main reasons for switching between motivational styles are said to be frustration and satiation.

Reversal theory was first developed in the 1970s by Apter and Smith (Smith and Apter 1975; Apter 1976), and influences from **phenomenology**, humanistic psychology and clinical experience can be seen. However, the theory is in no way derivative, as it arose in large part from dissatisfaction with existing theories dealing with aspects of motivation and mental health such as anxiety (Apter 1976). It is presented as an integrative theory, capable of bridging the gap between biological and social explanations of human experience, and applying structural quantitative models to the study of mental life.

The development of the MSP and related instruments

The Apter MSP has 14 sub-scales. In addition to the eight styles shown in Figure 8, there are two more pairs which are polar opposites (arousal-avoidance and arousal-seeking; optimism and pessimism) plus two scales which represent tendencies rather than psychological needs (arousability and effortfulness). While arousal-seeking is a 'need to experience excitement, thrills or other intense feelings, and to search for problems or stimulation which might raise arousal to a satisfactorily high level', arousability is defined as a 'tendency to be easily emotionally aroused, whether one desires this or not' (Apter, Mallows and Williams 1998, 9).

Each scale has five items and respondents are asked to rate themselves on a six-point scale – ranging from 'never' to 'always' – by making an estimate of how they experience things in general, trying not to let present feelings sway their judgement. Sample items are 'feel rebellious', 'look for thrills' and 'give to those in need'.

In addition to the 14 sub-scale totals, Apter, Mallows and Williams (1998) propose a further 10 derived measures. Six of these are measures of 'dominance' (calculated by subtracting one sub-scale from its paired opposite) and four are measures of 'salience' (calculated by adding sub-scales).

Apter has developed three additional related instruments for use in business contexts. The first of these is a shortened version of the MSP with norms for managers in the UK and the US. The other two are the Apter Team Contribution System (ATCS) and the Apter Work Impact System (AWIS), neither of which are in the public domain. The purpose of the ATCS is to uncover problem areas within team functioning by allowing team members to compare how they see themselves with how they are seen by others. The AWIS allows comparisons to be made between corporate values, employee needs, employee satisfaction and managerial perception of employee satisfaction.

Critical evaluation of reversal theory

Reversal theory certainly makes predictions about thinking, learning and behaviour and has generated a substantial volume of research since its first publication by Smith and Apter (1975). For many, it has face validity, unlike theories which claim that motivation is **homeostatically** controlled or which assume the existence of personality types or traits. It has the virtue of taking subjective meaning as seriously as psychophysiological states and it is a systemic theory which acknowledges the interaction of emotion, cognition and volition.

The theory is an evolving one and Apter (2001, 307) acknowledges the need for 'a systematic developmental underpinning for the theory' as well as the 'need to develop specific techniques that would allow people to come more in control of their own reversal processes' (2001, 306). This is a difficult area, since Apter has posited an unconscious biological basis for reversal without fully accounting for its adaptive value. There is, nonetheless, an impressive amount of empirical evidence which supports reversal theory. Apter and Heskin (2001) have summarised the research evidence which supports the basic propositions of the theory, including some studies in which reversal was monitored during educationally relevant activities such as studying statistics and reading.

While Apter does not claim that his four domains are the only way of conceptualising psychological needs, he does (2001, 39) claim exhaustiveness in the sense that for a given pair of motivational states, 'one or the other will be active during the whole of waking life'. He allows that a pair of states may be more or less central or peripheral in awareness, but not that both may disappear altogether from consciousness. However, it is not clear whether this is a logical or empirical claim, and if the latter, whether it is falsifiable.

Apter does not seem to allow for the simultaneous activation of pairs of states such as goal-oriented (*telic*) and activity-oriented (*paratelic*). Yet if simultaneous activation does not occur, it is difficult to explain behaviour where both are required, such as the performance of musicians and stand-up comics, where the experience of flow is at once enjoyment and achievement.

Apter's treatment of arousal-avoidance and arousal-seeking is not fully consistent, since these are assimilated within the telic-paratelic dimension in much of his writing, but treated as a separate dimension in the MSP. The MSP approach is more convincing, since while peace and quiet may generally help people to focus on goal achievement, this is not always so.

Reversal theory is based on clear definitions and has a clear structure, despite the use of invented terms to refer to the poles of two dimensions ('telic' and 'paratelic' in the case of the means-end dimension and '*autic*' and '*alloic*' as applied to relationships). While some features of the theory can be questioned, Apter (2001) has set it out in a highly coherent form, with four basic assumptions and 10 basic propositions.

Although it is a theory of personality rather than of learning, reversal theory does provide a conceptual framework for asking questions in a systematic way about approaches to learning, especially about motivation, feelings about learning and personal style. Its dimensions are not new, but the concept of reversal is refreshingly novel and provides a real challenge to theorists who seek to pigeonhole individuals in terms of fixed characteristics.

It is helpful to consider reversal theory in the context of other theories and models of thinking, learning and personal style. Apter's telic-paratelic dimension is conceptually linked with **extrinsic** versus **intrinsic motivation** and with convergent versus divergent thinking. A telic orientation may also be what motivates some learners to approach study with the aim of gaining high examination marks, while some students who do not take their studies seriously may have a paratelic orientation. Deep absorption in studying a subject can be an end in itself or be motivated by a serious academic ambition, while 'surface' learners may become more interested if teachers find ways of making learning more enjoyable. There is a family resemblance between Apter's conformist-negativistic dimension, Sternberg's (1998) hierarchic and anarchic thinking styles and Kirton's distinction (1989) between adaptors and innovators. Apter's concept of autic mastery reflects values of individualism and competitiveness, while alloic sympathy reflects values of social belonging and cooperation.

Most importantly, the key concept of reversal has major implications for how we think about learning styles. It leads us to expect reversals between learning styles as well as some degree of individual consistency over time, and it strongly suggests that productive learning styles can be fostered by creating learning environments though which important values are conveyed and in which reversals through boredom and satiation are less likely to occur.

Evaluation of the MSP and of related instruments

The MSP items are written in simple language, with a readability level of about 9 years. Most are clearly expressed, but some (especially those beginning with 'I like…') can be read in more than one way. For example, I may respond that I always 'like to be liked', meaning that being liked is a common experience for me; or I may, by the same response, mean that I always like the experience of being liked, even though I do not have it very often.

The MSP is fairly robust in psychometric terms, with internal consistency of the 14 sub-scales in the range 0.64 to 0.89 for the UK version and test–retest correlations in the range 0.73 to 0.92 over a 12-week period (Apter, Mallows and Williams 1998). The most stable sub-scales were those for other-oriented affection, optimism, excitement and fun.

Figure 8
Possible motivational
style reversals in four
experiential domains

Need	Achievement	Means-ends domain	Fun
Style	Serious	←——————→	Playful
Need	Fitting in	Rules domain	Freedom
Style	Conforming	←——————→	Challenging
Need	Power	Transactions domain	Love
Style	Competitive	←——————→	Affectionate
Need	Individuation	Relationships domain	Transcendence
Style	Self-oriented	←——————→	Other-oriented

In terms of reversal theory, it is appropriate that each pole of a dimension should be rated separately, but if the poles are indeed opposites, one would expect this to be confirmed by factor analysis, with the polar opposites having positive and negative loadings on a particular factor. However, Apter, Mallows and Williams (1998) did not find this pattern with the main five dimensions, and only 'optimism' and 'pessimism' items loaded in this way (positively and negatively) on a single factor. They did, however, find that with very few exceptions, all the items in a given sub-scale loaded on the same factor. The predicted association between the paratelic and arousal-seeking scales was found, but not the corresponding association between the telic and arousal-avoidance scales. In general, it cannot be said that factor analysis has shown the MSP to adequately measure the 'binary oppositions' on which reversal theory is built.

There are other serious concerns as to whether the MSP does full justice to the theory on which it is based. It does not provide a measure of the frequency of reversals, nor does it indicate the extent of change. The method of calculating 'salience' is also questionable. A person who self-rates as 'seldom conforming' and 'seldom challenging' will gain a very low salience score, even though their thoughts may be filled with criticisms of society and the futility of trying to change it. The problem of assuming equal numerical intervals between ratings is illustrated by the fact that the same salience score will be obtained by someone who self-rates as 'always conforming' and 'never challenging' as by someone who self-rates as 'often conforming' and 'sometimes challenging'.

So far as concurrent validity is concerned, Apter, Mallows and Williams (1998) report on two studies in which extraversion was found to be positively correlated with the paratelic, arousal-seeking and autic mastery sub-scales. Neuroticism was strongly related to pessimism, as well as (negatively) to the paratelic, arousal-seeking and alloic mastery sub-scales. All of these relationships are consistent with theory and everyday experience. We are all familiar with lively, cheerful extroverts who like to be in control of events and to dominate others, as well as with fearful, nervous people who are not much fun, avoid taking risks and are not good team players. It is, however, rather paradoxical that some of the 'big five' personality dimensions (neuroticism, extraversion, openness to experience, agreeableness and conscientiousness) are used to validate the MSP when reversal theory is intended to provide a challenge to trait theories.

We conclude that better evidence in support of reversal theory is likely to come from process and observational reports of change over time, rather than from data collected through rating scales such as the MSP. We are unable to evaluate the Apter Team Contribution System (ATCS) and the Apter Work Impact System (AWIS), as there is, as yet, no published research about their construction and use.

Implications for pedagogy

The implications of reversal theory for learning have not been fully elaborated or widely researched, except in specialised fields such as sport and addiction. Nevertheless, the theory is intended to have wide application and to hold good across the lifespan and across cultures. Apter sees it as being relevant to groups and organisations as well as to individuals, and for this purpose, has set up a management consultancy, Apter International, with a website at www.apterinternational.com

Achievement, motivation, boredom, frustration and satiation are concepts of considerable interest to educators. Other key concepts in reversal theory which are especially relevant in learning and instruction are those of arousal seeking, arousal avoidance and cognitive synergy (including aesthetic experience and humour).

Table 15		Strengths	Weaknesses
Apter's Motivational Style Profile (MSP)	**General**	The theory provides a structure for understanding human behaviour and experience, not in terms of fixed personality 'types', but by outlining the dynamic interplay between 'reversing' motivational states.	The MSP is a measure of personality, not learning style alone.
	Design of the model	There are four domains of experience in which there is interaction between emotion, cognition and volition. These are: means-ends, rules, transactions and relationships. Reversal theory is about systems in nature, bridging between biology and lived experience.	Apter's claim that one of the four pairs of motivational states is always in operation is as yet unproven.
	Reliability	The MSP has acceptable levels of internal consistency and test–retest reliability.	
	Validity	There is an impressive amount of empirical evidence which supports reversal theory.	In general, it cannot be said that **factor analysis** has shown the MSP to measure adequately the 'binary oppositions' on which reversal theory is built.
	Implications for pedagogy	■ Reversal has major implications for how we think about learning styles, leading us to expect reversals between learning styles as well as some degree of individual consistency over time. ■ Productive learning can be fostered by creating learning environments in which reversals through boredom and satiation are less likely to occur.	The implications of reversal theory for learning have not been fully elaborated or widely researched, except in specialised fields such as sport and addiction.
	Evidence of pedagogical impact		None as yet.
	Overall assessment	A theory which poses a threat to fixed-trait models of learning style and which merits further research and development in educational contexts.	
	Key source	Apter 2001	

5.3
Jackson's Learning Styles Profiler (LSP)

Origins

The LSP is described as 'an applied neuropsychological model of learning styles for business and education' (Jackson 2002). Chris Jackson, an organisational psychologist now at the University of Queensland, developed it in the UK over 10 years, working in the research culture of Eysenckian personality theory and drawing on the psychobiological theories of Gray (1982) and Cloninger (1993).

Definitions, description and scope

For Jackson, learning styles are a sub-set of personality, having a biological basis and constituting *'the learnt basis of personality'* (2002, 12). Four learning styles are proposed, which resemble the Honey and Mumford (2000) styles, but are not claimed to be totally independent or to form part of a learning cycle. They are: *initiator, reasoner, analyst* and *implementer.*

There are 80 items in the LSP, randomly ordered, with 20 for each style. Respondents have to select from the options 'yes', 'no' and 'can't decide'. There is a computerised version of the LSP which provides feedback in the form of a percentile score for each style and a detailed profile containing advice for getting future learning experiences right and improving weaker learning styles. The four item-derived characteristics which, according to the *item analysis* reported in the manual, are the best indicators of each style are given in Table 16, together with the descriptors from the LSP manual (Jackson 2002).

The four LSP styles, with the strengths and weaknesses claimed for each in the LSP manual (Jackson 2002) are listed in Table 17.

The initiator style is thought to be linked with Gray's (1982) Behavioural Activation System (BAS), which initiates approach behaviour when there is a chance of reward, whereas the reasoner style is thought to have a basis in Gray's Behavioural Inhibition System (BIS), which inhibits behaviour in response to cues associated with punishment. Following Cloninger (1993), the analyst style is seen as a self-regulatory, goal-oriented tendency which serves to maintain interest in a problem so that it can be thoroughly understood. No neuropsychological basis is claimed for the implementer style, which is seen as a logically necessary addition if plans are to be carried out.

The LSP is intended for use with adults, and has been standardised in the UK on 1394 people aged between 20 and 60+. It is intended for use in a wide range of settings, but the emphasis so far has been placed on business organisations.

Evaluation

Reliability

Internal consistency reliability for each of the four scales is provided in the manual (Jackson 2002), on the basis of three studies, the largest of which involved 1524 people. In that study, the alphas were in the range 0.72 to 0.75. Test–retest reliability for 42 students over a 10-week period was: 0.85 for initiator, 0.47 for reasoner, 0.74 for analyst and 0.73 for implementer. In another study involving 61 students who were tested in their first and third college years, the figures were: 0.63 for initiator, 0.52 for reasoner, 0.75 for analyst and 0.73 for implementer. These figures can be taken as moderately encouraging, with the exception of the reasoner scale.

Validity

Factorial validity for the styles is claimed on the basis of a four-factor solution for 400 students. This reveals some problems with nearly half the items, either because of low loadings or because of higher loadings on other scales. The latter problem is most acute with the initiator scale, since six of the items are more closely aligned with the analyst scale. The items with the highest loadings on each factor are generally those listed in Table 16 below, with the exception of the initiator scale. In this case, the four items which appear in Table 16 all had higher loadings on the analyst scale. The four highest-loading initiator items emphasise spontaneity, fun and excitement, which is consistent with Jackson's summary descriptors. On balance, it seems that some further refinement of items is needed, especially in the initiator scale.

The initiator and reasoner styles are, on theoretical grounds, expected to act against each other. This idea is partially substantiated by a negative correlation of -0.28 between their respective scales. The opposition of introversion and extraversion is reflected in a negative correlation of -0.50 between the initiator and reasoner scales. As might be expected from inspection of the items, there is some overlap between the reasoner and analyst scales, reflected in a positive correlation of 0.38.

Although the LSP style names closely resemble those used by Honey and Mumford (2000) in their Learning Styles Questionnaire (LSQ), the construct validity of one or both instruments is called into question by a study involving 817 New Zealand workers. None of the correlation coefficients obtained were high. The percentages of shared *variance* for the four pairs of scales are shown in Table 18.

Jackson argues that this is a positive finding since other researchers such as Swailes and Senior (1999) and Duff and Duffy (2002) have concluded that the Honey and Mumford LSQ is a poor measure of learning. However, it is also possible that the style names chosen by Jackson are not good descriptors of the underlying constructs.

Table 16
Key characteristics
of each style

Initiator (sensation seeking, impulsive, extroverted)

Does not usually think carefully before doing anything

Generally does and says things without stopping to think

Mostly speaks before thinking things out

Considers all the advantages and disadvantages before making up his/her mind

Reasoner (intellectual, rational, objective, has 'theory of mind')

Rarely gets the feeling that it is useless trying to get anywhere in life

Rarely feels that he/she doesn't have enough control over the direction his/her life is taking

Rarely feels that he/she has little influence over the things that happen to him/her

Rarely finds life difficult to cope with

Analyst (introverted, responsible, cautious, wise, methodological, insightful)

Does not have a tendency to be inconsistent and untidy in his/her work

Rarely leaves things to the last minute

Does not have a tendency to 'let things slide'

Can always be fully relied upon

Implementer (expedient, realistic, practical)

Rarely philosophises about the purpose of human existence

Is not overcome by a sense of wonder when he/she visits historical monuments

Rarely discusses the causes and possible solutions of social and political problems with friends

Rarely pauses just to meditate about things in general

Table 17
Strengths and
weaknesses of the
different preferences

	Strengths	Weaknesses
Initiator	■ Engages problem ■ Centre of attention ■ Makes it happen	■ Leaps without looking ■ Focuses on self too much and on others too little ■ Can make mistakes
Reasoner	■ Inhibits further initiation behaviour to increase understanding ■ Identifies why things happen ■ Provides a model ■ Autonomous, self-reliant ■ Independent ■ Insightful	■ More interested in theory than in action ■ Doesn't understand realities of the problem
Analyst	■ Knows all about the issues ■ Great source of information ■ Sees the pros and cons ■ Wise, responsible and conscientious ■ Maintains behaviour; insight learning	■ Can't see the wood for the trees ■ Doesn't get started ■ Procrastinates
Implementer	■ Understands the realities ■ Very practical ■ Down to earth	■ Has little 'humanity' ■ Not enough imagination

Table 18
The extent to which
corresponding scales –
Jackson (LSP) and
Honey and Mumford
(LSQ) – measure the
same constructs

Corresponding measures (LSP and LSQ)	Percentage of shared variance
Initiator and activist	14
Reasoner and theorist	2
Analyst and reflector	4
Implementer and pragmatist	0

The latter interpretation receives some support when face validity is considered. The term *initiator* does not have the same connotation as the quality of impulsivity that comes through from the items in Table 16. *Reasoner* is not a good match for the quality of self-efficacy which the items in Table 16 convey, and *analyst* does not equate with personal organisation. The core construct items for *implementer* in Table 16 are negatively framed and clearly suggest reflection, which is not necessarily the opposite of practicality.

Correlations with a range of personality measures are also reported by Jackson as evidence of validity. These may be summarised as follows: initiators tend to have high scores on risk taking, dysfunctional impulsivity and **psychoticism**; reasoners have few neurotic worries, are usually happy, purposeful and confident; analysts tend to have low scores on psychoticism, they may be ambitious, but tend to lie; and implementers cannot be clearly identified by personality tests. These findings are not clear-cut, providing some support for the hypothesised constructs, but also suggesting that other theories and interpretations should be considered, especially for the reasoner and analyst scales.

Jackson argues that differences in the mean scores of various occupational groups support the construct validity of the LSP. This may be the case, but the argument stands just as well if different style names (with better face validity) are substituted for the originals. We might, for example, expect most engineers and computer people to have a greater sense of self-efficacy than male warehouse staff.

Predictive validity has so far been studied in only one 'real world' context, a sample of 59 sales staff in an unnamed blue-chip company. It was found that both the initiator and analyst scales were low positive predictors of job performance.

Implications for pedagogy

Most practical applications of the LSP to date have been in organisational contexts. Jackson sees uses for it in selection and appraisal, in planning professional development and team building, and in creating learning cultures.

There is a positive emphasis in the computer-generated recommendations for personal development which result from completing the questionnaire. The feedback is very detailed and contains suggestions for building on strengths, dealing with challenging situations and remedying maladaptive learning. The relevance, practicality and value of this feedback have yet to be evaluated.

Jackson sees some learning styles, behaviours and strategies as being more easily modified than others. According to 131 raters, the analyst style is the most conscious in origin, which accords with its theoretical status as self-regulatory, goal-oriented and 'interest maintaining'. The raters thought that the initiator style is the most instinctive in origin, which suggests that impulsive, pleasure-seeking behaviour is the most difficult to change.

Overall, Jackson takes the view that for both individuals and organisations, it is desirable to build up multiple strengths, rather than encouraging people to work only in ways which come most naturally to them.

Conclusions

The LSP is a sophisticated instrument, but has some relatively weak aspects. The quantity and quality of statistical data accompanying its first publication in 2002 is most impressive and Jackson is to be commended for making it open to scrutiny on the internet. It is understandable that with such a new instrument, no published empirical studies by independent researchers are available at the time of writing.

However, as indicated above, there are a number of theoretical, social, managerial and pedagogical questions which need to be addressed. While certain small technical adjustments to the LSP are desirable, there are more fundamental issues concerning its further development and use. It seems to suffer from a tension between *a priori* theorising and lived experience. Each scale includes a number of rather loosely associated variables and often the generic label is not the most appropriate one.

Jackson's theoretical stance is not rigid, and it is noteworthy that he does not see a problem in acknowledging that learning styles are influenced to varying degrees by biology as well as by experience and conscious control. By encouraging self-awareness about preferences, behaviour and beliefs, Jackson is promoting a positive attitude to personal evelopment. It is possible that this approach will prove more fruitful in organisational psychology, education and training than the many existing commercial applications which rely on theories of fixed personality traits.

Table 19

Jackson's Learning
Styles Profiler (LSP)

	Strengths	Weaknesses
General	■ The LSP is a sophisticated instrument in terms of its theory base and computerised format. ■ Designed for use in business and education.	
Design of the model	The model describes four styles: Initiator, Analyst, Reasoner and Implementer.	It is possible that the style names chosen by Jackson are not good descriptors of the underlying constructs.
Reliability	The test–retest reliability of three scales is satisfactory.	The Reasoner scale has poor test–retest reliability.
Validity	■ The authors claim *factorial validity* on the basis of a four-factor solution. ■ Some evidence of *concurrent validity* is provided by correlations with other measures of personality.	Some further refinement of items is needed, especially in the Iinitiator scale.
Implications for pedagogy	■ There is a positive emphasis in the computer-generated recommendations for personal development which result from completing the questionnaire. ■ The feedback is very detailed and contains suggestions for building on strengths, dealing with challenging situations and remedying maladaptive learning.	It is desirable, both for individuals and organisations, to build up multiple strengths rather than for people to work only in ways which come most naturally to them.
Evidence of pedagogical impact		The relevance, practicality and value of the personal feedback have yet to be evaluated.
Overall assessment	The theoretical model and the LSP, for which UK norms exist, have promise for wider use and consequential refinement in organisational and educational contexts.	
Key source	Jackson 2002	

Section 6

Flexibly stable learning preferences

Introduction

One of the most influential models of learning styles was developed by David Kolb in the early 1970s. His theory of experiential learning and the instrument which he devised to test the theory – the Learning Style Inventory (LSI) – have generated a very considerable body of research. The starting point was his dissatisfaction with traditional methods of teaching management students, which led him to experiment with experiential teaching methods. He then observed that some students had definite preferences for some activities (eg exercises), but not others (eg formal lectures): 'From this emerged the idea of an inventory that would identify these preferences by capturing individual learning differences' (Kolb 2000, 8).

For Kolb and for those who have followed in his tradition, a learning style is not a fixed trait, but 'a differential preference for learning, which changes slightly from situation to situation. At the same time, there is some long-term stability in learning style' (2000, 8). Kolb goes so far as to claim that the scores derived from the LSI are stable over very long periods; for example, the learning style of a 60 year old will bear a close resemblance to that individual's learning style when he or she was an undergraduate of 20. It is, however, difficult to accept this claim when the necessary longitudinal research has still to be carried out.

Be that as it may, Kolb's four dominant learning styles – diverging, assimilating, converging and accommodating, each located in a different quadrant of the cycle of learning – have been enormously influential in education, medicine and management training. Here it is more relevant to see Kolb as the main inspiration for large numbers of theorists and practitioners who have used his original ideas to generate their own questionnaires and teaching methods.

For example, Honey and Mumford (2000) make explicit their intellectual debt to Kolb's theory, although they also make it clear that they produced their own Learning Styles Questionnaire (LSQ) because they found that Kolb's LSI had low face validity with managers. They also made changes to Kolb's nomenclature by substituting *reflector*, *theorist*, *pragmatist* and *activist* for Kolb's rather more unwieldy terms: reflective observation, abstract conceptualisation, active experimentation and concrete experience. But as De Ciantis and Kirton (1996, 810) have pointed out: 'the descriptions [of the four styles] they represent are, by design, essentially Kolb's'.

Honey and Mumford (2000) also give pride of place in their model to the learning cycle, which for them provides an ideal structure for reviewing experience, learning lessons and planning improvements. For Honey (2002, 116), the learning cycle is:

flexible and helps people to see how they can enter the cycle at any stage with information to ponder, with a hypothesis to test, with a plan in search of an opportunity to implement it, with a technique to experiment with and see how well it works out in practice.

In the US, McCarthy (1990) has developed a detailed method of instruction called 4MAT, which is explicitly based on Kolb's theory of the cycle of learning, and which is receiving support from increasing numbers of US practitioners. We describe and evaluate 4MAT in Coffield *et al.* 2004 (Section 4) when discussing learning styles and pedagogy (see also Section 8 and Figure 13 of this report).

In much the same way as Honey and Mumford were inspired by Kolb's pioneering work, Allison and Hayes (1996) latched onto two notions ('action' and 'analysis') in Honey and Mumford's LSQ when they were devising their own Cognitive Style Index (CSI). For Allinson and Hayes, style is defined as an individual's characteristic and consistent approach to processing information, but they readily admit that a person's style can be influenced by culture, experience or a particular context. At first reading, it may appear that Allinson and Hayes' fundamental dimension of style is brain-based, with *action* being characteristic of right-brain orientation, and *analysis* being characteristic of left-brain orientation. Their claim, however, is not substantiated by any research and so, in our view, Allinson and Hayes are more appropriately placed within the Kolbian 'family' of learning theorists.

6.1
Kolb's Learning Style Inventory (LSI)

Introduction

David Kolb, Professor of Organisational Behaviour at Case Western Reserve University in Cleveland in the US, is widely credited with launching the modern learning styles movement in 1984 with the publication of *Experiential learning: experience as the source of learning and development*. That book summarised 17 years of research into the theory of experiential learning and its applications to education, work and adult development. Kolb describes in this text how the LSI was created to assess individual orientations towards learning; and, because the LSI grew out of his theory of experiential learning, it is necessary to understand that theory and the place of the LSI within it.

It has proved to be a highly productive approach as can be gauged from the fact that in 2000, Kolb produced a bibliography of research on his experiential learning theory and the LSI which contains details of 1004 studies in the fields of education (430), management (207), computer studies (104), psychology (101) and medicine (72), as well as nursing, accounting and law (see Mainemelis, Boyatzis and Kolb 2002). Kolb claims (1999) that an appreciation of differing learning styles can help people to work more effectively in teams, resolve conflict, communicate at work and at home, and choose careers. The effects of the experiential learning theory and the LSI have been widespread and the instrument itself has been translated into Arabic, Chinese, French, Italian, Russian, Spanish and Swedish.

Definitions and description

According to Kolb (1984, 41): 'learning is the process whereby knowledge is created through the transformation of experience. Knowledge results from the combination of grasping experience and transforming it'. He proposes that experiential learning has six characteristic features.

1
Learning is best conceived as a process, not in terms of outcomes.

2
Learning is a continuous process grounded in experience.

3
Learning requires the resolution of conflicts between **dialectically** opposed modes of adaptation to the world. For Kolb, learning is by its very nature full of tension, because new knowledge is constructed by learners choosing the particular type of abilities they need. Effective learners need four kinds of ability to learn: from concrete experiences (CE); from reflective observations (RO); from abstract conceptualisations (AC); and from active experimentations (AE). These four capacities are structures along two independent axes as shown in Figure 9, with the concrete experiencing of events at one end of the first axis and abstract conceptualisation at the other. The second axis has active experimentation at one end and reflective observation at the other. Conflicts are resolved by choosing one of these adaptive modes, and over time, we develop preferred ways of choosing.

4
Learning is a holistic process of adaptation to the world.

5
Learning involves transactions between the person and the environment.

6
Learning is the process of creating knowledge: '[which] is the result of the transaction between social knowledge and personal knowledge' (1984, 36).

Kolb describes the process of experiential learning as a four-stage cycle. This involves the four adaptive learning modes mentioned above – CE, RO, AC and AE – and the transactions and the resolutions among them. The tension in the abstract-concrete dimension is between relying on conceptual interpretation (what Kolb calls 'comprehension') or on immediate experience (apprehension) in order to grasp hold of experience. The tension in the active-reflective dimension is between relying on internal reflection (intention) or external manipulation (extension) in order to transform experience.

It is out of this structure that Kolb defines four different types of knowledge and four corresponding learning styles. He explains the process (1984, 76–77) as follows:

As a result of our hereditary equipment, our particular past life experience, and the demands of our present environment, most people develop learning styles that emphasise some learning abilities over others. Through socialisation experiences in family, school and work, we come to resolve the conflicts between being active and reflective and between being immediate and analytical in characteristic ways, thus leading to reliance on one of the four basic forms of knowing: divergence, achieved by reliance on apprehension transformed by intention; assimilation, achieved by comprehension transformed by intention; convergence, achieved through extensive transformation of comprehension; and accommodation, achieved through extensive transformation of apprehension.

In this way, Kolb (2000, 5) arrived at four basic learning styles, as shown in Figure 9.

In the latest version of the LSI, the previous titles of diverger, assimilator, converger and accommodator have been changed to 'the diverging style', etc to respond to the criticism that people tend to treat their learning style as static. The main characteristics of the four styles are summarised below.

■ *Type 1: the converging style* (abstract, active) relies primarily on abstract conceptualisation and active experimentation; is good at problem solving, decision making and the practical application of ideas; does best in situations like conventional intelligence tests; is controlled in the expression of emotion and prefers dealing with technical problems rather than interpersonal issues.

■ *Type 2: the diverging style* (concrete, reflective) emphasises concrete experience and reflective observation; is imaginative and aware of meanings and values; views concrete situations from many perspectives; adapts by observation rather than by action; interested in people and tends to be feeling-oriented.

■ *Type 3: the assimilating style* (abstract, reflective) prefers abstract conceptualisation and reflective observation; likes to reason inductively and to create theoretical models; is more concerned with ideas and abstract concepts than with people; thinks it more important that ideas be logically sound than practical.

■ *Type 4: the accommodating style* (concrete, active) emphasises concrete experience and active experimentation; likes doing things, carrying out plans and getting involved in new experiences; good at adapting to changing circumstances; solves problems in an intuitive, trial-and-error manner; at ease with people but sometimes seen as impatient and 'pushy'.

For more information on the strengths and weaknesses of each style, see Jonassen and Grabowski (1993).

Figure 9
Kolb's four learning styles

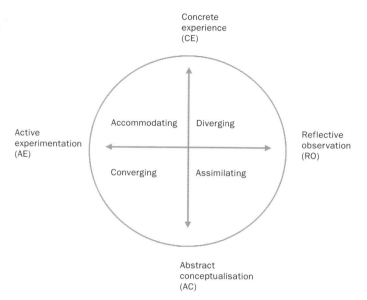

Concrete
experience
(CE)

Active
experimentation
(AE)

Accommodating   Diverging

Reflective
observation
(RO)

Converging   Assimilating

Abstract
conceptualisation
(AC)

Figure 10
The experiential
learning theory
of growth
and development

Source: Kolb (2000)

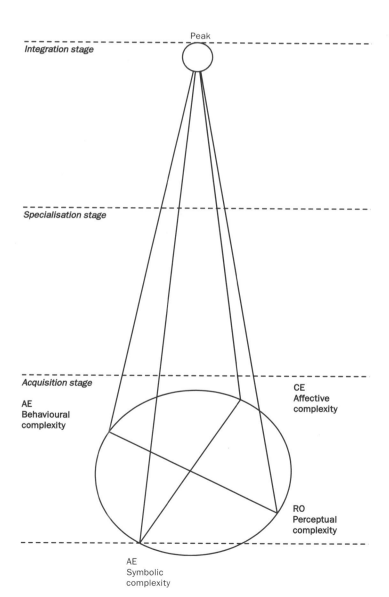

Peak

Integration stage

Specialisation stage

Acquisition stage

AE
Behavioural
complexity

CE
Affective
complexity

RO
Perceptual
complexity

AE
Symbolic
complexity

This detailed explanation of Kolb's theory, which essentially maintains that learning is a process involving the resolution of dialectical conflicts between opposing modes of dealing with the world (ie action and reflection, concreteness and abstraction), leads to Kolb's definition of learning styles (1981, 290): 'Learning styles represent preferences for one mode of adaptation over the others; but these preferences do not operate to the exclusion of other adaptive modes and will vary from time to time and situation to situation'.

In the most recent exposition of his theory, Kolb discusses three orders of learning styles from the specialised to the balanced. The first order refers to the four basic learning styles described earlier: diverging, assimilating, converging and accommodating. The second order combines the abilities of two basic learning styles; for example, the diverging and the accommodating styles. The third-order learning styles are exhibited by people who have integrated the four basic styles, who learn in a holistic way, 'using the abilities associated with all four learning modes' (Kolb, Boyatzis and Mainemelis 2001, 243). Exploratory research into these second- and third-order styles has only just begun and there are no systematic studies as yet.

Figure 10 shows the relevance of Kolb's theory for growth and development and helps to explain how individuals progress through the three developmental stages of acquisition, specialisation and integration. The model, in the shape of a cone, has the four learning modes at the base, which represents the lower stages of development, while the peak of development comes when learners can draw on all four learning modes.

Kolb claims that learning styles play a significant role in at least five main fields – behaviour/personality, educational specialisation, professional career, current job and adaptive competencies. The most relevant field to explore here is that of educational specialisation. Kolb argues that our educational experiences shape our learning styles and so we should not be surprised to find relations between specialisation and learning styles. So, for example, undergraduate students of business, management and education administration are found by Kolb to have accommodative learning styles; engineering and economics students are convergers; history, English and psychology students are divergers; mathematicians, sociologists, educational researchers, theologians and chemists are predominantly assimilators; while physicists are on the border between convergers and assimilators. In his own words (1984, 88): 'people choose fields that are consistent with their learning styles and are further shaped to fit the learning norms of their field once they are in it'.

It is important to recognise that Kolb conceives of learning styles *not* as fixed personality traits, but as adaptive orientations that achieve stability through consistent patterns of transaction with the world. In Kolb's own words (2000, 8), a learning style is a 'differential preference for learning, which changes slightly from situation to situation. At the same time, there's some long-term stability in learning style'.

Origins

Kolb is explicit in acknowledging the intellectual origins of his theory of experiential learning and of the LSI; his model is based on research in psychology, philosophy and physiology. For example, the relevance of brain research to this theory is exemplified in the finding (1984, 16) that 'the modes of knowing associated with the left and right hemispheres correspond directly with the distinction between concrete experiential and abstract cognitive approaches to learning'.

The three main figures on whose work Kolb has built his theory of experiential learning are John Dewey, Kurt Lewin and Jean Piaget. For instance, from Dewey's pragmatism he draws the notion of experience as an organising focus for learning; from Lewin's social psychology, the idea of action research; and from Piaget's genetic **epistemology**, the dialectic between assimilation and accommodation. Other figures whose ideas are incorporated into Kolb's model include Vygotsky, Guilford, Freire and Jung. Recently, Garner (2000) has criticised Kolb for claiming that his learning styles are virtually synonymous with Jung's personality types. His review of the evidence points to 'only occasional weak connections' (2000, 343) between the two approaches; moreover, he argues that Kolb has ignored the role of subordinate abilities which are so important in Jung's work.

From these sources, Kolb produced the first systematic and comprehensive exposition of the theory of experiential learning; and, as has already been mentioned, this theory forms the basis of his new typology of individual learning styles. Although his theory is rooted in the research of other thinkers, his own contribution in detailing the characteristics of experiential learning, the structural foundations of the learning process, and in creating the LSI to assess individual learning styles deserves to be regarded as original and significant.

The Learning Style Inventory (LSI)

The first version of the LSI appeared in 1976, the second in 1985, and the third in 1999 (following an experimental version in 1993); the later versions represent a response to criticisms of, for example, the internal consistency of the scales. The 1999 inventory uses a forced-choice ranking method to assess an individual's preferred modes of learning (AC, CE, AE and RO) and is described by Mainemelis, Boyatzis and Kolb (2002, 8) in the following way:

Individuals are asked to complete 12 sentences that describe learning. Each sentence (eg 'I learn best from') has four endings (eg AC = 'rational theories', CE = 'personal relationships', AE = 'a chance to try out and practice', and RO = 'observation'). Individuals rank the endings for each sentence according to what best describes the way they learn (ie '4 = most like you', '1 = least like you'). Four scores, AC, CE, AE and RO, measure an individual's preference for the four modes, and two dimensional scores indicate an individual's relative preference for one pole or the other of the two dialectics, conceptualising/experiencing (AC–CE) and acting/reflecting (AE-RO).

Kolb does not recommend that the LSI should be used for individual selection purposes because such inventories cannot measure individuals with complete accuracy: 'For this reason we do not refer to the LSI as a test but rather an experience in understanding how you learn' (Kolb, quoted by Delahoussaye 2002, 30). Earlier, Kolb (1981, 290–291) had argued his case in more detail:

When it is used in the simple, straightforward, and open way intended, the LSI usually provides an interesting self-examination and discussion that recognises the uniqueness, complexity and variability in individual approaches to learning. The danger lies in the reification of learning styles into fixed traits, such that learning styles become stereotypes used to pigeonhole individuals and their behaviour.

Reliability

The psychometric properties of the LSI have been the subject of criticism and controversy since the first version was issued in 1976. Freedman and Stumpf, for instance, argued (1978, 279) that 'the test–retest reliabilities suggest that the LSI is rather volatile, unlike the theoretical constructs being investigated'. Kolb responded by saying that because the four learning styles assessed by the LSI are theoretically interdependent and situationally variable, the two standard tests of reliability (test–retest and split-half techniques) would show lower coefficients than when measuring stable psychological traits.

Kolb went on to claim that the reliability coefficients for the two combined scores AC–CE and AE–RO were 'reasonable', but those for the four basic scales were 'somewhat less satisfactory'. He issued (1981, 293) the 'cautious recommendation … that researchers should rely on the combination scores AC–CE and AE–RO and use the single scales primarily for qualitative description'. Such caution did not, however, satisfy Stumpf and Freedman (1981, 297) who countered that the learning styles which Kolb claimed were dominant and preferred 'should be stable over a few weeks given comparable learning environments'. Their review of the literature and their own research revealed medium to low reliabilities which led them to pose (1981, 298) the pertinent question: 'How is someone classified as an assimilator to know whether the classification is due to personal characteristics, situational factors or measurement error?'. In 2002, Kolb was still claiming that test–retest studies of the LSI suggested that learning styles are relatively stable over time. He did, however, concede that:

cross-sectional studies suggest that learning style does change as a function of career path and life experience. For example, engineers who remain bench engineers throughout their career retain the converging (abstract and active) learning style typical of the engineering profession, but engineers who become managers become more concrete because of the interpersonal job demands of that role.
(Kolb, quoted by Delahoussaye 2002, 34)

Within the vast and growing literature devoted to this topic, the authors of this report moved from empirical studies which testified to the reliability (and validity) of the LSI (eg Marshall and Merritt 1986; Heffler 2001) to others which criticised the test–retest reliability of the 1985 version of the LSI as being no higher than the earlier version of 1976 (eg Wilson 1986; Veres, Sims and Shake 1987; Cornwell, Manfredo and Dunlap 1991; Newstead 1992; Lam 1997) to still others which provided decidedly mixed support (eg Geiger and Pinto 1991, 1992). To give but one example of the complexity of the issues, Ruble and Stout (1992) found that, while 56% of their respondents maintained the same learning style at the second test, 16% changed to the opposite learning style; for example, from assimilator to accommodator. Similarly, Loo (1997) reported that 13% of his sample made a dramatic change to the opposite style, with approximately half maintaining the same learning style. Moreover, in a study of 95 workers in Hong Kong, Lam (1997, 142) argued that the 1985 version of the LSI 'does not provide a reasonably stable measure of learning style when used with a nonwestern sample'.

The long history of public dispute over the reliability of the LSI can be portrayed as the action of two opposing factions of supporters and detractors. But this complex picture is made more complicated still by one of the sharpest groups of critics having a change of heart as a result of research with a modified version of the 1985 version of the LSI. In a number of studies, Veres, Sims and their colleagues had criticised the 1985 version because the minor improvements in test–retest reliability as compared to the 1976 version were not sufficient to support Kolb's theory (Sims *et al.* 1986; Veres, Sims and Shake 1987; Sims, Veres and Shake 1989). However, when they changed the instrument by randomly presenting the order of the sentence endings to eliminate a probable response bias, the test–retest reliabilities 'increased dramatically' (Veres, Sims and Locklear 1991, 149). As a result, they now recommend that researchers should use the modified version of the LSI to study learning styles.

Their stance is supported by Romero, Tepper and Tetrault (1992) who likewise, in order to avoid problems with scoring the LSI, developed new scales which proved to have adequate levels of reliability and validity. In the technical specifications of the 1999 version of the LSI, Kolb (2000, 69) uses the data produced by Veres, Sims and Locklear (1991) to claim that its reliability has been 'substantially improved as a result of the new randomized self-scoring format'.

Validity

The continuing conflict over the reliability of the LSI is replicated with respect to its validity and shows little sign of the kind of resolution which the theory of experiential learning suggests is necessary for learning to take place. The latest version of the guide to the LSI (Kolb 2000) contains one general paragraph on the topic of validity. This refers the reader to the vast bibliography on the topic, but does not provide any detailed statistics or arguments beyond claiming that in 1991, Hickox reviewed the literature and concluded that '83.3 per cent of the studies she analyzed provided support for the validity of Experiential Learning Theory and the Learning Style Inventory' (Kolb 2000, 70). In sharp contrast, Freedman and Stumpf (1978, 280) reported that in studies of undergraduates following different courses, 'on average, less than 5 percent of between-group variance … can be accounted for by knowledge of learning style'. While they accepted that the LSI has sufficient face validity to win over students, factor analysis provided only weak support for the theory; furthermore, they claimed that the variance accounted for by the LSI may be simply a function of the scoring system.

Further confusion arises because for every negative study, a positive one can be found. For example, Katz (1986) produced a Hebrew version of the LSI and administered it to 739 Israeli students to investigate its construct validity. Factor analysis provided empirical support for the construct validity of the instrument and suggested that 'Kolb's theory may be generalised to another culture and population' (Katz 1986, 1326). Yet in direct contradiction, Newstead's study (1992, 311) of 188 psychology students at the University of Plymouth found that, as well as disappointingly low reliability scores, 'the factor structure emerging from a factor analysis bore only a passing resemblance to that predicted by Kolb, and the scales did not correlate well with academic performance'.

Again, Sims, Veres and Shake (1989) attempted to establish construct validity by examining the LSI and Honey and Mumford's LSQ for convergence. The evidence, based on both instruments being administered to 279 students in two south-eastern US universities, was 'disappointingly sparse' (1989, 232). Goldstein and Bokoros (1992, 710) also compared the two instruments and found a 'modest but significant degree of classification into equivalent styles'.

A more serious challenge to Kolb's theory and instrument is provided by De Ciantis and Kirton (1996) whose psychometric analysis revealed two substantial weaknesses. First, they argued (1996, 816) that Kolb is attempting, in the LSI, to measure 'three unrelated aspects of cognition: style, level and process'. By 'process', they mean the four discrete stages of the learning cycle through which learners pass; by 'level', the ability to perform well or poorly at any of the four stages; and by 'style', the manner in which 'each stage in the learning process is approached and operationalised' (1996, 813). So, as they concluded: 'each stage can be accomplished in a range of styles and in a range of levels' (1996, 817). The separation of these three cognitive elements – style, level and process – is a significant advance in precision over Kolb's conflation of styles, abilities and stages and should help in the selection of an appropriate learning strategy.

De Ciantis and Kirton go further, however, by casting doubt on Kolb's two bipolar dimensions of reflective observation (RO)-active experimentation (AE) and concrete experience (CE)-abstract conceptualisation (AC). Interestingly, the two researchers elected to use Honey and Mumford's LSQ in their study of the learning styles of 185 managers in the UK and the Republic of Ireland, because they considered it more reliable than Kolb's LSI. Kolb's four learning styles emerged from their factor analysis, but in a different configuration, with CE at one pole and RO at the other; and AC at one pole and AE at the other.

More recently, Wierstra and de Jong (2002) have again empirically analysed the two-dimensional model behind the 1985 version of the LSI and have suggested yet another configuration. They argue that there has been no conclusive evidence for the existence of Kolb's two dimensions – AC-CE and RO-AE – and indeed, other researchers have found different two-dimensional structures or no two-dimensional structure at all (eg Cornwell, Manfredo and Dunlap 1991; Geiger and Pinto 1992). Their own research found two configurations of the relations between the four constructs, both of them different from the structure proposed by Kolb. Their preferred solution, which is suggested by all the types of analysis they carried out and which is not influenced by the problem of the 'ipsative' scoring system (see below for explanation) is 'a one-dimensional bipolar representation: (AC+RO) versus (AE+CE) or "reflective learning versus learning by doing"' (Wierstra and de Jong 2002, 439). This finding now needs to be replicated with other samples, but there is no doubt that, for the present, their research and that of De Ciantis and Kirton constitute a serious challenge to the construct validity of the LSI.

General issues

Another recurrent criticism of the LSI has concerned the scoring method. There are, in effect, two separate issues which are sometimes combined by some commentators. First, all three versions of the LSI employ the forced-choice method which Kolb chose deliberately, *partly* to increase the ecological validity of the instrument (ie the learner is forced to make a choice between different ways of learning in accordance with Kolb's theory), and *partly* to avoid the 'social desirability response' set. To control for this response, Kolb chose four words 'of equally positive social desirability' (1981, 293), although it is questionable whether this objective has been achieved.

Second, the LSI is what is technically described as 'ipsative': that is, the interdependence of the four learning modes is built into the test. To explain in more detail, a learner is forced to assign one of the four scores (1, 2, 3 or 4) to one of four endings to a sentence so that the total score for each learner for each sentence is always 10 (ie 1+2+3+4). For example, 'When I learn: I am happy (1). I am fast (3). I am logical (2). I am careful (4)'. For Wierstra and de Jong (2002, 432), 'ipsativity obscures the real relation between the four learning modes and it hampers research into the dimensionality of the test'.

Mainemelis, Boyatzis and Kolb (2002, 10) responded to these problems by arguing as follows: 'In the LSI, the four scale scores (AC, CE, AE, RO) are clearly ipsative, but the two dimensional scores (AC-CE and AE-RO) are not … learning styles in the LSI are determined on the basis of the two non-ipsative dimensional scores and not the four ipsative scale scores'.

Implications for pedagogy

Kolb argues that his theory of experiential learning provides a useful framework for the design and management of all learning experiences and, moreover, he makes three practical suggestions. Both types of contribution are briefly explored here.

According to Kolb (1984, 196), the main weakness of current pedagogy is 'the failure to recognise and explicitly provide for the differences in learning styles that are characteristic of both individuals and subject matters'. As a result of studying the instructional preferences of students of business and architecture, Kolb produced a table which lists in great detail the characteristics of learning environments that help or hinder learners with four different learning styles. For example, the students scoring highest in active experimentation were, it is claimed, helped in their learning by small-group discussions, projects, peer feedback and homework, but not by lectures.

Kolb's first practical suggestion is that teachers and learners should explicitly share their respective theories of learning, a process which would create four benefits.

■ Students would understand why the subject matter is taught as it is and what changes they would need to make to their learning styles to study this subject.

■ Teachers would identify the range of learning styles among the student body and would modify their teaching accordingly.

■ Both teachers and students would be 'stimulated to examine and refine their learning theories' (Kolb 1984, 202).

■ Through dialogue, teachers would become more empathetic with their students and so more able to help them improve their knowledge and skills. Freedman and Stumpf (1978) make, however, the reasonable point that such dialogues will not always take place in ideal conditions – that is, in small classes which provide individual attention from a tutor who is trained in the theory and practice of learning styles.

The need to individualise instruction is the second practical conclusion that Kolb draws from his research into learning environments. This is, of course, easier said than done, particularly in further education with large group sizes and a modular curriculum, but Kolb believes that information technology (IT) will provide the breakthrough, together with a shift in the teacher's role from 'dispenser of information to coach or manager of the learning process' (1984, 202). Kolb's *Facilitator's guide to learning* presents a table which 'summarizes learning strengths and preferred learning situations that have been discussed in learning style research' (Kolb 2000, 17). No further details about the research are given. The table claims, for example, that those whose strength lies in learning by experiencing prefer games and role plays, whereas those whose strength lies in learning by reflecting prefer lectures.

Finally, Kolb is concerned about the growing specialisation in US higher education and does not want students to be equipped only with the learning styles appropriate for particular careers. Instead, he argues for 'integrative development', where students become highly competent in all four learning modes: active, reflective, abstract and concrete (see Kolb *et al.* 1986 on integrative learning for managers). So Kolb's aim is to produce balanced learners with a full range of learning capacities, rather than simply matching instruction to existing learning styles.

Empirical evidence for pedagogical impact

The literature on learning styles contains many discussions of the significance and relevance of Kolb's theory and practical concerns for pedagogy (eg Claxton and Murrell 1987; Sharp 1997). Unfortunately, that section of the literature which consists of experimental studies of the fit between learning styles and teaching methods is rather small, the size of the samples is not large, and the findings are contradictory and inconclusive. Some studies – some negative and others more supportive – will now be described to give a flavour of the range. Sugarman, for example, views Kolb's theory of experiential learning 'as a model of effective teaching' (1985, 264). She also raises the interesting question as to whether all courses should begin with concrete experience as this is the first stage in Kolb's learning cycle and he claims that the most effective learning emanates from personal experiences. Such a proposal may run up against the expectations of students, but unfortunately there is no testing of the idea by Sugarman.

Empirical investigations of the relationship between learning styles and teaching methods have, however, produced some surprising findings. McNeal and Dwyer (1999), for instance, used Kolb's LSI to ascertain the learning styles of 154 US nursing students who were then assigned *either* to a group where the teaching agreed with their learning style, *or* where it did not, *or* to a control group. The hypothesis was that teaching which was consistent with the learning style of the learners would enhance their learning, but no significant differences were found in the achievement of the three groups.

Similarly, Buch and Bartley (2002, 7) administered both Kolb's LSI and a new instrument devised by the authors – the Preferred Delivery Mode Self-Assessment – to 165 employees in a large US financial institution. The workers had to choose between five different teaching methods – computer, TV, print, audio or classroom. Buch and Bartley's review of research into the relationship between learning style and training delivery mode led them to hypothesise that accommodators and convergers would prefer computers, divergers would prefer classrooms and assimilators would choose print. The results, however, showed that 'all learners, regardless of learning style, prefer the traditional approach to learning, face-to-face classroom delivery' (2002, 9). Was this because the workers felt more comfortable with a teaching method which they had known since early childhood? Or did they prefer the classroom to modern technology for social reasons, or because they did not want to be challenged by new methods? No definitive answers are provided by the study.

Another study explored the interesting question: would knowledge of learning styles and the provision of 'prescriptive study strategies' improve the academic achievement of adult graduate students? Ehrhard (2000) explored this hypothesis with 148 students: they were divided into an experimental group, who were sent a personalised learning profile and study strategies that were appropriate for their learning type, and a control group who received nothing. The scores for the two groups were similar. So knowledge of learning style backed up by some supportive advice did not appear, in this case, to be sufficient to improve learning. On the other hand, students who were given Kolb's theory and LSI as a framework to discuss their learning, often reported an 'increased sense of self-esteem and self-understanding' (Mark and Menson, quoted by Claxton and Murrell 1987, 31).

More positively still, Katz (1990) in a quasi-experimental study of 44 occupational therapy students in the US and 50 in Israel, hypothesised that students whose learning styles matched the teaching method would perform better (ie more effectively) and would need less time to study outside class (ie more efficiently). The findings in both countries supported the premise that 'the better the match is between students' individual characteristics and instructional components, the more effective or efficient the learning program is' (Katz 1990, 233). But even this conclusion needed to be qualified as it applied only to higher-order cognitive outcomes and not to basic knowledge.

Further support is provided by Sein and Robey (1991) who administered Kolb's LSI to 80 undergraduate computer students in the US and then assigned them randomly to one of two different training methods. The results appear to indicate that 'performance can be enhanced by tailoring instructional methods to accommodate individual preferences in learning style' (1991, 246). However, no control group was used and no indication was given of the size of the effect.

How is one to make sense of such conflicting evidence, based as it is on rather small samples? Fortunately, there are two reviews of the literature which provide a little help. Cavanagh and Coffin evaluated the literature on 'matching' and found 'relatively little empirical work to indicate the exact nature and magnitude of the change that can be expected in a student's learning' (1994, 109). The age of the learner appears to be crucial, as there was evidence that matching improved academic performance in primary education in the US; but the evidence in higher education generally, and in nursing more particularly, was inconclusive. Crucially, they concluded that little is known about the interaction of learning styles with organisational and resource issues. Their advice (1994, 109) is that 'just varying delivery style may not be enough and ... the unit of analysis must be the individual rather than the group'.

The second, more recent, review by Smith, Sekar and Townsend found that: 'For each research study supporting the principle of matching instructional style and learning style, there is a study rejecting the matching hypothesis' (2002, 411). Indeed, they found eight studies supporting and eight studies rejecting the 'matching' hypothesis, which is based on the assumption that learning styles, if not a fixed characteristic of the person, are at least relatively stable over time. Kolb's views at least are clear: rather than confining learners to their preferred style, he advocates stretching their learning capabilities in other learning modes. Grasha (1984) reviewed the literature on matching and concluded that no single dimension of learners should dictate teaching methods.

Conclusion

In a recent article, Mainemelis, Boyatzis and Kolb (2002) summarise the evidence for and against the LSI by reference to two unpublished doctoral dissertations in the US. The first, by Hickox, analysed 81 studies and concluded that 'overall 61.7 per cent of the studies supported the Experiential Learning Theory (ELT), 16.1 per cent showed mixed support and 22.2 per cent did not support ELT' (cited by Mainemelis, Boyatzis and Kolb 2002, 12). The second meta-analysis by Iliff of 101 quantitative studies found that '49 studies showed strong support for the LSI, 40 showed mixed support and 12 studies showed no support' (cited by Mainemelis, Boyatzis and Kolb 2002, 12). Iliff also concluded that the balance of the evidence suggested that the statistical standards set for predictive validity had not been met by the LSI, while recognising that the LSI was developed as a self-assessment exercise and not as a predictive test. It seems difficult, if not impossible, to move beyond this continuing debate, with some researchers advocating the use of the LSI, and others denouncing it, while still others (eg Loo 1999) recognise the weaknesses of the instrument, and at the same time, argue for its usefulness as a pedagogical tool.

In response to earlier criticism, Kolb (2000) claims that the latest version of the LSI has further improved the test–retest reliability, but as yet there is no independent body of evidence to confirm or deny that statement. In the meantime, Kolb and his associates have developed two new instruments: the Adaptive Style Inventory (ASI) which aims to measure flexibility in learning – 'the degree to which individuals change their learning style to respond to different learning situations in their life' (Mainemelis, Boyatzis and Kolb 2002, 11); and the Learning Skills Profile (LSP) – to assess levels of skill development in interpersonal, information, analytical and behavioural skills. This latest instrument (LSP) means that learning *styles* must now be distinguished from learning *skills*. According to Kolb (2000, 50), the former are the ways we prefer to absorb and incorporate new information, while the latter are more situational and subject to intentional development: 'A skill is a combination of ability, knowledge and experience that enables a person to do something well'. Despite this recent surge of creativity, it is still difficult to resist the conclusion that the statistical sophistication used to analyse the data is not matched by the theoretical sophistication used to improve the concept of learning styles.

An overall evaluation of Kolb's contribution therefore needs to differentiate between the theory of experiential learning and the instrument, the LSI, that is designed to measure individual learning styles. Kolb has not only explicitly based his four learning styles on a theory, he also developed that theory which has been very widely taken up by researchers, tutors and trainers in, for example, education, counselling, management and business more generally. There is now a massive international literature devoted to the topic, which shows no signs of waning.

On the other hand, the controversies over the psychometric properties of the first two versions of the LSI continue unabated, while it is still too early to pass judgement on the third version. What, however, cannot be contested is that Kolb's instrument has created a whole school of adapters and revisers who have used the LSI as the basis from which to develop their own version of a learning styles instrument. Of these, Honey and Mumford (2000) are the best known. But whether the continuing proliferation of 'eponymous questionnaires that overlap considerably' is good for the development of the (in)discipline is an important issue raised by Furnham (1992, 437). The unending controversies over the psychometric shortcomings of the LSI have, however, had one unfortunate consequence: they 'have discouraged conceptual development and testing of the experiential learning theory' (Romero, Tepper and Tetrault 1992, 172).

The debate over the most appropriate measure of reliability of the LSI is not just a technical issue; for some commentators, like Garner (2000, 346), it is a reflection of deeper theoretical contradictions in Kolb's work because 'the actual nature of what is being measured is constantly shifting from "flexible" to "stable"'. Garner's argument is that Kolb has responded to criticism by claiming that his learning styles exhibit 'stable flexibility', but they are presented in his published work as highly stable and essentially fixed. Similarly, Garner finds unconvincing Kolb's reference to the importance of context as a means of avoiding the charge of stereotyping: 'Kolb *attributes learning styles to the learners themselves* and, although he recognises the influence of the environment, he makes no attempt to describe exactly what this influence is or how it can be best understood or measured' (Garner 2000, 343; original emphasis).

Kolb clearly believes that learning takes place in a cycle and that learners should use all four phases of that cycle to become effective. Popular adaptations of his theory (for which he is not, of course, responsible) claim, however, that all four phases should be tackled and in order. The manual for the third version of the LSI is explicit on this point: 'You may begin a learning process in any of the four phases of the learning cycle. Ideally, using a well-rounded learning process, you would cycle through all the four phases. However, you may find that you sometimes skip a phase in the cycle or focus primarily on just one' (Kolb 1999, 4). But if Wierstra and de Jong's (2002) analysis, which reduces Kolb's model to a one-dimensional bipolar structure of reflection versus doing, proves to be accurate, then the notion of a learning cycle may be seriously flawed.

There is also a general, and largely unacknowledged, problem with some of the best summaries and descriptions of Kolb's learning styles, when they turn to a discussion of the relevance of the styles for teaching or instruction. For example, Jonassen and Grabowski, in a highly detailed and fine-grained analysis of Kolb's contribution, base their two pages of advice to tutors on implications which they have 'drawn logically from descriptive information regarding the trait' (1993, 259) rather than on findings from research. The five studies which they review, before offering their advice, include commentators who 'believe' in one practice or who 'recommend' another. There does not yet appear to be sufficient experimental evidence about Kolb's learning styles on which to base firm recommendations about pedagogy.

Finally, it may be asked if too much is being expected of a relatively simple test which consists of nine (1976) or 12 (1985 and 1999) sets of four words to choose from. What is indisputable is that such simplicity has generated complexity, controversy and an enduring and frustrating lack of clarity.

Table 20
Kolb's Learning Style
Inventory (LSI)

	Strengths	Weaknesses
General	■ Learning styles are not fixed personality traits, but relatively stable patterns of behaviour. ■ 30 years of critique have helped to improve the LSI, which can be used as an introduction to how people learn.	Should not be used for individual selection.
Design of the model	■ Learning styles are both flexible and stable. ■ Based on the theory of experiential learning which incorporates growth and development.	Three elements need to be separated: ■ process = the four stages of the learning cycle ■ level = how well one performs at any of the four stages ■ style = how each stage is approached.
Reliability	Changes to the instrument have increased its reliability.	Long, public dispute over reliability of LSI. Third version is still undergoing examination.
Validity		■ The construct validity of the LSI has been challenged and the matter is not yet settled. ■ It has low predictive validity, but it was developed for another purpose – as a self-assessment exercise.
Implications for pedagogy	■ In general, the theory claims to provide a framework for the design and management of all learning experiences. ■ Teachers and students may be stimulated to examine and refine their theories of learning; through dialogue, teachers may become more empathetic with students. ■ All students to become competent in all four learning styles (active, reflective, abstract and concrete) to produce balanced, integrated learners. ■ Instruction to be individualised with the help of IT.	■ The notion of a learning cycle may be seriously flawed. ■ The implications for teaching have been drawn logically from the theory rather than from research findings.
Evidence of pedagogical impact		■ There is no evidence that 'matching' improves academic performance in further education. ■ The findings are contradictory and inconclusive. No large body of unequivocal evidence on which to base firm recommendations about pedagogy.
Overall assessment	One of the first learning styles, based on an explicit theory. Problems about reliability, validity and the learning cycle continue to dog this model.	
Key source	Kolb 1999	

6.2
Honey and Mumford's Learning Styles Questionnaire (LSQ)

Introduction

In the late 1970s, Alan Mumford was in charge of senior management development at the Chloride Organisation and invited Peter Honey, a chartered psychologist, to join him in studying the then relatively neglected topic of how managers learn. They began by administering Kolb's Learning Style Inventory (LSI), which was the first, and for some time the only, available diagnostic tool for exploring how individuals learn. Because the LSI was found to have low face validity with managers, Honey and Mumford spent four years experimenting with different approaches to assessing individual differences in learning preferences before producing the Learning Styles Questionnaire (LSQ) in 1982. So instead of asking people directly how they learn, as Kolb's LSI does – something which most people have never consciously considered – Honey and Mumford give them a questionnaire which probes general behavioural tendencies rather than learning. The new instrument was designed to be used as a starting point for discussion and improvement. Peter Honey has continued working in the same vein, producing a series of manuals for trainers and self-help booklets for learners (eg Honey 1994).

The links with Kolb's work remain strong, however, because the four learning styles are connected to a revised version of Kolb's experiential learning cycle. So, for example, activists are said to have a predilection for experiencing; reflectors for reviewing experiences or mulling over data; theorists for drawing conclusions; and pragmatists for planning the next steps (see Figure 11). Honey and Mumford's intention is that learners should become proficient in all four stages of the learning cycle.

Definitions and descriptions

Honey and Mumford (1992, 1) define a learning style as being 'a description of the attitudes and behaviour which determine an individual's preferred way of learning'. The four learning styles are described as those of activists, reflectors, theorists and pragmatists and the following lists in Table 21 give a brief summary of the strengths and weaknesses of each style:

The authors are keen to emphasise (2000, 43) that 'no single style has an overwhelming advantage over any other. Each has strengths and weaknesses but the strengths may be especially important in one situation, but not in another'. They are also careful not to exaggerate the significance of personal learning styles and explicitly acknowledge that they constitute only one factor in a range of influences which include past experiences of learning, the range of opportunities available, the culture and climate for learning and the impact of the trainer/teacher, among many other factors.

Moreover, it is emphasised that the LSQ should be used for personal and organisational development and not for assessment or selection, an approach which, it is argued, encourages respondents to behave honestly. Honey and Mumford also provide answers to some of the most frequently posed questions about learning styles, the most significant of which are briefly discussed here.

■ *Are there only four learning styles?*
The figure of four is defended because 'they are easy to remember, they reinforce the stages people need to go through to become balanced learners and they are widely understood, accepted and used by learners...' (Honey and Mumford 2000, 19).

■ *Can learning style preferences change?*
Learning styles 'are modifiable at will' – for example, to strengthen an underdeveloped style; or 'by a change of circumstances' (Honey and Mumford 2000, 19) – for example, a change of job to a firm with a different learning culture.

■ *How accurate are self-perceptions?*
It is admitted that 'self-perceptions can be misleading [and that] the answers are easy to fake if someone is determined to give a misleading impression' (Honey and Mumford 2000, 20). The latter is considered less likely if people have been assured that the LSQ is a tool for personal development.

■ *Why does the LSQ allow a binary choice – tick or cross?*
'To keep it simple' (Honey and Mumford 2000, 21). This does not obviate the difficulty many people find in being forced to respond 'Yes' or 'No' to such items as 'I tend to be open about how I'm feeling' or 'I'm always interested to find out what people think'.

■ *Aren't labels misleading/stereotyping?*
The labels 'are a convenient oversimplification ... [and] a starting point for discussion on how an individual learns. That discussion will remove any misleading judgements' (2000, 21). This presupposes that the LSQ is always used by trainers/tutors who are knowledgeable about the strengths and limitations of the approach, who are aware of the dangers of labelling and stereotyping and who discuss the results of the LSQ individually with the learners. Indeed, elsewhere, Honey and Mumford (2000, 41) argue that a trainer needs to be '...adept at interpreting the questionnaire and counselling interested parties in its implications'.

Table 21
Strengths and
weaknesses

Source: Honey and
Mumford (2000)

Style	Strengths	Weaknesses
Activists	■ Flexible and open-minded ■ Ready to take action ■ Like to be exposed to new situations ■ Optimistic about anything new and therefore unlikely to resist change	■ Tendency to take the immediately obvious action without thinking through possible consequences ■ Often take unnecessary risks ■ Tendency to do too much themselves and to hog the limelight ■ Rush into action without sufficient preparation ■ Get bored with implementation/consolidation/follow through
Reflectors	■ Careful ■ Thorough and methodical ■ Thoughtful ■ Good at listening to others and assimilating information ■ Rarely jump to conclusions	■ Tendency to hold back from direct participation ■ Slow to make up their minds and reach a decision ■ Tendency to be too cautious and not take enough risks ■ Not assertive; not particularly forthcoming and have no 'small talk'
Theorists	■ Logical, 'vertical' thinkers ■ Rational and objective ■ Good at asking probing questions ■ Disciplined approach ■ Grasp of the 'big picture'	■ Restricted in lateral thinking ■ Low tolerance for uncertainty, disorder and ambiguity ■ Intolerant of anything subjective or intuitive ■ Full of 'shoulds, oughts and musts'
Pragmatists	■ Eager to test things out in practice ■ Practical, down to earth, realistic ■ Businesslike – get straight to the point ■ Technique-oriented	■ Tendency to reject anything without an obvious application ■ Not very interested in theory or basic principles ■ Tendency to seize on the first expedient solution to a problem ■ Impatient with indecision ■ More task-oriented than people-oriented

Table 22
LSQ retest correlations,
by learning style

Style	
Theorists	
	0.95
Reflectors	
	0.92
Pragmatists	
	0.87
Activists	
	0.81

Figure 11
Dimensions of Honey
and Mumford's
learning cycle

Source: Honey and
Mumford (2000)

Activist
Stage 1
Having an
experience

Reflector
Stage 2
Reviewing the
experience

Theorist
Stage 3
Concluding
from the
experience

Pragmatist
Stage 4
Planning the
next steps

Measurement by authors

Description of measure

The *Manual of learning styles* was published in 1982, revised in 1992 and then replaced in 2000 by *The learning styles helper's guide* and the LSQ. According to Honey, their learning styles 'have been translated into dozens of languages, are now used throughout the world, in all sectors of commerce and education, and enjoy high face validity' (Honey and Mumford 2000, foreword). The current version of the LSQ consists of 80 items which probe preferences for four learning styles with 20 items for each style.

The manual for the LSQ (Honey and Mumford 1992) contains a variety of suggestions to help people strengthen an underutilised style, including keeping a learning log to encourage people to review their experiences, to draw out the lessons they have learned from them and to form plans to do something better/different. The objectives of the LSQ are clear throughout – to offer practical help to individuals, and especially directors and managers, either in playing to their strengths as learners or in developing as all-round learners or both. Such practical help follows from the belief of Honey and Mumford that, as preferences have been learned, they can be modified and improved upon. The key issue for Mumford (1987, 59) is that the LSQ enables managers to 'improve their learning processes, not just diagnose them'.

Reliability and validity

In the final chapter of *The learning styles helper's guide* (2000), Honey and Mumford provide some statistical data on the LSQ. With regard to reliability, a test–retest study of 50 people, with an interval of 2 weeks between tests, provided a correlation of 0.89. In more detail, the correlations for the four styles are shown in Table 22, above.

The authors claim that the face validity of the LSQ is not in doubt, but no other type of validity has been explored by them. One exercise has also been completed to estimate how many people have a strong preference for one style, where 'strong' means the top 30% of scores. The results from a random sample of 300 managers were as follows.

- With 1 strong preference
  35%

- With 2 strong preferences
  24%

- With 3 strong preferences
  20%

- With 4 strong preferences
  2%

- With 0 strong preferences
  19%

These results could be presented as meaning that a majority (59%) of these managers have either one or two strong preferences and that only 2% appear to be well-rounded learners. Alternatively, it could be claimed that almost two-thirds (65%) do not exhibit one strong preference and so the labelling of people as 'theorists' or 'pragmatists' is only likely to be accurate in one out of three cases.

Finally, norms are given for various occupational groups (eg civil servants, police inspectors), for males and females (which suggest that there are no significant gender differences) and for a small number of countries (which indicate that differences exist between Scandinavian countries and Italy). It has to be borne in mind, however, that the samples on which these conclusions are based are generally very small; for example, the gender differences are explored with random samples of 117 females and 117 males. The only exception is that the general norms are based on scores from 3500 people.

External evaluation

Since its development, the LSQ has attracted considerable interest, application and research. Its arrival on the scene was welcomed at first as an improvement on Kolb's LSI, but evaluation by a number of researchers has become increasingly critical. A brief account is now given of the findings from the major research studies of the LSQ, followed by Honey's response to the criticisms and a final comment by the present authors.

Psychologists like Furnham (1992, 1996b; Furnham, Jackson and Miller 1999) have explored the correlation between classic personality variables such as extraversion and the four learning styles proposed by Honey and Mumford. He concluded (1999, 1115) that 'learning styles is (sic) a sub-set of personality' and so need not be measured independently. Jackson and Lawty-Jones (1996) confirmed Furnham's findings and suggested that learning styles represent the components of personality which are related to learning. In Furnham, Jackson and Miller's study (1999) of 203 telephone sales employees, it is important to note that the percentage of variance explained by both personality and learning styles was only about 8%. The authors comment (1999, 1120): 'This is not a large amount and indicates that the majority of variance was unrelated to individual differences in personality and learning style'. Perhaps the research emphasis should be directed to whatever explains the remaining 92% of the variance. The LSQ, however, in Furnham's research proved to be more predictive of supervisor ratings in the workplace than Eysenck's Personality Inventory.

The earliest studies of the psychometric properties of the LSQ by Allinson and Hayes (1988, 1990) claimed that its temporal stability and internal consistency were well established and offered some evidence of construct validity, but not of concurrent or predictive validity. The overall evaluation of the LSQ by Allinson and Hayes amounted to a cautious welcome as the following quotation (1990, 866) makes clear:

Although the questionnaire appears to be a stable and internally consistent measure of two behavioural or attitudinal dimensions, it is still not clear that it provides a satisfactory alternative to Kolb's inventory as a method of assessing learning styles. More evidence of its validity is necessary before it can be adopted with confidence.

In 1999, Swailes and Senior surveyed 329 British managers, using cluster and factor analysis, to assess the validity of the LSQ. Their findings indicated a three-stage learning cycle of action, reflection and planning as opposed to the four stages in Honey and Mumford's model. Moreover, they noted the poor discrimination of some LSQ items, claiming that over one-third of the items failed to discriminate between learning styles. They conclude (1999, 9–10) that the scale scores 'do not appear distinctive enough to allow individuals to be categorized on the basis of their learning style profiles', and they recommend that the LSQ be redesigned to overcome the weaknesses they identify.

Sadler-Smith (2001a) examined the claims of Swailes and Senior by administering the LSQ to 233 business and management undergraduates in the UK, and used confirmatory factor analysis to test the Honey and Mumford model against competing explanations. His data indicates that 'the LSQ does not measure two bipolar dimensions of learning style as might be anticipated from its origins in the theory by Kolb (1984). Rather, the LSQ and Honey and Mumford's version of the learning cycle appear to consist of four uni-polar elements' (Sadler-Smith 2001a, 212). In an important rejoinder, Swailes and Senior quoted Mumford as stating in a personal communication that 'the LSQ is not based upon Kolb's bi-polar structure as the academic community seems to think' (2001, 215). Unfortunately, no alternative theoretical structure has so far been suggested by Honey and Mumford.

More recently still, Duff (2001) and Duff and Duffy (2002) have usefully summarised the estimates from a number of research studies of the psychometric properties of the LSQ. A study by Fung, Ho and Kwan (1993) is omitted from what follows because a short form of the LSQ was used which was probably responsible for relatively low reliability scores. On the other hand, a study of the learning styles and academic performance of engineering and business students by Van Zwanenberg, Wilkinson and Anderson (2000) is included because its findings are consonant with those of the other researchers, including Duff and Duffy (2002).

First, Duff and Duffy (2002) examined the internal consistency reliability of the LSQ (ie the extent to which the items in the questionnaire are measuring the same thing) by summarising the findings of previous research as well as by conducting their own studies. The results from Allinson and Hayes (1988), Sims, Veres and Shake (1989), Tepper *et al.* (1993), Jackson and Lawty-Jones (1996), De Ciantis and Kirton (1996) and Van Zwanenberg, Wilkinson and Anderson (2000) are remarkably consistent: they show only a moderate internal consistency reliability of the order of 0.52 to 0.78, when 0.8 is usually regarded as the acceptable criterion of reliability. Duff and Duffy also used both exploratory and confirmatory factor analysis in order to identify the four learning styles and two bipolar dimensions proposed by Honey and Mumford, but they failed to do so. Moreover, learning style proved to be only a weak predictor of academic performance. Mumford (2003) objected to this inference because the course design and methods are likely to dictate the learning style. If, for example, a course is biased towards theorist preferences, then in order to pass, most students, regardless of their real preferences, will learn in that way. It would then be unsurprising if the LSQ scores were poor predictors. Duff and Duffy (2002, 160) concluded as follows:

Caution should be employed if adopting the LSQ to select appropriate instructional materials or to categorise individual students. The findings indicate the LSQ is not a suitable alternative to either [Kolb's] LSI or LSI-1985.

Honey (2002b) countered that these academic criticisms miss the point and are 'unhelpful in undermining confidence in a diagnostic [tool] that has proved to be helpful to so many people for 20 years'. Moreover, he argued that the academics are treating the LSQ as a psychometric instrument which it was never intended to be:

The LSQ is simply a checklist that invites people to take stock of how they learn. It is purely designed to stimulate people into thinking about the way they learn from experience (which most people just take for granted). There is nothing remotely sophisticated about it: it is an utterly straightforward, harmless self-developmental tool.

Honey (2002c) summed up as follows: 'The LSQ is therefore merely a starting point, a way to get people who haven't thought about how they learn to give it some consideration and to realise, often for the first time, that learning is learnable'. Finally, he challenged the academics by asking what questionnaire they would recommend and, if they are unable to do so, what questionnaire they have themselves designed.

Table 23
Activities and preferences

Source: Honey and Mumford (2000)

Activists react positively to:	■ Action learning ■ Business game simulations	■ Job rotation ■ Discussion in small groups	■ Role playing ■ Training others ■ Outdoor activities
Reflectors react positively to:	■ E-learning ■ Learning reviews	■ Listening to lectures or presentations ■ Observing role plays	■ Reading ■ Self-study/self-directed learning
Theorists react positively to:	■ Analytical reviewing ■ Exercises with a right answer	■ Listening to lectures ■ Self-study/self-directed learning	■ Solo exercises ■ Watching 'talking head' videos
Pragmatists react positively to:	■ Action learning ■ Discussion about work problems in the organisation	■ Discussion in small groups ■ Problem-solving workshops	■ Group work with tasks where learning is applied ■ Project work

Recently, Honey and Mumford's LSQ was used by Price and Richardson (2003) to examine the relationships between learning style and performance and different instructional methods. They also studied the usefulness of the LSQ in predicting students' preferences among instructional models, and students' performance, study techniques and recall processes. The LSQ consistently failed to predict all these aspects of students' performance and preferences. Price and Richardson concluded (2003, 294) that '…tests of generalised individual differences are inappropriate for understanding performance in task-specific and context-dependent situations'.

Implications for pedagogy

When it comes to matching learning activities with learning style preferences, Honey and Mumford claim (2000, 28) that: 'Our research into a number of different training methods showed the following positive correlations'. Unfortunately, what follows is not a set of correlations, but a list of activities which match each of the four learning styles, a list which is reproduced above in Table 23. No further information is given either about the research or the correlations.

It is also clear from Honey and Mumford (2000) that the two main uses for the LSQ, as envisaged by the authors, are to devise personal development plans and to show the activist manager, the reflector manager, the theorist manager and the pragmatist manager how to help their staff learn by, for example, choosing activities that are congruent with the preferred style of the learners. Honey and Mumford argue (2000, 52) that 'managers, if they encourage learning at all, will tend to do so in ways consistent with their own learning styles'. An approach which improves the quality of support for workplace learning is to be welcomed, particularly given the findings of research which show that 'a major factor affecting a person's learning at work is the personality, interpersonal skills, knowledge and learning orientation of their manager' (Eraut et al. 1999, 29).

Empirical evidence of pedagogical impact

No empirical evidence of pedagogical impact is quoted in the guide to the LSQ (Honey and Mumford 2000) and we have found no other such studies.

Conclusions

The research summarised above has clearly cast doubt both on the psychometric robustness of the LSQ and its ability to predict performance. If trainers in firms and FE and HE tutors are to continue to use the LSQ, they need to be aware of these deficiencies and of the dangers of labelling individuals; and they also have to make the prior professional decision either to concentrate on trying to change the learning styles of individuals, or the learning culture of the organisation, or any of the many other factors which affect learning. If the LSQ is used, as Honey suggests, purely as a stimulus to discussion with a knowledgeable tutor about how people can become more effective learners, then perhaps little harm and some good will be done. The original intention of the authors needs to be kept in mind – namely, to help managers who want to improve their own performance as well as the performance of the people they are responsible for. A more satisfactory outcome, however, would be a revision of the LSQ to answer the criticisms which have been made of it.

Perhaps the more fundamental problem is the implicit assumption that one instrument of 80 statements can capture all the complexities and the multifaceted nature of learning as well as the cycle of learning. In addition, Honey and Mumford based their LSQ on Kolb's model, but because they found its bipolar structure untenable, they designed the LSQ so that the style preferences are aligned to the stages in the learning cycle. They have not, however, produced an alternative to Kolb's bipolar theory. For all these criticisms, the LSQ remains very popular as a self-development tool with practitioners, is used extensively – for instance, by industrial trainers and FE tutors – and can now be completed online.

Table 24
Honey and Mumford's
Learning Styles
Questionnaire (LSQ)

	Strengths	Weaknesses
General	LSQ probes the attitudes and behaviours which determine preferences with regard to learning. To be used for personal/organisational development and not for assessment/selection. Not a psychometric instrument, but a checklist about how people learn.	Danger of labelling people as 'theorists' or 'pragmatists', when most people exhibit more than one strong preference.
Design of the model	Based on Kolb's model, with new terms for style preferences which are aligned to the four stages in the learning cycle.	Evaluation by researchers has become increasingly critical, eg percentage of *variance* explained by personality and learning style put at 8% (Jackson and Lawty-Jones 1996).
Reliability		Only moderate internal consistency has been found.
Validity	Face validity is claimed by authors.	Validity not assessed by authors. More evidence is needed before LSQ is acceptable.
Implications for pedagogy	■ To help managers/ employees to devise personal development plans. ■ To show managers how to help their staff learn. ■ To be used as a starting point for discussion and improvement with a knowledgeable tutor. ■ Suggestions made to help people strengthen an under-utilised style.	All the suggestions are derived logically or from practice with using the LSQ; they have not been rigorously tested to see if they work.
Evidence of pedagogical impact	No evidence quoted by authors.	No evidence found by researchers.
Overall assessment	Has been widely used in business, but needs to be redesigned to overcome weaknesses identified by researchers.	
Key source	Honey and Mumford 2000	

6.3
The Herrmann 'whole brain' model and the Herrmann Brain Dominance Instrument (HBDI)

Introduction

Ned Herrmann developed his 'whole brain' concept while he was in charge of management education for General Electric. Throughout his education and professional career, he was actively involved with the creative arts as well as with science and technology. Having developed a format of self-assessment by questionnaire, followed by group learning activities, he left General Electric in 1982 to set up the Ned Herrmann Group. The group is now established in more than a dozen countries, offering services in personal, interpersonal, staff and organisational development. These services are derived from the profiling procedure built into the Herrmann Brain Dominance Instrument (HBDI). At the time of writing, over 1m mental preference profiles have been analysed by occupational category and in other ways, including international comparisons of management style. The 'whole brain' model has been applied in many contexts, including personal growth, counselling, group processes, teaching and learning, decision making and management.

Origins and description of the model

The HBDI provides, on the basis of 120 items, a four-category classification of mental preferences or thinking styles (sometimes also referred to as 'learning styles'). The first version was developed in 1982, after Herrmann had achieved only limited success in identifying electroencephalographic (EEG) correlates of specialised left- and right-brain functions. He was inspired by the widely publicised split-brain research carried out by Roger Sperry, winner of the Nobel Prize (Sperry 1964). However, following MacLean (1952), Herrmann (1989) also took into account hypothesised functions of the brain's **limbic system**, which is located beneath the surface layers (or cerebral cortex). The four categories in Herrmann's model can be summarised as follows.

A Theorists (cerebral, left: the *rational* self)
Theorists are said to find it difficult to accommodate the feeling self and the humanitarian style.

B Organisers (limbic, left: the *safe-keeping* self)
Organisers are said to find it difficult to accommodate the experimental self and the innovatory style.

D Innovators (cerebral, right: the *experimental* self)
Innovators are said to find it difficult to accommodate the safe-keeping self and the organising style.

C Humanitarians (limbic, right: the *feeling* self)
Humanitarians are said to find it difficult to accommodate the rational self and the theoretical style.

Although Herrmann began with a brain-based theory of hemisphere dominance, he later accepted that this was an oversimplification with inadequate empirical support and recommended (1989, 63) that A, B, C, D quadrant terminology be used instead: 'The whole-brain model, although originally thought of as a physiological map, is today entirely a metaphor.' The metaphor is expressed in many different ways, using a range of descriptors based on the 120 items in the HBDI, and in Appendix E of *The creative brain* (1989), Herrmann devotes 14 pages to graphic representations of his model, each differing in the labels used. Two of these representations locate the 'whole brain' model within the surrounding culture (ethnic, family, social and organisational) and environment (physical, geographic, economic, temporal and motivational). Table 25 is a representation which illustrates how people who strongly prefer one of the four categories (or quadrants) are said to differ in their approach to learning. Virtually the same representation appears in Herrmann (1996), where it is described as a model of learning styles.

The quadrant model and the concept of 'dominance' is not meant to imply that most people have a strong preference for one quadrant only. In fact, Herrmann states that this is true of only 7% of the population studied. The most common pattern (for 60%) is to have strong preferences in two quadrants, followed by strong preferences in three quadrants (30%). Only about 3% of those assessed have what is termed a 'quadruple dominant' or 'whole brain' profile. Herrmann states (1989, 89–90) that these people 'are capable of developing an extraordinarily balanced view of any given situation. They can also communicate easily with people who favor one of the other quadrants, and act as translators among people of different mental preferences.'

Another feature of Herrmann's model is the idea that certain combinations of preference are more harmonious than others, especially the 'left-brain' combination of A and B quadrants and the 'right-brain' combination of D and C quadrants. Conflict is more likely to arise between 'diagonal' quadrants – that is, *experimental* as opposed to *safe-keeping* tendencies and *rational* as opposed to *feeling* appraisals (D/B and A/C).

The 'whole brain' model is not based on biological determinism. Indeed, Herrmann (1989, 20–21) is persuaded that 'the way a person uses the specialised brain results from socialisation – parenting, teaching, life experiences, and cultural influences – far more than from genetic inheritance'. He believes that it is in the interest of individuals and organisations to develop sufficient flexibility to respond, against their natural preferences, to meet particular situational demands; and, where necessary, to make longer-lasting value-based adjustments, especially if this can release latent creativity in an individual or in an organisation.

Table 25
'Whole brain'
learning and design
considerations
Source:
Herrmann (1989)

Quadrant A: upper left

Learns by:
Acquiring and quantifying facts
Applying analysis and logic
Thinking through ideas
Building cases
Forming theories

Learners respond to:
Formalised lecture
Data-based content
Financial/technical case discussions
Textbooks and bibliographies
Programmed learning
Behaviour modification

Quadrant D: upper right

Learns by:
Taking initiative
Exploring hidden possibilities
Relying on intuition
Self-discovery
Constructing concepts
Synthesising content

Learners respond to:
Spontaneity
Free flow
Experiential opportunities
Experimentation
Playfulness
Future-oriented case discussions
Visual displays
Individuality
Aesthetics
Being involved

Quadrant B: lower left

Learns by:
Organising and structuring content
Sequencing content
Evaluating and testing theories
Acquiring skills through practice
Implementing course content

Learners respond to:
Thorough planning
Sequential order
Organisational and administrative case
discussions
Textbooks
Behaviour modification
Programmed learning
Structure
Lectures

Quadrant C: lower right

Learns by:
Listening and sharing ideas
Integrating experiences with self
Moving and feeling
Harmonising with the content
Emotional involvement

Learners respond to:
Experiential opportunities
Sensory movement
Music
People-oriented case discussions
Group interaction

The Herrmann Brain Dominance Instrument (HBDI)

The HBDI is a self-report instrument covering the following types of preference and performance rating:

- handedness
- strong and weak school subjects
- work elements (eg administrative, innovating, teaching/training)
- key descriptors (eg verbal, emotional, factual)
- hobbies (eg fishing, photography, travel)
- energy level (eg day person, night person)
- motion sickness (frequency and connection with reading)
- adjective pairs (forced choice: eg controlled/creative)
- introversion/extraversion (nine-point scale)
- 20 questions (five-point scale: eg 'I dislike things uncertain and unpredictable').

The Flesch-Kincaid readability level of the 20 questions is 12–13 years and the vocabulary demand of the work element, key descriptor and adjective pair items is such that Herrmann provides a 43-item glossary. This suggests that the instrument will be inaccessible, without personal mediation, to people with low levels of basic literacy.

Reliability

The only reliability statistics published by the Herrmann Group (1989) are test–retest figures, based on a sample of 78 individuals (see below). The figures are remarkably high (except for quadrant B), but it should be noted that no information is provided about the interval between the two assessments, or about the feedback that may have been provided after the first assessment. The test–retest study formed part of a doctoral dissertation by Ho (unreferenced):

A the *rational* self:
0.86

B the *safe-keeping* self:
0.73

C the *feeling* self:
0.97

D the *experimental* self:
0.94

- introversion/extraversion rating:
0.73.

While short-term test–retest reliability is perhaps more important than internal consistency in an instrument of this kind, it is clear that there is a pressing need for a rigorous independent study of the reliability of the HBDI.

Validity

Herrmann's categories appear to have good face, factorial and construct validity and are claimed to have catalytic validity when applied in education and in the business field. However, there have been very few studies of reliability or validity carried out by independent researchers, and we have not been able to locate any longitudinal studies.

As the descriptors in the feedback from a scored personal profile include many of those used in the HBDI itself, there is a high probability that respondents will judge the instrument to have good face validity. Our own impression is that this is the case, as clusters of items seem to relate to one's life experience. The many individual and group case illustrations provided by Herrmann in his books also have an authentic quality.

Factorial validity has been established through the analysis of four data sets, three carried out by Bunderson (a nationally known American psychometrician contracted by Herrmann for the purpose) and one by Ho (unreferenced). These are presented in some detail in Appendix A of Herrmann (1989).

Two factor analyses were based on the HBDI items alone. The first of these was performed on an early, 91-item version of the HBDI, with a sample consisting of 439 people, including managers, other professionals and students. Nine factors were extracted, the first two being bipolar and corresponding to the main hypothesised dimensions. The most significant item loadings are presented in Table 26.

The factor loadings were used to establish 12 sets of item parcels, which were then re-analysed, this time yielding a two-factor solution which provided an even better match to Herrmann's theoretical model and led to a revision of the item scoring system. A higher-order left-right dominance factor was also found, supporting Herrmann's concept of a closer affinity between quadrants associated with the same half of the brain (ie A with B; C with D).

The factor analytic study by Ho (unreferenced) drew on a sample of 7989 people. This used the current 120-item HBDI and yielded five factors, including a handedness factor, which was unrelated to the other four. The first four factors again confirmed Herrmann's model and are presented in Table 27.

Table 26
Summary of positive
and negative
loading items on
two HBDI factors

Factor 1: safe-keeping preferences versus creative synthesis

Preferring:	■ Specific instructions
	■ Step-by-step methods
	■ Detailed planning
	■ Administration
	■ Organisation
	■ Avoidance of uncertainty

As opposed to:	■ Conceptual thinking
	■ Dealing with creative aspects
	■ Desire to synthesise
	■ Desire to express ideas

Factor 2: analytical problem solving versus interpersonal/empathetic

Preferring:	■ Analytical
	■ Logical
	■ Technical
	■ Mathematical problem solving

As opposed to:	■ Interpersonal aspects
	■ Dealing with emotion
	■ Intuition
	■ Making decisions based on first impressions and hunches

Table 27
Item loadings on the
four main HBDI factors
(120-item version)

A quadrant factor: rational, logical

Preferring:	■ Logical
	■ Rational
	■ Mathematical activities/style

As opposed to:	■ Emotional
	■ Spiritual
	■ Musical
	■ Artistic
	■ Reading
	■ Arts and crafts
	■ Introvert
	■ Feeling activities/style

D quadrant factor: creative, innovative

Preferring:	■ Innovating
	■ Conceptualising
	■ Creating
	■ Imaginative
	■ Original
	■ Artistic activities/style

| **As opposed to:** | ■ Controlled |
| | ■ Conservative activities/style |

B quadrant factor: safe-keeping

Preferring:	■ Order
	■ Planning
	■ Administration
	■ Organisation
	■ Reliability
	■ Detail
	■ Low level of uncertainty

As opposed to:	■ Holistic thinking
	■ Conceptualising
	■ Synthesis
	■ Creating
	■ Innovating

C quadrant factor: people-oriented

Preferring:	■ Interpersonal
	■ Verbal
	■ People-oriented
	■ Emotional
	■ Musical activities/style

As opposed to:	■ Analytical
	■ Technical
	■ Logical
	■ Mathematical activities/style

Construct and concurrent validity

The other two factor analytic studies were designed to establish construct validity and involved a considerable number of other instruments as well as the HBDI. The second of these analyses was based on the current version of the HBDI. Cognitive ability measures, the Myers-Briggs Type Indicator (MBTI), Kolb's Learning Style Inventory (LSI) and 11 other measures of thinking styles and learning strategies were included. The sample comprised 182 students.

The analysis yielded two higher-order factors. The first was a bipolar factor, contrasting the Herrmann C and A quadrants, with significant loadings on extraversion-introversion, a preference for learning in groups, learning through personal experience, visual imagery and Kolb's 'concrete experience' scale. Bunderson (cited by Herrmann 1989) suggested that there is conceptual congruence between this bipolar factor and Witkin's dimension of field dependence-independence. The second factor had relatively lower loadings, but contrasted Herrmann's D and B quadrants and had something in common with the Myers-Briggs perceiving-judging and intuition-sensing categorisation, as well as with six other measures suggesting a non-verbal, divergent thinking preference.

It is of interest that one of the HBDI factors was more closely related to measures from the MBTI than from Kolb's LSI. In an earlier factor analytic study by Bunderson, the largest single factor also contrasted the D and B quadrants and had relatively high loadings from the same two Myers-Briggs measures (perceiving-judging: 0.61; and intuition-sensing: 0.69). The correlation between the HBDI and the Myers-Briggs measures of extraversion-introversion was 0.73. Bunderson suggested that the overlap between the two instruments was such that the item clusters 'may ultimately be explainable by a common set of constructs' (cited by Herrmann 1989, 377).

At a conceptual level, Herrmann's model shares important features with those of theorists other than those mentioned above. Gregorc's Mind Styles Model has four quadrants which correspond closely to those of Herrmann, but which are differently organised in that *abstract sequential* qualities, resembling those of Herrmann's *theorists*, are diametrically opposed to those of Herrmann's *innovators*, and *concrete sequential* qualities, resembling those of Herrmann's *organisers*, are contrasted with those of his *humanitarians*. The lack of factor analytic support for Gregorc's model (see Section 3.1) contrasts with the relatively strong support provided by Bunderson for that of Herrmann.

Among the theorists whose models are conceptually related to that of Herrmann are Allinson and Hayes (1996), who contrast left-brained *analysis* with right-brained *intuition*. McCarthy's 4MAT model (1990) includes what she calls 'right mode' and 'left mode' phases. Kirton (1976) distinguishes between *adapters* and *innovators* just as Herrmann does between *organisers* and *innovators*. Sternberg's descriptions (1999) of *legislative, executive* and *judicial* thinking styles bring to mind Herrmann's *innovators, organisers* and *theorists* respectively.

It is also possible that there is some connection between the opposition of the B and D quadrants in Herrmann's model and motivational features in the Dunn and Dunn model (Dunn and Griggs 2003) and in Apter's (2001) model of motivational styles. It is likely that Herrmann's creative *innovators* are sometimes non-conforming and do not welcome structure, unlike *organisers*. In Apter's terms, Herrmann's B-D axis offers possibilities of reversal within the *means-ends* and *rules* domains, while the A-D axis offers reversal within the *transactions* and *relationships* domains. Herrmann's interest in the need to develop stylistic flexibility fits well with Apter's concept that reversing between opposites increases the likelihood of psychological satisfaction.

Herrmann's concept of harmonious and conflicting combinations of quadrant preference receives some support from the distribution of double dominance profiles found in a large UK sample (Martin 2003). 'Harmonious' combinations (A-B and C-D) are the most common patterns in the database of 3400 profiles (62%), followed by the upper (A-D) and lower (B-C) pairings (31%) and then by the conflicting diagonal pairings (A-C and B-D) which occur in only 7% of cases.

Gender, ethnic and occupational differences

Although Herrmann (1996) had no theoretically based reasons for predicting gender effects, it soon became clear that there are very substantial gender differences on the HBDI. These boil down to a strong male preference for the A (theorist) quadrant and a strong female preference for the C (humanitarian) quadrant. The same pattern is apparent in Martin's (2003) UK sample, where the gender ratios are often greater than 3:1 for dominant profiles. It is not clear how far these large gender-related differences are socio-culturally determined, or indeed whether they are self-presentational rather than behavioural. However, there is a striking similarity between what is revealed by the HBDI and Baron-Cohen's portrayal (2003) of 'systematising' (male) and 'empathetic' (female) brains.

It is abundantly clear from the Herrmann Group's international database that ethnic differences are minimal or non-existent. Herrmann (1996) presents virtually identical mean profiles for Blacks, Hispanics, Native Americans, Asians and Whites.

Table 28	Profile type	Descriptor	Occupational group
Illustrative occupational group norms	A	Rational	Chemical engineer; actuary
Source: Herrmann (1996)	B	Safe-keeping	Assembly-line processor; bank clerk
	C	Feeling	Nurse; primary school teacher
	D	Experimental	Artist; entrepreneur
	AB	Left brained	Production engineer; bank manager
	CD	Right brained	Minister of religion; psychologist
	AD	Cerebral	Physicist; forestry manager
	BC	Limbic	Secretary; homemaker
	Multi-dominant	Balanced	Director; customer service manager

However, major differences have been found between typical profiles in different occupations. These are summarised by Herrmann (1996) in the form of the average profile patterns drawn from a database of over 113,000 returns – certainly sufficient to demonstrate that the differences are real. Some examples are given in Table 28.

The visual presentation used by Herrmann permits only an eyeball analysis of the size of the differences summarised in Table 28, but they appear to be very substantial. It would be good to see further statistical analyses of occupational differences broken down by age, gender and social class.

Implications for teaching and learning

Like many other theorists, Herrmann (1996, 151) makes the reasonable assumption that 'every classroom represents a complete spectrum of learning style preferences'. Both in educational and in business settings, he claims that there is up to 50% wastage because of a lack of alignment between learners and courses. His recommended solution is 'whole brain teaching and learning', whereby each key learning point is taught in three or four different ways, while peripheral matter is removed. He describes an application of this approach in teaching creative thinking, in which the use of metaphor plays a central part. After an initial interest in the subject has been established, the phases of *preparation*, *verification*, *incubation* and *illumination* correspond to the A, B, C and D quadrants of experience, with didactic and experiential approaches complementing each other. As well as providing a wide range of creative materials and individual and group activities to encourage people to move beyond their comfort zones, the leaders set up problem-solving activities, first in groups of homogeneous learning style, then in heterogeneous pairs, and eventually in heterogeneous communities of six, so that participants can encounter 'both the enhancements and challenges of having different mental modes at work in the same group' (1989, 234).

Herrmann does not speculate on the implications for teaching and learning of the very substantial gender differences revealed by the HBDI, other than to point out the advantages of working in gender-balanced (and therefore more stylistically balanced) teams. This is clearly an area where further investigation is needed, especially in areas of educational practice traditionally dominated by one gender or the other.

The main thrust of the Herrmann Group's work with business organisations is to help them make better use of their creative potential, and at the same time, to achieve greater synergy between all stylistic approaches. Herrmann (1996) presents a four-quadrant classification of 77 creative thinking processes. Again, he argues for diversity in approach, to increase the overall level of learner engagement and chances of success. For example, attribute listing, the Delphi method, interactive brainstorming and creative dramatics each appeal to different styles of thinking, and if four creative methods of problem solving (or even all 77) are made available, individuals and groups will gravitate to the processes which they understand and which work for them.

In chapter 9 of *The creative brain*, Herrmann (1989) offers many constructive and detailed suggestions for expanding mental preferences by changing frames of reference in terms of values, reasoning and decision making. He claims that shifting into opposing modes may be resisted, but can provide enormous pleasure, making mental life more creative as well as more varied and interesting.

Herrmann admits that it is not easy to involve top management in new learning, but his study of international and gender differences in the profiles of 773 chief executive officers (CEOs) provides food for thought, not least for multinational companies. He found that CEOs were generally strongest in the *experimental* 'D' quadrant, especially in Australia, where conceptualising and creative aspects were highly ranked and teaching and training were valued more highly than elsewhere. The UK sample ranked conceptualising, creative aspects, interpersonal aspects and writing much lower than their US counterparts, while giving higher priority to planning, implementation, analytical thinking and organisation. Gender differences were not marked, but were in line with the general tendency for women to be rather more interested in people than in analytic thinking.

Empirical evidence of impact

Martin (1994) describes the Herrmann 'whole brain' approach to teaching and learning and how it appeared to benefit a large client company in the UK. However, apart from the impressive business portfolio of the Ned Herrmann Group and the six pages of testimonials from participants in Applied Creative Thinking courses, there is very little published research evidence to convince sceptics of the potential value of the Herrmann approach for large-scale use in post-16 education and training. Nevertheless, its inclusive and optimistic stance and the fact that it does not rely on gimmicky techniques are very positive features.

Conclusion

It is highly likely that any four-category or two-dimensional model of approaches to thinking and learning will be oversimplistic for certain purposes. However, Herrmann is aware of this and certainly does not seek to label and confine individuals or organisations. He positively encourages change and growth, whether for short-term adaptive purposes or for the longer term, on the basis of more mature values and attitudes.

With his model and the HBDI, Herrmann has provided a creative space which has already been enriched through empirically-checked revisions. It almost certainly needs further work if it is to be used with a wider constituency of younger, less experienced and less literate post-16 learners than those to be found at higher levels of responsibility in the business world.

The psychometric properties of the HBDI appear to be sound, but there is a pressing need for up-to-date independent study of the instrument and of its many possible uses.

There are good reasons to recommend the use of the HBDI as a means of individual and group reflection on thinking and learning preferences. It is more detailed and situation-focused than many of its competitors, while accommodating many of the constructs which receive incomplete or less reliable and valid coverage in other instruments. Herrmann's model is concerned with thinking, feeling and doing as an individual and in social contexts. It addresses both long-established habits and personality traits as well as situationally-dependent preferences. As it is concerned with process rather than product, it is largely independent of cognitive ability. It is possible to envisage considerable benefits to be derived from its use by policy-makers and course designers as well as in organisations concerned with education and training. The design and delivery of lifelong learning experiences may then more effectively promote 'whole person' and 'whole organisation' balance.

The HBDI is a transparent instrument and should not be used 'for making a decision about a person that is beyond the control of that person' (Herrmann 1989, 341). It is presented as a tool for learning, for use in a climate of openness and trust. However, like other such tools (for example Kolb's LSI, Honey and Mumford's LSQ and McCarthy's 4MAT), its potential to improve the quality of teaching and learning, formal and informal, has not yet been substantiated in a rigorous manner, other than to the satisfaction of its proponents.

Table 29
Herrmann's Brain
Dominance Instrument
(HBDI)

	Strengths	Weaknesses
General	■ The HBDI and new ways of using it effectively have been developed over more than 20 years. ■ The 'whole brain' model is compatible with several other models of learning style.	
Design of the model	■ It is based on theory which, although originally brain-based, incorporates growth and development, especially in creativity. ■ Learning styles as defined by the HBDI are not fixed personality traits, but to a large extent, learned patterns of behaviour.	■ As with most self-report instruments, it is possible to complete it with the intention of presenting a particular profile. ■ Some will find the HBDI items hard to read and understand.
Reliability and validity	Internal evidence suggests that the HBDI is psychometrically sound, and new analyses can draw on an enormous international database.	There are very few independent studies of the reliability and validity of the HBDI.
Implications for pedagogy	■ HBDI-based feedback does not seek to attach permanent labels to the individual. ■ Herrmann provides rich accounts of how people think and learn, valuing diversity and arguing for mutual understanding. ■ Teachers, students, managers and workers may be stimulated to examine and refine their ideas about communication and learning. ■ Herrmann argues that all learners need to develop stylistic flexibility and, where appropriate, extend their range of competence.	The pedagogical implications of the 'whole brain' model have not yet been fully explored and tested.
Evidence of pedagogical impact		Although well established in the business world, the use of the HBDI has yet to be extensively validated in education.
Overall assessment	A model which, although largely ignored in academic research, offers considerable promise for use in education and training. It is more inclusive and systemic than many others, taking an optimistic, open and non-labelling stance towards the development of people and organisations.	
Key source	Herrmann 1989	

6.4
Allinson and Hayes' Cognitive Style Index (CSI)

Introduction

Christopher Allinson and John Hayes (working in the Leeds University Business School) developed the CSI after identifying two factors ('action' and 'analysis') in Honey and Mumford's LSQ. Finding problems with many existing ways of measuring cognitive style, they decided to produce an easy-to-use instrument with a three-point rating scale, in order to measure a single dimension with *intuition* at one extreme and *analysis* at the other.

The CSI was designed for use in adult organisational contexts and as a research tool on a national and international basis. It has been translated into Finnish (Löfström 2002) and several other languages. Cross-cultural studies have been carried out by its authors (Allinson and Hayes 2000), by Hill *et al.* (2000) and by Sadler-Smith, Spicer and Tsang (2000).

Definitions and theoretical basis

Allinson and Hayes see *intuition-analysis* as the most fundamental dimension of cognitive style. The 38 items of the CSI were chosen to reflect their belief (1996, 122) that:

Intuition, characteristic of right-brain orientation, refers to immediate judgment based on feeling and the adoption of a global perspective. Analysis, characteristic of left-brain orientation, refers to judgment based on mental reasoning and a focus on detail.

They follow Mintzberg (1976) in linking right-brained intuition with the need of managers to make quick decisions on the basis of 'soft' information, while left-brained analysis is seen as the kind of rational information processing that makes for good planning (Hayes and Allinson 1997). They regard 'brainedness' as 'a useful metaphor' and claim that a left-brain oriented person 'tends to be compliant, prefers structure and is most effective when handling problems that require a step-by-step solution', while a right-brain oriented person 'tends to be non-conformist, prefers open-ended tasks and works best on problems favouring a holistic approach' (Allinson and Hayes 2000, 161).

Although they accept Tennant's (1988, page 89) definition of cognitive style as 'an individual's characteristic and consistent approach to organizing and processing information', Allinson and Hayes readily admit that cognitive style can be shaped by culture, altered by experience and overridden for particular purposes. Nevertheless, their starting position seems to be that the cognitive style concept may prove useful in work settings, not so much because styles can be modified, but rather through fitting people to jobs and, where economically feasible, adjusting job demands to what best suits the individual.

Description

There are 38 items in the CSI, ordered in such a way that nine of the first 10 items are about analytic qualities and nine of the last 10 are about intuitive qualities. Respondents have to respond to each item by choosing between 'true', 'uncertain' and 'false'. It is possible to derive from the high-loading items in Table 30 (taken from a factor analysis by Löfström 2002) a basic understanding of the multifaceted constructs *analysis* and *intuition*.

Close study of the CSI items reveals that many items relate to behaviour with and without time pressure; some emphasise decisive action rather than organised inaction; some focus on spontaneity rather than obeying rules; some are about valuing or ignoring detail; and others are about risk taking or risk avoidance.

Measurement by authors

Reliability

To establish test reliability and validity, Allinson and Hayes (1996) analysed data collected from 945 adults, 45% of whom were students and 55% of whom were employed adults (most of them managers). Item analysis yielded excellent internal consistency, with alphas in the range 0.84 to 0.92 across seven sub-samples. In a later cross-cultural study (Allinson and Hayes 2000), similar results were obtained, with the single exception of a sample of 39 Nepalese managers. In their 1996 study, they report excellent test–retest reliability over a 4-week period (r_{tt}=0.90)[11] for a subgroup of 30 management students.

Validity

On the basis of factor analyses using six 'parcels' of intercorrelated items, Allinson and Hayes (1996) claim that the CSI measures a single dimension. They do not say whether they considered and rejected other factor structures.

Although they expected the CSI to measure something different from reasoning ability, Allinson and Hayes report that intuitive students performed significantly better than analytic students on the Watson-Glaser Critical Thinking Appraisal (r=–0.25). They acknowledge that more research is needed to understand the relationships between cognitive style, intellectual ability and educational achievement.

The best evidence the authors provide of construct validity is a high negative correlation (–0.81) between the CSI and an 'action' factor score derived from Honey and Mumford's LSQ. They also report moderate correlations with the following measures from the MBTI: 0.57 with introversion; 0.57 with thinking as opposed to feeling; 0.47 with sensing as opposed to intuition; and 0.41 with judging as opposed to perceiving.

11
The symbol r_{tt} indicates a test–retest correlation coefficient.

Table 30	**Analysis type**	■ I find detailed, methodological work satisfying.
Items which best characterise *analysis* and *intuition*		■ I am careful to follow rules and regulations at work.
Source: Löfström (2002)		■ When making a decision, I take my time and thoroughly consider all relevant factors.
		■ My philosophy is that it is better to be safe than risk being sorry.
	Intuition	■ I make decisions and get on with things rather than analyse every last detail.
		■ I find that 'too much analysis results in paralysis'.
		■ My 'gut feeling' is just as good a basis for decision making as careful analysis.
		■ I make many of my decisions on the basis of intuition.

Suggestive evidence of predictive validity was also reported. Analytic-style junior managers working in a bureaucratic structure reported higher job satisfaction than intuitives (r=0.29), and analytic-style basic grade primary school teachers were more positive about job climate than intuitives.

Allinson and Hayes (1996) predicted that intuition rather than analysis would be more strongly associated with seniority in business organisations. They found that within two companies (construction and brewing), senior managers and directors came out as significantly more intuitive than lower-level managers and supervisors. The effect sizes were 0.43 and 0.41 respectively. Similarly, Allinson, Chell and Hayes (2000) found that 156 successful entrepreneurs were rather more intuitive than:

■ an opportunity sample of 257 managers and

■ the senior construction and brewery managers previously studied.

In these comparisons, the effect sizes were small to moderate (0.27, 0.09 and 0.41 respectively). However, in a later study of mentors and protégés in police, medical and engineering contexts, Armstrong, Allinson and Hayes (2002) found that mentors (who generally worked at much higher levels of responsibility than protégés) came out as more analytic than protégés (effect size 0.31). This raises two important questions:

■ how far success in different types of organisation depends on different qualities and

■ how far people respond differently to questionnaires such as the CSI depending on their understanding of the focus of the enquiry.

External evaluation

Reliability

Using a Canadian sample of 89 business undergraduates, Murphy *et al.* (1998) found that the CSI had good internal consistency (alpha=0.83). Further confirmation of good internal consistency was provided by Sadler-Smith, Spicer and Tsang (2000) in a large-scale study which included sub-samples of management and staff in the UK and in Hong Kong. The highest level of internal consistency found was 0.89 for 201 personnel practitioners, and the lowest was 0.79 for 98 owner-managers in Hong Kong. Overall, only two items failed to correlate well with the total score. Test–retest stability over 3 weeks for 79 individuals in Murphy's study was extremely high at 0.89.

Validity

The idea that the CSI measures a single dimension has received much less support than empirically based criticism. Sadler-Smith, Spicer and Tsang (2000) followed the 'parcelling' procedure recommended by Allinson and Hayes and were able to support a single-factor model. However, Spicer (2002) pointed out that the 'analytic' and 'intuitive' item sets identified by Allinson and Hayes (1996) were far from being polar opposites and Löfström (2002) found that a two-factor model provided a good fit to the data she obtained from 228 working adults. Hodgkinson and Sadler-Smith (2003) drew attention to bias in the item-parcelling procedure used in earlier studies and, after exploratory and confirmatory factor analysis with large samples (total n=939), reported unequivocal support for a model with *analysis* and *intuition* as two moderately correlated factors.

Although Sadler-Smith, Spicer and Tsang (2000) failed in their attempt to validate the CSI against Riding's computerised Cognitive Styles Analysis (CSA), the near-zero correlation reported should not be taken as a criticism of the CSI, as Riding's instrument has since been shown to be seriously flawed (Peterson, Deary and Austin 2003a). In another study with undergraduates, Sadler-Smith (1999a, 1999b) obtained low, but statistically significant, correlations between the CSI and the *meaning* and *achieving* sub-scales of a short form of Entwistle's ASSIST (1998).

Sadler-Smith, Spicer and Tsang (2000) related CSI scores to levels of responsibility in two local government organisations. In their large sample of 501 workers, there was a clear and consistent trend across four levels of responsibility, with senior managers presenting as the most intuitive and managed staff as the most analytic. The effect size when these two groups are compared is very large (1.06). Hill *et al.* (2000) found similar results in the UK and Finland, but not in Poland. In a Finnish study of 102 managers and 126 managed workers in small and medium-sized enterprises (SMEs) in the service sector and production industry, Löfström (2002) also found that managers were as a group more intuitive than those they managed.

The 'matching' hypothesis

In a study of 142 manager–subordinate dyads in two large manufacturing organisations, Allinson, Armstrong and Hayes (2001) investigated the hypothesis that similarity in cognitive style would help to produce positive relationships. This turned out not to be the case, since the more intuitive the style of managers was relative to the style of their subordinates, the more they were seen as non-dominant and nurturing and were liked and respected. The differences on these measures between the extremes of intuitive manager with analytic subordinate and analytic manager with intuitive subordinate were moderate to large (effect sizes between 0.72 and 0.98). It is worth noting that this study focused on comfortable feelings rather than performance.

Another context in which the matching hypothesis has been studied is that of mentoring (Armstrong, Allinson and Hayes 2002). In this case, rather different findings were obtained, which may reflect important differences between managerial supervision and mentoring. The main finding was that when mentors were more analytic than their protégés, a close match in cognitive style was associated with perceived psychosocial advantages on the part of protégés and perceived practical career-development action by mentors. Overall, perceived similarity in personality, ability and behaviour was correlated with mutual liking, and liking was in turn associated with the delivery and receipt of psychosocial and career support. However, in this study, there was no evidence that intuitive mentors were liked more than analytic ones. This suggests that advantages may be derived from pairing analytic mentors with analytic protégés, but that pairing according to mutual liking rather than cognitive style may, where practicable, be generally more effective.

This is an interesting area of research, in which a tentative interpretation is that differences in cognitive style can be stimulating and productive in manager–subordinate relationships when the manager is seen as a person who gets things done. However, in the mentoring situation, people who have many qualities in common may work together more effectively.

Implications for managers and teachers

A number of cross-cultural comparisons of the CSI style of managers have yielded substantial differences. The study by Allinson and Hayes (2000) is typical, reporting moderate and large effect sizes for differences between highly intuitive British managers and more analytical samples in India, Jordan, Nepal, Russia and Singapore. They suggest that managers need training in how to recognise and deal with such differences. They also suggest that companies should select staff for international work on the basis of cognitive style and should exercise 'caution in the transfer of management practices from one part of the world to another' (2000, 168). All this begs the question as to whether achieving a stylistic match (however contrived) is worth the effort. Perhaps we need to ask a more serious question: is there any basis for the assumption that an intuitive management style is the most effective response to information overload in rapidly changing business conditions?

As we have seen, and irrespective of culture, the weight of evidence suggests that within a particular organisation, managers are likely to be more intuitive than their subordinates. Allinson and Hayes (2000) also found that British managers are generally more intuitive than undergraduate management students (effect size 0.52). What does this mean? One interpretation is that as they become more experienced, people change in style to accommodate to new situations and responsibilities. On this basis, managers who are promoted into contexts where rapid decisions have to be made come to base those decisions on 'gut feeling' or 'big picture' thinking, grounded, one would hope, in a wealth of experience. Similarly, lower-level workers in rule-bound organisations may learn to stick with or adopt an analytic coping style, keeping to the book and attending to detail.

Another interpretation is that successful managers delegate time-consuming analytic tasks and therefore no longer need to use the analytic abilities they actually have. A less reassuring interpretation is that some managers enjoy risk taking and change for its own sake and even welcome situations where there is no time for considered planning. Without longitudinal research which considers change, development and outcomes in a range of contexts, we cannot determine causality and are therefore unable to draw out practical implications. However, although we know little about the flexibility of intuitive and analytic styles at different levels of responsibility, it may be advantageous for an organisation to plan how best to use and develop the diverse skills of people with preferred intuitive and analytic approaches.

While successful managers often say they are intuitive in approach, there seems to be clear evidence that to succeed in management and business-related courses in HE contexts, analytic qualities are required. Armstrong (2000) found that 190 analytic students obtained significantly higher degree grades than 176 intuitive students, although the effect size was rather small (0.26). This result is consistent with Spicer's (2002) finding that for 105 students across 2 years, there was a low positive correlation between analytic style and academic achievement.

In an exploratory study involving 118 management students and their final-year dissertation supervisors, Armstrong (2002) found that analytic supervisors were better for students than intuitive supervisors. Students rated the quality of supervision provided by analytic supervisors as being better and also obtained higher grades (effect size 0.44). Analytic students who had analytic supervisors obtained substantially higher grades than intuitive students with intuitive supervisors (effect size 0.64). This finding could reflect the fact that analytic supervisors take time to help students with every part of a structured linear task which requires analysis, synthesis and evaluation

Armstrong (2000) draws attention to the apparent paradox that if business organisations appoint graduates on the basis of degree level, they may be rejecting many candidates with good management potential. Unfortunately, we do not have any studies which track the development of successful managers and entrepreneurs over time. Therefore we do not know whether the expertise of such people is built on an initially intuitive approach or on the successful application of analytic skills in earlier life. It would be unwise to make radical changes in HE pedagogy and assessment practice without evidence that placing a higher value on intuitive performance leads to more successful career and business outcomes. However, degree courses could usefully seek to develop a broader range of competencies than the 'systematic analysis and evaluation of information resulting in cogent, structured and logically flowing arguments' (Armstrong 200, 336).

Conclusions

Despite the claims of its authors, the CSI has been shown to measure two related, albeit multifaceted, constructs. We believe that the basically sound psychometric properties of the CSI would be further improved if the revised two-factor scoring system proposed by Hodgkinson and Sadler-Smith (2003) were generally adopted.

The multifaceted nature of the CSI means that people will respond not only in terms of underlying style, but in terms of the opportunities their work affords as well as what they believe to be socially desirable responses for people in similar situations. For example, not many office workers will admit to not reading reports in detail, or to not following rules and regulations at work. Similarly, few managers will assess themselves as having less to say in meetings than most other participants, and students deep into their dissertations are unlikely say that they find formal plans a hindrance. If responses to the CSI are situation-dependent, it is difficult to sustain the idea that their short-term consistency is brain-based, other than in extreme cases.

The popularised stereotype of left- and right-brainedness creates an unhelpful image of people going through life with half of their brains inactive. If British managers are among the most right-brained in the world, this would mean that they would be virtually inarticulate, unable to use the left-brain speech and language areas and unable to deal with the simplest computations. While this is clearly a caricature, the idea that the CSI measures a consistent single dimension based on consistently associated functions within each brain hemisphere does not do justice to what is known about the enormous flexibility of human thought.

The relationship between CSI scores and cognitive abilities needs further investigation, preferably on a longitudinal basis. Intellectually able students are usually flexible in their thinking and learning and can therefore adopt an analytic approach when necessary (as in university contexts and when appropriate in the early stages of a career). If, in addition to good reasoning and problem-solving abilities, they have the confidence, creativity and drive to become high achievers in the business world, it is likely that their approach to decision making will become more 'intuitive' in the sense that it is based on expertise.

It is too early to assess the potential catalytic value of the CSI in improving the quality of learning for individuals or organisations. Although the CSI was not designed for pedagogical purposes, it may be that future research will show that it helps people become more aware of important qualities in themselves and others, leading to measurable benefits in communication and performance. So far, however, the 'matching' hypothesis has not been upheld in studies with the CSI, so there are no grounds for using it to select or group people for particular purposes. At the same time, it is clear from the amount of interest it has received since publication in 1996 that it is well regarded as a means of asking pertinent questions about how adults think, behave and learn in the world of work.

Table 31

Allinson and Hayes'
Cognitive Styles Index
(CSI)

	Strengths	Weaknesses
General	Designed for use with adults.	
Design of the model	A single bipolar dimension of intuition-analysis, which authors contend underpins other aspects of learning style.	The proposed single dimension is very broad and made up of diverse, loosely associated characteristics.
Reliability	*Internal consistency* and *test–retest reliability* are high, according to both internal and external evaluations.	
Validity	■ The CSI correlates with scales from other instruments, including four from the Myers-Briggs Type Indicator. ■ Analysis is associated with more job satisfaction in junior roles than intuition, while intuition is associated with seniority in business and with success in entrepreneurship.	■ There is unequivocal evidence that intuition and analysis, although negatively related, are not opposites. ■ The authors acknowledge that more research is needed to understand the relationships between cognitive style, intellectual ability and educational achievement.
Implications for pedagogy	■ Intuitive managers are generally better liked, irrespective of the style of their subordinates. ■ Matched styles are often effective in mentoring relationships. ■ One study showed that *analytic* qualities in university dissertation supervisors are desirable. ■ If it were to be shown that placing a higher value on intuitive performance by university students led to more successful career and business outcomes, changes in HE pedagogy and assessment would be indicated.	It is not clear how far findings are context-dependent. Implications are, at best, interesting suggestions which need to be tested empirically.
Evidence of pedagogical impact	None as yet	
Overall assessment	Overall, the CSI has the best evidence for reliability and validity of the 13 models studied. The constructs of analysis and intuition are relevant to decision making and work performance in many contexts, although the pedagogical implications of the model have not been fully explored. The CSI is a suitable tool for researching and reflecting on teaching and learning, especially if treated as a measure of two factors rather than one.	
Key source	Allinson and Hayes 1996; Hodgkinson and Sadler-Smith 2003	

Section 7

Learning approaches and strategies

Introduction

During the 1970s, a body of research on learning explored a holistic, active view of *approaches* and *strategies* – as opposed to *styles* – that takes into account the effects of previous experiences and contextual influences. This body of work has been led for over 25 years in the UK by Noel Entwistle at the University of Edinburgh. It draws on the work of Marton and Säljö (1976) in Sweden and Pask (1976) in the UK. In northern Europe, Vermunt's model of learning styles, from which his Inventory of Learning Styles (ILS) is derived, is influential, again in higher education. We review Entwistle's and Vermunt's models in detail below (Sections 7.1 and 7.2).

In this broader view, contextual factors influence learners' approaches and strategies and lead to a multifaceted view of teaching. This emphasis encourages a broad approach to pedagogy that encompasses subject discipline, institutional culture, students' previous experience and the way the curriculum is organised and assessed. Theorists within this family of learning research tend to eschew 'styles' in favour of 'strategies' and 'approaches' because previous ideas about styles promoted the idea of specific interventions either to 'match' existing styles or to encourage a repertoire of styles.

In Entwistle's model, for example, a strategy describes the way in which students choose to deal with a specific learning task. In doing this, they take account of its perceived demands. It is therefore less fixed than a style, which is a broader characterisation of how students prefer to tackle learning tasks generally. For Entwistle (1998), this definition of strategy makes it difficult to develop a general scale that can measure it.

Researchers within this family refer to underlying personality differences and relatively fixed cognitive characteristics. This leads them to differentiate between styles, strategies and approaches, with the latter being derived from perceptions of a task and cognitive strategies that learners might then adopt to tackle it.

An influential researcher within this field has been Pask (1976) who argues that there are identifiable differences between students' strategies, so that some learners adopt a *holist* strategy and aim from the outset to build up a broad view of the task, and to relate it to other topics and to real-life and personal experience. The opposite strategy is a *serialist* one, where students attempt to build their understanding from the details of activities, facts and experimental results instead of making theoretical connections.

Deep and *surface* strategies are linked closely to holist and serialist approaches. Pask makes his holist/serialist distinction from a theory of learning derived from what he calls a conversation between two representations of knowledge. Student understanding has to be demonstrated by applying that knowledge to an unfamiliar problem in a concrete, non-verbal way, often using specially designed approaches. Pask's development (1976) of scientific experiments, apparatus and procedures for eliciting evidence of different types of understanding and the processes students use to gain understanding are too technical and complex to be presented easily here.

Drawing on research on concept learning by Bruner and colleagues in the 1950s, Pask and his colleagues analysed transcripts of students presenting oral accounts of their reasons for approaching tasks in particular ways. From this, Pask identified two distinct learning strategies:

- **serialists (partists)** followed a step-by-step learning procedure, concentrating on narrow, simple hypotheses relating to one characteristic at a time

- **holists (wholists)** tended to form more complex hypotheses relating to more than one characteristic at a time.

This distinction led Pask to identify 'inevitable learning pathologies'. For example, holists search for rich analogies and make inappropriate links between ideas, a pathology that Pask calls 'globetrotting'. Serialists often ignore valid analogies and so suffer from 'improvidence'. Both pathologies hinder students in their attempt to understand the learning materials.

In his later work, Pask reinforced the distinction between strategies and styles and identified two extreme and therefore incomplete styles: comprehension and operation learning. In summary, comprehension learners tend to:

- pick up readily an overall picture of the subject matter (eg relationships between discrete classes)

- recognise easily where to gain information

- build descriptions of topics and describe the relations between topics.

If left to their own devices, operation learners tend to:

- pick up rules, methods and details, but are not aware of how or why they fit together

- have a sparse mental picture of the material

- be guided by arbitrary number schemes or accidental features of the presentation

- use specific, externally-offered descriptions to assimilate procedures and to build concepts for isolated topics.

Some learners use both types of strategy in a 'versatile' approach.

The theoretical dichotomy between holist and serialist strategies was not enough to identify the styles empirically, leading Pask to invent two tests that aimed to measure them: the Spy Ring History Test and the Smuggler's Test. Although Pask's work has been influential in this family of learning styles, both in concepts and methodology, his two tests have not gained credence as reliable or easily usable instruments outside science disciplines (see Entwistle 1978b for a summary of the original tests and problems with them). We have not therefore analysed the tests in this report as a discrete model of learning styles.

Another crucial influence in this family is the work of Marton and Säljö who identified (1976, 7–8) two different levels of processing in terms of the learning material on which students' attention is focused:

in the case of surface-level processing, the student directs his (sic) attention towards learning the test itself (the sign), ie., he has a reproductive conception of learning which means he is more or less forced to keep to a rote-learning strategy. In the case of deep-level processing, on the other hand, the student is directed towards the intentional content of the learning material (what is signified), ie. he is directed towards comprehending what the author wants to say, for instance, a certain scientific problem or principle.

It is important to distinguish between a logical and an empirical association between approaches and outcomes for students' learning. Although it is possible to present a clear theoretical case that certain approaches affect learning outcomes, unexpected or idiosyncratic contextual factors may disrupt this theoretical association. According to Ramsden (1983), empirical study of different contexts of learning highlights the effects of individuals' decisions and previous experiences on their approaches and strategies. He argues that some students reveal a capacity to adapt to or shape the environment more effectively so that the capacity is learnable. In terms of pedagogy, 'students who are aware of their own learning strategies and the variety of strategies available to them, and who are skilled at making the right choices, can be said to be responding intelligently ... or metacognitively in that context' (1983, 178).

7.1
Entwistle's Approaches and Study Skills Inventory for Students (ASSIST)

Introduction

Working largely within the field of educational psychology, Noel Entwistle and his colleagues at Lancaster University and the University of Edinburgh have developed a conceptual model and a quantitative and qualitative methodology. These aim to capture students' approaches to learning, their intellectual development, a subject knowledge base and the skills and attitudes needed for effective approaches to learning. The purpose of this work is to produce:

*A **heuristic** model of the teaching-learning process [which can] guide departments and institutions wanting to engage in a process of critical reflection on current practice ... [so that] the whole learning milieu within a particular department or institution can be redesigned to ensure improvement in the quality of student learning* (Entwistle 1990, 680)

During its evolution over 30 years, the model has sought to encompass the complex 'web of influence' that connects motivation, study methods and academic performance with the subtle effects of teaching, course design, environment and assessment methods on intentions and approaches to learning. The model has also been influenced by parallel work in Australia, the Netherlands and the US (see Entwistle and McCune 2003 for a detailed account of these links and their impact on the concepts and measures used in Entwistle's work). Five versions of an inventory have evolved, aiming to measure undergraduate students' approaches to learning and their perceptions about the impact of course organisation and teaching:

- the Approaches to Studying Inventory (ASI) in 1981

- the Course Perception Questionnaire (CPQ) in 1981

- the Revised Approaches to Studying Inventory (RASI) in 1995

- the Approaches and Study Skills Inventory for Students (ASSIST) in 1997

- the Approaches to Learning and Studying Inventory (ALSI) (currently being developed).

There is a strong emphasis on development in Entwistle's work, both in relation to the underlying concepts and the inventories used. The ASSIST was derived from evaluations of other measures – the ASI, CPQ and RASI (for an account of this evolution, see Entwistle and McCune 2003; Entwistle and Peterson 2003). More than 100 studies have addressed the theoretical and empirical tasks of evaluating the effectiveness of the inventories and their implications for pedagogy in universities. The studies can be categorised broadly as being concerned with:

- the theoretical and conceptual development of a rationale for focusing on approaches and strategies for learning

- refinements to the reliability and validity of a particular inventory to measure approaches to and strategies of learning

- the implications for pedagogy

- theoretical development of the inventories used and/or their relationship to others.

Most of the studies reviewed for this report fall into the first two categories and there appear to be no empirical evaluations of changes to pedagogy arising from use of the inventory.

In order to make theories of learning more credible outside educational psychology, Entwistle and his colleagues have related psychological concepts to some of the wide range of variables that affect approaches and strategies to learning. These include the traditions and ethos of subject disciplines, institutional structures and cultures, curriculum organisation, and students' past experience and motivation. In order to persuade teachers and students to develop sophisticated conceptions of both teaching and learning, Entwistle (1990, 669) believes that researchers have to recognise that 'general theories of human learning are only of limited value in explaining everyday learning. It is essential for the theories to have ecological validity, for them to apply specifically to the context in which they are to be useful'. The ecological validity of the inventories and an underpinning model of learning are thought to be especially important if lecturers are to be persuaded to take student learning seriously and to improve their pedagogy.

Unlike other inventories reviewed in this report, those of Entwistle and Vermunt are the only two that attempt to develop a model of learning within the specific context of higher education. The research has influenced staff development programmes in HE institutions in Australia, South Africa, Sweden and the UK. Entwistle has written a large number of chapters and papers for staff developers and academics outside the discipline of education. The overall intention of theoretical development, systematic development of the inventories, and establishing evidence of their validity and reliability, is to create a convincing case that encourages lecturers to change their pedagogy and universities to support students in developing more effective approaches to learning.

Entwistle is currently engaged on a project as part of the ESRC's Teaching and Learning Research Programme (TLRP). This focuses on enhancing teaching and learning environments in undergraduate courses and supports 25 UK university departments in thinking about new ways to 'encourage high quality learning' (see www.tlrp.org). This work takes account of the ways in which intensifying political pressures on quality assurance and assessment regimes in the UK affect learning and teaching.

The inventory that arises from Entwistle's model of learning is important for our review because a significant proportion of first-level undergraduate programmes is taught in FE colleges. Government plans to extend higher education to a broader range of institutions make it all the more important that pedagogy for this area of post-16 learning is based on sound research.

Definitions and description

The research of Entwistle and his colleagues draws directly on a detailed analysis of tests and models of learning styles developed by Pask, Biggs and Marton and Säljö (see the introduction to this section). This research derives from a number of linked concepts that underpin Entwistle's view of learning and it is therefore important to note that terms in italics have a precise technical use in Entwistle's work.

- The learner's intentions and goals determine four distinct *educational orientations*: academic, vocational, personal and social.

- These orientations relate to *extrinsic and intrinsic motivation* and while discernible, these different types of motivation fluctuate throughout a degree course.

- Students hold *conceptions of learning* that tend to become increasingly sophisticated as they progress through a degree course; for example, unsophisticated students may see learning as increasing knowledge or acquiring facts, while more sophisticated students recognise that learning requires the abstraction of meaning and that understanding reality is based on interpretation (Entwistle 1990).

- Students' orientations to, and conceptions of, learning and the nature of knowledge both lead to and are affected by students' typical *approaches to learning*.

Students' conceptions of learning are said to develop over time. An influential study by Perry (1970) delineated progression through different stages of thinking about the nature of knowledge and evidence. While this development takes on different forms in different subject disciplines, there are four discernible stages which may or may not be made explicit in the design of the curriculum or by university teachers:

- *dualism* (there are right and wrong answers)

- *multiplicity* (we do not always know the answers, people are entitled to different views and any one opinion, including their own, is as good as another)

- *relativism* (conclusions rest on interpretations from objective evidence, but different conclusions can justifiably be drawn)

- *commitment* (a coherent individual perspective on a discipline is needed, based on personal commitment to the forms of interpretation that develop through this perspective).

Entwistle (1998) draws directly on Perry to argue that students' *conceptions of learning* are linked to their progress through these stages of thinking about knowledge and evidence. Yet this development takes time and it cannot be assumed, for example, that first-year undergraduates can readily use relativist thinking, even though many curricula and assessment tasks assume that they can. Drawing on Marton and Säljö's ideas about *deep* and *surface* learning (1976), Entwistle argues that if students have a sophisticated conception of learning and a rich understanding of the nature of knowledge and evidence, they adopt a *deep* approach in order to reach their own understanding of material and ideas. If, on the other hand, they see learning as memorising or acquiring facts, and their intention is merely to meet course requirements or to respond to external injunctions, they are likely to adopt a *surface approach*. A surface approach relies on identifying those elements within a task that are likely to be assessed and then memorising the details.

However, students do not only adopt deep and surface approaches. The structure of a curriculum and the demands of **summative assessment** exert a strong influence on approaches to learning. Entwistle argues that summative assessment in higher education usually encourages a *strategic approach* where students combine deep and surface approaches in order to achieve the best possible marks. Students using this approach become adept at organising their study time and methods, attend carefully to cues given by teachers as to what type of work gains good grades or what questions will come up in examinations. If this argument is valid, it is likely that the increased use of explicit, detailed assessment criteria used in many courses will encourage this strategic approach.

Students' *approaches to learning* emerge in subtle, complex ways from *orientations*, *conceptions* of learning and types of knowledge and different *motives*. All these factors fluctuate over time and between tasks. Entwistle argues that consistency and variation in approaches can therefore be evident simultaneously. However, he maintains that students show sufficient consistency 'in intention and process across broadly similar academic tasks to justify measuring it as a dimension' (Entwistle, Hanley and Hounsell 1979, 367). Studies, such as those by Pask (1976), demonstrate students' consistency in experimental situations and normal studying, but qualitative studies by Marton and Säljö (eg 1976) show evidence of variability, where students adapt their approaches according to the demands of a specific task.

This evidence leads Entwistle to argue that a focus on process rather than intention affects the degree of consistency or variability of students' approaches. Entwistle differentiates between a *'style'* – as a broader characteristic of a student's preferred way of tackling learning tasks; and *'strategy'* – as a description of the way that a student chooses to tackle a specific task in the light of its perceived demands. Entwistle draws on Pask's distinction between holist and serialist strategies to argue that distinct learning styles underlie strategies. These styles are based on relatively fixed predispositions towards *comprehension* learning and *operation* learning (see the introduction to Section 7 for explanation).

Strategy is defined (Entwistle, Hanley and Hounsell 1979, 368; original emphasis) as the way 'a student *chooses* to deal with a specific learning task in the light of its perceived demands' and style 'as a broader characterisation of a student's *preferred* way of tackling learning tasks generally'.

Entwistle argues (1990, 675) that stylistic preferences are often strong:

perhaps reflecting cerebral dominance of left (serialist) or right (holist) hemispheres of the brain, combined with firmly established personality characteristics of the individual. Strong stylistic preferences may be rather difficult to modify, implying that choice in both materials and methods of learning is important for allowing students to learn effectively.

It is not clear what evidence Entwistle draws upon to link comprehension and operation learning directly to ideas about brain hemispheres or personality.

Evidence from studies that explore the effects of personality on studying leads Entwistle to argue that it is possible to identify three distinct personality types in higher education courses:

- *non-committers* (cautious, anxious, disinclined to take risks)
- *hustlers* (competitive, dynamic, but insensitive)
- *plungers* (emotional, impulsive and individualistic).

Over time, he argues (1998), these might develop towards an ideal fourth type – the *reasonable adventurer* who combines curiosity and the ability to be critical and reflective. Entwistle, McCune and Walker (2001, 108) argue that:

the intentions to learn in deep or surface ways are mutually exclusive, although the related learning processes may sometimes become mixed in everyday experience. The combination of deep and strategic approaches is commonly found in successful students, but a deep approach on its own is not carried through with sufficient determination and effort to reach deep levels of understanding.

Defining features of approaches to learning and studying are represented in Table 32:

Table 32	**Deep approach**	**Seeking meaning**
Defining features of approaches to learning and studying	Intention – to understand ideas for yourself	By:
Source: Entwistle, McCune and Walker (2001)	■ Relating ideas to previous knowledge and experience	
	■ Looking for patterns and underlying principles	
	■ Checking evidence and relating it to conclusions	
	■ Examining logic and argument cautiously and critically	
	■ Being aware of understanding developing while learning	
	■ Becoming actively interested in the course content	

	Surface approach	**Reproducing**
	Intention – to cope with course requirements	By:
	■ Treating the course as unrelated bits of knowledge	
	■ Memorising facts and carrying out procedures routinely	
	■ Finding difficulty in making sense of new ideas presented	
	■ Seeing little value or meaning in either courses or tasks set	
	■ Studying without reflecting on either purpose or strategy	
	■ Feeling undue pressure and worry about work	

	Strategic approach	**Reflective organising**
	Intention – to achieve the highest possible grades	By:
	■ Putting consistent effort into studying	
	■ Managing time and effort effectively	
	■ Finding the right conditions and materials for studying	
	■ Monitoring the effectiveness of ways of studying	
	■ Being alert to assessment requirements and criteria	
	■ Gearing work to the perceived preferences of lecturers	

As Entwistle's research has progressed, he and his colleagues have related the degree of variability in students' approaches to contextual factors such as task demands, perceptions of course organisation, workload, environment and teaching. This has led to the development of in-depth qualitative methods to explore the nuances of individual students' approaches and conceptions of learning.

A conceptual map of the various components of effective studying encompassed by the ASSIST (Figure 12) shows the relationships between holist and serialist modes of thinking. These include students' strategic awareness of what Entwistle calls the assessment 'game' and its rules, and their ability to use relevant aspects of the learning environment such as tutorial support. Entwistle, McCune and Walker (2001) argue that qualitative research into everyday studying is needed to counter the way that psychometric measures oversimplify the complexity of studying in different environments.

Description of measure

The first of Entwistle's inventories, the 1981 Approaches to Studying Inventory (ASI) drew directly upon Biggs' Study Behaviour Questionnaire (1976), which was developed in Australia. Entwistle and his colleagues emphasise the evolutionary nature of the inventories in relation to development of the model of learning. Following their own and external evaluations of the validity and reliability of the ASI and the Revised ASI in 1995, together with the development of a Course Perception Questionnaire (Ramsden and Entwistle 1981), the ASSIST was developed in 1997. The most recent inventory is the Approaches to Learning and Studying Inventory (ALSI), currently being developed for a project exploring how specific changes in the teaching and learning environment affect approaches to studying. However, because the ALSI is still being developed, this review focuses on the ASSIST.

Entwistle has also drawn on related developments by other researchers, including Vermunt's Inventory of Learning Styles (ILS; see Section 7.2). Across the field of research within the learning approaches 'family', successive inventories have built on the earlier ones. Entwistle and McCune (2003) argue that development might be done to refine the conceptualisation of original scales, to add new ones in order to keep up with more recent research, or to adapt an inventory to suit a particular project or improve its user-friendliness.

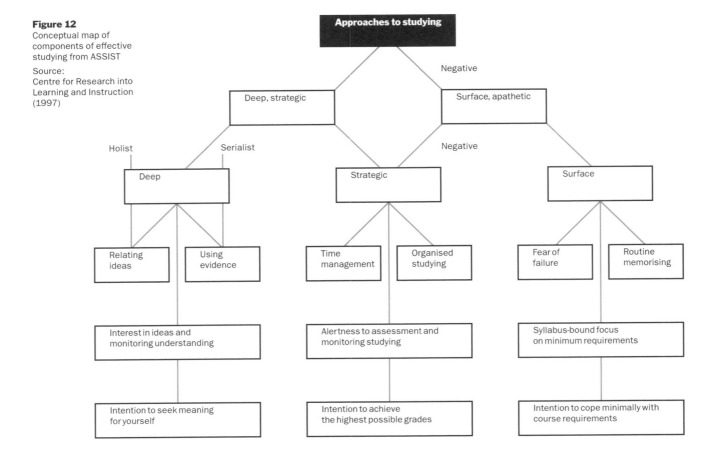

Figure 12
Conceptual map of components of effective studying from ASSIST

Source:
Centre for Research into Learning and Instruction (1997)

In addition to items refined from factor analyses, the ASSIST had new scales to improve the descriptions of studying and reactions to teaching, and to include metacognition and **self-regulation** in the strategic approach. *Meaning* and *reproducing orientations* from the ASI were recategorised in the ASSIST as *conceptions of learning* – namely, whether students see the purpose of learning as *transforming* or *reproducing* knowledge. *Approaches* were redefined as *deep, strategic* and *surface apathetic*. ASSIST also introduced new items to take account of perceptions of environment, workload and the organisation and design of the course. Items are presented in three sections, as follows.

1
What is learning? – this section comprises six items to test whether students see learning as being about, for example, 'making sure you remember things well' or 'seeing things in a different and more meaningful way'.

2
Approaches to studying – this section comprises 52 items based on comments about studying made by students in previous studies, covering deep, surface and strategic approaches, and reproducing, meaning and achievement orientations. Students have to agree or disagree with statements such as 'I go over the work I've done carefully to check the reasoning and that it makes sense' and 'Often I find myself questioning things I hear in lectures and read in books'.

3
Preferences for different types of course organisation and teaching – this section comprises eight items asking students to say how far they like, for example, 'exams which allow me to show that I've thought about the course material for myself'.

Students have to rank each statement according to:

■ how close the statement is to their own way of thinking, in order to reveal their ideas about learning

■ their relative disagreement or agreement with comments about studying made by other students, in order to reveal their approaches to studying and preferences for different types of course and teaching.

Each statement is ranked 1–5 on a Likert scale and students are encouraged to avoid choosing '3'. (It is not clear why the inventory does not use a four-point scale instead). A time limit is not suggested and students are asked to 'work through the comments, giving your *immediate* response. In deciding your answers, think in terms of this *particular lecture course*. It is also important that you answer *all* the questions: check you have' (CRLI 1997; original emphasis).

Evaluation by authors

Most of the internal and external evaluations of Entwistle's inventories have focused on the ASI and RASI: because of the evolutionary nature of the inventories, we review the earlier inventories for their accounts of validity and reliability, together with the small number of evaluations of ASSIST.

Reliability

The ASI was developed through a series of pilots, with item analyses (Ramsden and Entwistle 1981). In an earlier study, Entwistle, Hanley and Hounsell (1979) claimed high alpha coefficients of reliability as the basis for retaining the six best items for each scale in the final version of ASI. However, it is worth noting that seven out of 12 of these have coefficients below 0.7. We have re-ordered the scales in relation to each approach and type of motivation as shown in Table 33:

Table 33
Reliability of ASI sub-scales

Adapted from data presented in Entwistle, Hanley and Hounsell (1979)

Deep-level approach	8 items, 0.60
Comprehension learning	8 items, 0.65
Surface-level approach	8 items, 0.50
Operation learning	8 items, 0.62
Organised study methods	6 items, 0.72
Strategic approach	10 items, 0.55
Achievement motivation	6 items, 0.59
Intrinsic motivation	6 items, 0.74
Extrinsic motivation	6 items, 0.70
Fear of failure	6 items, 0.69
Disillusioned attitudes	6 items, 0.71

In an evaluation of the ASSIST, a study of 817 first-year students from 10 contrasting departments in three long-established and three recently established British universities offered the following coefficients of reliability for three approaches to studying: deep approach (0.84); strategic approach (0.80) and surface apathetic approach (0.87) (CRLI 1997).

Another study involved 1284 first-year students from three long-established and three recently established British universities, 466 first-year students from a Scottish technological university and 219 students from a 'historically disadvantaged' South African university of predominantly Black and Coloured students. It aimed to analyse the factor structure of ASSIST at sub-scale level and to carry out cluster analysis to see how far patterns of sub-scale scores retained their integrity across contrasting groups of students. High coefficients of reliability were found for sub-scales of a deep approach (0.84), a surface apathetic approach (0.80) and a strategic approach (0.87) (Entwistle, Tait and McCune 2000). The study also compared sub-scale factor structure for students who did well and those who did relatively poorly in summative assessments.

Validity

In a study of 767 first-year, second-term students from nine departments in three universities in the UK, separate factor analyses were carried out on the ASI for arts, social science and science students. According to Entwistle, this confirmed a robust three-factor structure: deep approach and comprehension learning; surface approach with operation learning; organised study methods and achievement-oriented learning (Entwistle, Hanley and Hounsell 1979). There was also evidence in this study that the ASI enabled some prediction of the departments in which students would be likely to adopt surface or deep approaches.

In a study in 1981, Ramsden and Entwistle administered the ASI with the Course Perceptions Questionnaire to 2208 students from 66 academic departments in six contrasting disciplines in British polytechnics and universities. Factor analysis confirmed the construct validity of the three orientations (meaning, reproducing and achievement). From analysis of responses to the Course Perceptions Questionnaire, they concluded that there were correlations between students' higher-than-average scores on meaning orientation and high ratings of good teaching, appropriate workload and freedom in learning. These contextual factors were linked to those in the ASI to form new items in the ASSIST.

In relation to the ASSIST, the Centre for Research into Learning and Instruction (CRLI) (1997,10) claimed that factor analysis of items in ASSIST is confirmed from diverse studies and that 'these factors, and the aspects of studying they have been designed to tap ... [provide] well-established analytic categories for describing general tendencies in studying and their correlates'.

Entwistle also evaluated the predictive validity of the ASI by seeing how well it could discriminate between extreme groups, self-ranked as 'high' and 'low achieving'. He found a prediction of 83.3% for the low-achieving group and 75% for the high-achieving group. In Ramsden and Entwistle (1981), similar results were obtained with moderate correlations between academic progress, organised study methods and a strategic approach. A deep approach did not appear to be the strongest predictor of high achievement in either study.

Cluster analysis of ASSIST in Entwistle, Tait and McCune (2000) examined patterns of study between individuals responding to items in similar and different ways. Analysis suggested interesting signs of dissonance between students' intentions to adopt particular approaches, their ability to apply them, and the effects of environmental factors on their ability to carry out their intentions. The importance of exploring similarities and dissonance between and across groups led the authors to argue that interpretation should combine factor and cluster analyses of responses to an inventory with analysis of findings from other studies.

As research on the inventories has progressed, analysis of validity has combined the use of the inventory with qualitative data from interviews with students. More recent work has aimed to establish the ecological validity of the methodology as a whole by combining quantitative and qualitative methods (see McCune and Entwistle 2000). For example, the authors argue that the ASSIST measures the extent to which students adopt a particular approach at a given time and shows patterns within groups. It also 'confirms and extends our understanding of patterns of study behaviours in relation to academic achievement and indicates the general influences of methods of teaching and assessment' (CRLI 1997, 12).

Yet ASSIST does not show how individuals develop skills and approaches over time. In addition, although inventories are important, Entwistle and his colleagues argue that researchers using them need a close understanding of their evolution and of how conceptually related categories in inventories derive from different mental models of learning (Entwistle and McCune 2003). Combining quantitative and qualitative methodology and understanding their respective purposes are also important. Inventories need to be supplemented with methods that can explore the idiosyncratic nature of students' learning and personal development, such as case studies of students' activities and attitudes over time (McCune and Entwistle 2000). For example, deep learning approaches vary greatly between a student's first- and final-year experiences, between different subjects and institutional cultures.

Entwistle and his colleagues argue then, that combining psychometric measures with in-depth, longitudinal or shorter qualitative studies creates a robust methodology. In addition, the goal of ecological validity, achieved through detailed transcription and analysis of interviews, 'allows staff and students to grasp the meaning of terms from their own experience, rather than facing technical terms that seem less relevant to their main concerns' (Entwistle 1998, 85). In recent work, Entwistle and colleagues have used detailed case studies to explore how teachers' sophisticated conceptions of teaching in higher education evolve over time (eg Entwistle and Walker 2000).

External evaluation

Reliability

In a review of seven external studies and that of Ramsden and Entwistle (1981), Duff (2002, 998) claims that extensive testing of the ASI over 20 years, across samples and contexts, has produced scores that 'demonstrate satisfactory internal consistency reliability and construct validity'. For example, using the Revised ASI with 365 first-year business studies students in a UK university, Duff (1997, 535) concluded that the RASI 'has a satisfactory level of internal consistency reliability on the three defining approaches to learning' proposed by Entwistle, with alpha coefficients of 0.80 for each approach.

Richardson (1992) applied a shorter 18-item version of the 64-item ASI over two lectures held 2 weeks apart, to two successive cohorts of 41 and 58 first-year students on social science degree courses (n=99). He concluded that the broad distinction between a meaning orientation and a reproducing orientation is reliable, with alpha coefficients of 0.72 for meaning and 0.73 for reproducing. He presented test–retest reliability with coefficients of 0.83 on meaning, 0.79 on reproducing and 0.79 on achieving. Richardson argued that the ASI has good test–retest reliability, but that the internal consistency of its 16 sub-scales is variable (see below).

Further support for the ASI as a reliable measure of broad orientations is offered by Kember and Gow (1990) who claim that, despite some small differences over factor structures relating to 'surface orientation', 1043 Hong Kong students revealed cultural differences in surface orientation where related constructs indicate a 'narrow orientation'. This new orientation meant that students were dependent on tasks defined by the lecturer and wanted to follow tasks in a systematic, step-by-step approach.

We have not found any external studies of reliability for the ASSIST.

Validity

In contrast to claims by Entwistle and his colleagues about the validity of the ASI, there is less agreement in external evaluations. For example, in a review of seven external studies and two by Entwistle and Ramsden, Richardson found problems with construct validity for many of the 16 sub-scales and individual items of the ASI generally. He argued that the ASI provided a convenient way of characterising students' approaches to learning within different contexts, but an ongoing problem for researchers had been to retrieve the original constituent structure of the ASI. Although factor analyses in both internal and external studies of the ASI have retrieved the basic distinction between meaning and reproducing orientations, 'dimensions concerning achieving orientation and styles and pathologies have been much less readily identifiable' (Richardson 1992, 41). He concluded (1997) that meaning and reproducing orientations constitute a valid typology of approaches to studying and that there is evidence of gender and age differences in orientations.

Problems with construct validity in the ASI are confirmed by Sadler-Smith (1999a), while other studies question the construct validity of some items for students of other cultures (see Meyer and Parsons 1989; Kember and Gow 1990). Kember and Gow argue that the test needs to be more culturally specific in terms of construct validity. There has also been disagreement about whether it offers predictive validity in correlating orientations and final assessment among 18–21-year-old undergraduates (Richardson 1992). However, Entwistle argues that the inventories were developed to describe different approaches to studying, not to predict achievement as such. In addition, the absence of standardised assessment criteria in higher education makes predictive validity difficult to demonstrate (Entwistle 2002).

In response to problems with construct and predictive validity, Fogarty and Taylor (1997) tested the ASI with 503 mature, 'non-traditional' (ie without entry qualifications) entrants to Australian universities. Their study confirmed problems with internal consistency reliability for seven of the sub-scales, with alpha coefficients in the range 0.31 to 0.60. In a similar vein to other studies that advocate a focus on broad orientations, the authors argued (1997, 328) that it 'may be better to concentrate on the meaning and reproducing orientations rather than on the various minor scales'. In terms of predictive validity, they found a negligible correlation between reproduction orientation and poor academic performance among their sample, but also a lack of correlation between a deep approach and good performance. This led them to argue that students unfamiliar with study may have appropriate orientations, but lack appropriate study skills to operationalise them.

Another study (Kember and Gow 1990) explored relationships between, on the one hand, performance and persistence; and on the other, approaches and orientation as measured by the ASI. In a study of 779 students divided between internal and external courses, **discriminant analysis** evaluated which of the sub-scales could distinguish between those who persist and those who do not. For both internal and external students, the surface approach was the variable that discriminated between non-persisters and persisters [discriminant coefficients of 0.71 (internal students) and 0.94 (external students)]. The other variable was fear of failure. Persistence was therefore partly related to fear of failure, while a surface approach was more likely to lead to dropping out.

In a study of 573 Norwegian undergraduates following an introductory course in the history of philosophy, logic and philosophy of science, Diseth (2001) evaluated the factor structure of the ASSIST. His study found evidence of the deep and surface approaches, but was less positive for items about course perception and assessment demands. In another test with 89 Norwegian psychology students, he found no links between general intelligence measures and approaches to learning. However, he noted (Diseth 2002) that straightforward correlations between achievement and the approaches that students adopt are not sufficient to predict success in assessment: instead, a surface approach had a statistically significant **curvilinear** link to examination grade: the highest level of achievement related to a low or moderate surface approach. The more that students used a surface approach, the more their achievement declined.

A strategic approach is also associated with high achievement, suggesting a need to differentiate between deep and surface approaches *to learning* and a strategic approach *to studying* (Entwistle and McCune 2003). This also suggests the need for lecturers, and students themselves, to be realistic about the importance of strategic approaches in students' responses to teaching and curriculum and assessment design. For example, the pressures of 'credential inflation' for achieving ever higher grades and levels of qualification are likely to encourage strategic approaches.

There has recently been a large upsurge of interest in describing and measuring the study strategies of students in higher education. This interest arises from both political and pedagogical goals: for example, policy decisions such as the training and certification of teachers in universities demand empirical evidence about appropriate pedagogy (see Entwistle and McCune 2003). In addition, current proposals to use student evaluations of their courses as the basis for league tables of universities derive heavily from the Course Perceptions Questionnaire developed for quite different purposes in the 1980s.

The growing influence of Entwistle's work raises new difficulties and criticisms, not least that inventories come to be separated from their underlying rationale for learning and used for different purposes than those intended by their designers. Notwithstanding these problems, there is a 'surprising lack of critique' in ideas surrounding deep and surface approaches to learning in higher education (Haggis 2003). One effect is that their increasing influence in mainstream academic debates can lead to the separation of individual elements from the underlying model, which then become identified as separate aspects of learning. Through 'a process of gradual reification as the ideas move into wider circulation, [the term] "deep approaches to learning" becomes "deep learning" and, ultimately, "deep learners"'(Haggis 2003, 91). This conceptual separation of the model from its inventory and the tendency to label people is a problem of all the inventories.

In addition, Haggis argues (2003, 91) that as the model and its scientific methodology become more influential, it 'appears to be seen as describing a kind of "truth" about how students learn in which research has "identified" both the categories and the relationships between them'. This 'truth' also becomes reified as other researchers interpret the implications of the model. For example, a number of interpretations of the research findings mistakenly claim that 'without exception', deep approaches are 'more likely' to result in high-quality learning outcomes (see Haggis 2003, 91).

A more fundamental difficulty, according to Haggis, is the assumption among supporters of the model that changing learning environments can induce students to see higher education differently. A mass system of higher education involves more students from 'non-traditional' backgrounds, and so assumptions in Entwistle's model about approaches and strategies become less valid. Haggis argues that the focus in the model on changing individuals' understanding contains implicit cultural biases that no longer fit mass participation in an expanding, underfunded system. She also argues that the model is epistemologically confused, because it combines human subjectivity and qualitative explanation with what proponents of the 'approaches model' claim are 'exceptionally rigorous' methods of scientific research. Taken together, these problems have, according to Haggis, created a narrow conception of the difficulties facing students and teachers in higher education. Haggis (2003) contends that alignment of the model to current political imperatives in higher education runs the risk of creating a single unifying framework that is becoming immune from critique and which creates passive learners.

Implications for pedagogy

The body of work on Entwistle's model and inventories has three broad implications for improving pedagogy. The inventory and its model could be used as:

- a diagnostic tool for lecturers and students to use in order to discuss approaches to learning and how they might be developed

- a diagnostic tool for course teams to use in talking about the design and implementation of the curriculum and assessment, including forms of support such as study skills courses

- a theoretical rationale, based on extensive empirical research, for discussion among lecturers (eg on teacher training and staff development courses) about students' learning and ways of improving their approaches.

In contrast to a belief in the relatively fixed nature of stylistic preferences, Entwistle, his colleagues and other supporters of the model argue that students, teachers and institutions can all change students' approaches to learning. Combining quantitative and qualitative methodology suggests that approaches to learning do not reflect inherent, fixed characteristics of individuals. Instead, Entwistle and his colleagues argue that approaches are responsive to the environment and to students' interpretations of that environment. However, there remains a conceptual and empirical tension between the stability of approaches across similar situations and their variability (Entwistle 2002).

Entwistle also claims that teaching can affect approaches to learning. For example, Ramsden and Entwistle (1981) showed that a deep approach is encouraged by students being given freedom in learning and by experiencing good teaching, with good pace, pitch, real-life illustrations, empathy with students' difficulties, tutors being enthusiastic and offering 'lively and striking' explanations. A surface approach is reinforced by the forms of summative assessment required in the course, a heavy workload and lecturers who foster dependency by 'spoon-feeding'. In recent work, Entwistle and his colleagues have explored how to create 'powerful learning environments' in order to change students' conceptions of learning. Referring to work by Perry on progression through different conceptions of knowledge (discussed in Section 7.1) and work by Vermunt and colleagues, Entwistle and Peterson (2003) argue that universities should encourage 'constructive friction' between the curriculum and teachers' and students' conceptions of knowledge. Drawing on constructivist and cognitive apprenticeship ideas about learning, they offer guidelines for promoting a deep approach to learning and more sophisticated conceptions of knowledge.

Perhaps the most useful contribution to understanding how to improve pedagogy in higher education is that this research provides:

a language of concepts and categories through which to discuss more precisely teaching and learning in higher education. Through that language, we should be able to explain to students how to become more effective learners. The research suggests that it is essential for students to become more aware of their own learning styles and strategies – to think out carefully what they are trying to achieve from their studying and to understand the implications of adopting deep and surface approaches to learning ... We should surely not leave effective study strategies to evolve through trial and error when we are now in a position to offer coherent advice.
(Entwistle 1989, 676)

Despite the potential of the model as a basis for better understanding about teaching, learning and approaches to study, Entwistle acknowledges that the recommendations he advocates have not been empirically tested. Instead, he offers a number of activities that can be logically deduced from his research to form a strategic approach to curriculum design, teaching and assessment. These activities include:

■ providing a clear statement of the purposes of a course

■ designing a course to take account of the students' current knowledge base in a subject and the level of understanding of the discipline that students show on entry

■ diagnostic testing of knowledge of the discipline and its concepts, with feedback to students as a basis for them to judge what they need to do to make progress

■ pitching teaching to previous knowledge, with remedial materials to overcome gaps and common misunderstandings

■ designing realistic assignment workloads

■ combining factual knowledge within problem-based curricula

■ making demands on students to adopt 'relativistic thinking' towards the end of a course rather than, unrealistically, from the outset

■ offering opportunities for peer discussion of course content and approaches to learning.

A number of universities have responded to Entwistle's work by developing study skills courses that encourage students to reflect on their approaches to learning. Entwistle argues that conventional study skills courses have limited value: 'taught as separate skills, they push students towards adopting surface approaches more strategically' (Martin and Ramsden, cited by Entwistle 1989, 676). The demands of formal, summative assessment also push students towards instrumental, reproduction learning.

There is a sense, though, in which Entwistle and his colleagues have not fully addressed the finding in their own and external evaluations that strategic approaches are important for students' achievement. Instead, there seems to be an underlying value judgement that perhaps most academics share – namely, that a deep approach is preferable to a strategic one. As more students take part in post-16 learning, it may be more realistic to foster good strategic approaches at the outset and then to build deeper approaches. Nevertheless, Haggis's (2003) warning about problems in relating the model to a mass system offers an important caveat in thinking about how to promote effective approaches to learning.

This warning is also pertinent, given that it is difficult to identify specific forms of support that can deal adequately with the complexity of individual students' approaches. For example, McCune and Entwistle (2000) found that some students, identified as having poor approaches to learning, were negative or indifferent to direct advice about study skills, even when they acknowledged problems in their approaches. A number of students showed little evidence of change in their approaches over time. These findings challenge the usefulness of generic study skills.

In addition, intensive individual attention to students' everyday learning does not seem realistic in the context of declining resources for contact between lecturers, support staff and students. Somehow, effective advice and support need to take account of the dynamic, idiosyncratic aspects of studying, students' motivation, the specific demands of subjects and disciplines, and particular academic discourses. The problem of how far teachers in a mass system with ever-expanding student/staff ratios can realistically diagnose and respond to individual needs is a significant one.

Implications for pedagogy

It is possible to offer a set of practical strategies that have been tested in empirical applications of ASI and ASSIST. Entwistle acknowledged, 14 years ago, that there was little evidence of individual departments in universities responding to his research findings (1989). In contrast, there is now growing interest in using the inventories to introduce changes in pedagogy. This leads, however, to the risk that the inventory becomes divorced from the complexity of the model of learning and also to the dangers of reification to which Haggis (2003) alerts us (see above).

Conclusions

Entwistle and his colleagues have spent almost 30 years refining the validity and reliability of their inventories to arrive at items that have reasonable predictive validity. They acknowledge the tendency for detailed, continuous refinements to make technical constructs less credible and less easy to use by researchers outside educational psychology. They have therefore supplemented their analysis of approaches to learning with data from qualitative studies to explore the consistency and variability of learning approaches within specific contexts (see McCune and Entwistle 2000; Entwistle and Walker 2000). In this respect, their methodology and the data their studies have produced offer a rich, authentic account of learning in higher education.

However, one feature of a positivist methodology, which aims for precise measures of psychometric traits, is that items proliferate in order to try to capture the nuances of approaches to learning. There are other limitations to quantitative measures of approaches to learning. For example, apparently robust classifications of meaning and reproduction orientations in a questionnaire are shown to be less valid when interviews are used with the same students. Richardson (1997) argued that interviews by Marton and Säljö show deep and surface approaches as different categories or forms of understanding, or as a single bipolar dimension along which individuals may vary. In contrast, questionnaires operationalise these approaches as separate scales that turn out to be essentially *orthogonal* to each other; a student may therefore score high or low on both. According to Richardson, this difference highlights the need for researchers to differentiate between methods that aim to reveal average and general dispositions within a group and those that aim to explain the subtlety of individuals' actions and motives.

Despite attempts to reflect the complexity of environmental factors affecting students' approaches to learning and studying, the model does not discuss the impact of broader factors such as class, race and gender. Although the model takes some account of intensifying political and institutional pressures in higher education, such as quality assurance and funding, sociological influences on participation and attitudes to learning are not encompassed by Entwistle's model.

There is also confusion over the theoretical basis for constructs in the ASI and ASSIST and subsequent interpretation of them in external evaluations. Two contrasting research traditions create these constructs: information processing in cognitive psychology; and qualitative interpretation of students' approaches to learning. Outside the work of Entwistle and his colleagues, a proliferation of instruments and scales, based on the original measure (the ASI), has led to the merging of constructs from both research traditions. Unless there is discussion of the original traditions from which the constructs came, the result is a growing lack of theoretical clarity in the field as a whole (Biggs 1993). Entwistle and his colleagues have themselves warned of this problem and provided an overview of the conceptions of learning, their history within the 'approaches to learning' model and how different inventories such as those of Entwistle and Vermunt relate to each other (Entwistle and McCune 2003).

There are a number of strengths in Entwistle's work. For example, he has shown that ecological validity is essential to prevent a tendency to label and stereotype students when psychological theory is translated into the practice of non-specialists. The issue of ecological validity illuminates an important point for our review as a whole, namely that the expertise and knowledge of non-specialists are both context-specific and idiosyncratic and this affects their ability to evaluate claims and ideas about a particular model of learning styles. High ecological validity makes a model or instrument much more accessible to non-specialists.

Entwistle's work has also aimed to simplify the diverse and sometimes contradictory factors in students' approaches to studying and learning, and to offer a theoretical rationale for them. He has attempted to reconcile ideas about the stability of learning styles with the idea that approaches are idiosyncratic and fluctuating and affected by complex learning environments. His work highlights the need for researchers to relate analysis and theoretical constructs to the everyday experience of teachers and students, and to make their constructs accessible (see also Laurillard 1979).

These features and the high output of work by Entwistle and his colleagues have made it credible with practitioners and staff developers within UK higher education. It has provided a model of learning with which academics who wish to be good teachers can engage: this is absent in teacher training for the further and adult education sectors, and for work-based trainers, where there is no influential theory of learning that could improve professional understanding and skills. Nevertheless, it is perhaps worth reiterating Haggis's warning (2003) that the model runs the risk of becoming a rigid framework that excludes social models of learning.

Finally, although Entwistle and his colleagues argue that researchers need to build up case studies by observing students studying and interviewing them about their approaches, it is not clear how far ASSIST is usable by university lecturers. Entwistle's concern to safeguard ideas about learning approaches from oversimplification in general use might be a reason for this. Nevertheless, notions such as 'deep', 'surface' and 'strategic' approaches to learning are now part of the everyday vocabulary of many HE teachers and the wealth of books on teaching techniques that draw directly on many of the concepts reviewed here is testimony to Entwistle's continuing influence on pedagogy in higher education. To use a term coined by Entwistle himself, the model has proved to be 'pedagogically fertile' in generating new ideas about teaching and learning in higher education.

Table 34
Entwistle's Approaches and Study Skills Inventory for Students (ASSIST)

	Strengths	Weaknesses
General	Model aims to encompass approaches to learning, study strategies, intellectual development skills and attitudes in higher education.	Complexity of the developing model and instruments is not easy for non-specialists to access.
Design of the model	Assesses study/learning orientations, approaches to study and preferences for course organisation and instruction.	There are dangers if the model is used by teachers without in-depth understanding of its underlying implications.
Reliability	Internal and external evaluations suggest satisfactory reliability and internal consistency.	■ Many of the sub-scales are less reliable. ■ Test–retest reliability not shown.
Validity	■ Extensive testing by authors of construct validity. ■ Validity of deep, surface and strategic approaches confirmed by external analysis.	■ Construct and predictive validity have been challenged by external studies. ■ Unquestioned preference for deep approaches, but strategic and even surface approaches may be effective in some contexts. ■ Rather weak relationships between approaches and attainment.
Implications for pedagogy	■ Teachers and learners can share ideas about effective and ineffective strategies for learning. ■ Course teams and managers can use approaches as a basis for redesigning instruction and assessment. ■ Model can inform the redesign of learning milieux within departments and courses.	■ The scope for manoeuvre in course design is variable outside the relative autonomy of higher education, especially in relation to assessment regimes. ■ There is a large gap between using the instrument and transforming the pedagogic environment. ■ As the terms 'deep' and 'surface' become popular, they become attached to individuals rather than behaviours, against the author's intention.
Evidence of pedagogical impact	Has been influential in training courses and staff development in British universities.	Not tested directly as a basis for pedagogical interventions.
Overall assessment	Potentially useful model and instrument for some post-16 contexts outside the success it has had in higher education, but significant development and testing will be needed.	
Key source	Entwistle 1998	

7.2
Vermunt's framework for classifying learning styles and his Inventory of Learning Styles (ILS)

Introduction

Jan Vermunt is an associate professor in the Graduate School of Education at Leiden University. He also has a part-time role as professor of educational innovation in higher education at Limburg University. His main areas of research and publication have been higher education, teaching and teacher education. He began his research on the regulation of learning (ie the direction, monitoring and control of learning) and on process-oriented instruction in the psychology department at Tilburg University in the late 1980s. Vermunt has published extensively in English and in Dutch, and his Inventory of Learning Styles (ILS) is available in both languages.

Definitions, description and scope

For Vermunt, the terms 'approach to learning' and 'learning style' are synonymous. He has tried to find out how far individuals maintain a degree of consistency across learning situations. He defines learning style (1996, 29) as 'a coherent whole of learning activities that students usually employ, their learning orientation and their mental model of learning'. He adds that 'Learning style is not conceived of as an unchangeable personality attribute, but as the result of the temporal interplay between personal and contextual influences'.

This definition of learning style seeks to be flexible and integrative and, in comparison with earlier approaches, strongly emphasises metacognitive knowledge and self-regulation. It is concerned with both declarative and procedural knowledge, including self-knowledge. It deals not only with cognitive processing, but also with motivation, effort and feelings (and their regulation). However its formulation was not directly influenced by personality theory.

Within Vermunt's framework, four learning styles are defined: meaning-directed, application-directed, reproduction-directed and undirected. Each is said (1996) to have distinguishing features in five areas:

- the way in which students cognitively process learning contents (what students do)

- the learning orientations of students (why they do it)

- the affective processes that occur during studying (how they feel about it)

- the mental learning models of students (how they see learning)

- the way in which students regulate their learning (how they plan and monitor learning).

The resulting 4x5 matrix is shown in Table 35 and suggests linked sets of behavioural, cognitive, affective, conative and metacognitive characteristics. However, it should be noted that the framework is conceived as a flexible one. Vermunt does not claim that his learning styles are mutually exclusive, nor that for all learners, the links between areas are always consistent with his theory. The case illustrations and quotations provided by Vermunt (1996) are captured in summary form as learner characteristics in Table 35. His four prototypical learning styles are set out in columns from left (high) to right (low) in terms of their presumed value as regards engagement with, and success in, academic studies.

Origins

Developed through his doctoral research project (1992), Vermunt's framework has clearly been influenced by several lines of research about deep, surface and strategic approaches to learning that date back to the 1970s, and by Flavell's ideas about metacognition (eg Flavell 1979). The work began with the qualitative analysis of interviews and later added a quantitative dimension through the development and use of the ILS (Vermunt 1994).

The Inventory of Learning Styles

Description of the measure

When the ILS was published, the original framework was simplified in that *affective* processes did not appear as a separate area. However, the area of learning orientations remains, encompassing long-term motivation and goals, and (to a lesser extent) dimensions of interest and confidence. The ILS is a 120-item self-rating instrument, using 5-point Likert scales. Its composition in terms of areas is shown in Table 36.

Reliability and validity

Statistical evidence to support the grouping of items into sub-scales has been provided. In two large-scale studies, Vermunt (1998) found that alpha values for the sub-scales were generally higher than 0.70. Confirmatory second-order factor analysis supported in almost every detail the grouping of sub-scales into Vermunt's hypothesised four learning styles, although there was some overlap between styles.

Table 35
Vermunt's learning styles
with illustrations of their
components

Source:
Vermunt (1990)

	Meaning-directed	Application-directed	Reproduction-directed	Undirected
Cognitive processing	Look for relationships between key concepts/theories: build an overview	Relate topics to everyday experience: look for concrete examples and uses	Select main points to retain	Find study difficult; read and re-read
Learning orientation	Self-improvement and enrichment	Vocational or 'real world' outcomes	Prove competence by getting good marks	Ambivalent; insecure
Affective processes	Intrinsic interest and pleasure	Interested in practical details	Put in time and effort; afraid of forgetting	Lack confidence; fear of failure
Mental model of learning	Dialogue with experts stimulates thinking and engagement with subject through exchange of views	Learn in order to use knowledge	Look for structure in teaching and texts to help take in knowledge and pass examinations. Do not value critical processing or peer discussion	Want teachers to do more; seek peer support
Regulation of learning	Self-guided by interest and their own questions; diagnose and correct poor understanding	Think of problems and examples to test understanding, especially of abstract concepts	Use objectives to check understanding; self-test; rehearse	Not adaptive

Table 36
Areas and sub-scales
of the ILS

Area	Sub-scale
Cognitive processing	Deep processing: ■ relating and structuring ■ critical processing Stepwise processing: ■ memorising and rehearsing ■ analysing Concrete processing
Learning orientation	■ Personally interested ■ Certificate-oriented ■ Self-test-oriented ■ Vocation-oriented ■ Ambivalent
Mental model of learning	■ Construction of knowledge ■ Intake of knowledge ■ Use of knowledge ■ Stimulating education ■ Cooperative learning
Regulation of learning	Self-regulation: ■ learning process and results ■ learning content External regulation: ■ learning process ■ learning results Lack of regulation

The fit between theory and empirical findings seems almost too good to be true. In Table 37, exemplars of each learning style are shown, constructed by taking the first item of each sub-scale with high factor loadings on each style factor. These exemplars certainly have a high degree of face validity as representing different approaches to study. It will be seen that there is some degree of overlap between styles, as well as two significant gaps which are consistent with Vermunt's theory. As application-directed learners are thought to use a mixture of self-regulation and external regulation, it is not surprising that there is no statement based on the sub-scale loadings for regulation for such learners. The second gap is that there is no statement about processing strategies for undirected learners, which is consistent with Vermunt's qualitative finding that such learners hardly ever engage in study-related cognitive processing.

The relevance of the ILS for use in the UK HE context has been established by Boyle, Duffy and Dunleavy (2003). The authors administered the 100-item (short form) version of the ILS to 273 students. They found that three of the four main scales have good internal consistency, while the fourth (learning orientation) had a borderline alpha value of 0.67. However, the reliability of the 20 sub-scales was rather less satisfactory than in Vermunt's 1998 study, with only 11 sub-scales having alpha values of 0.70 or above. Confirmatory factor analysis supported Vermunt's model of four learning styles, although the application-directed and undirected style measures showed less integration across components than the other two.

Despite its face and factorial validity and multidimensional structure, it has not been confirmed through independent research that the ILS is a good predictor of examination performance. With a sample of 409 psychology undergraduates, Busato *et al.* (2000) found that only the undirected style predicted academic success (negatively), and even then accounted for less than 4% of the variance over the first academic year. Both the meaning-directed style and openness (between which there was a *Pearson r* measure of 0.36) had virtually zero correlations with four outcome measures. Achievement motivation and the personality variable of conscientiousness were slightly better predictors in this study, but not nearly as good as performance on the first course examination on a introductory module.

In their UK study, Boyle, Duffy and Dunleavy (2003) also found that a factor measure of undirected learning style was a negative predictor of academic outcomes for 273 social science students, but it accounted for a mere 7% of the variance. On this occasion, meaning-directed style was a positive predictor, accounting for 5% of the variance, but neither reproduction-directed nor application-directed style yielded a significant correlation.

Evaluation

Vermunt's framework was not designed to apply in all post-16 learning contexts, but specifically to university students. However, he and his students are, at the time of writing, developing a new instrument to assess learning at work and a new version of the ILS for the 16–18-year-old group (Vermunt 2003). The new 16–18 instrument will take account of current teaching practices and will include an affective component.

The ILS asks about:

- how students attempt to master a particular piece of subject matter

- why they have taken up their present course of study

- their conceptions of learning, good education and cooperation with others.

By limiting his focus to higher education, Vermunt has been able to produce a reliable self-assessment tool, but this means that its relevance is largely unknown in other contexts, such as problem-based learning, vocational education, adult basic skills learning or work-based training. When an instrument modelled on the ILS was applied by Slaats, Lodewijks and Van der Sanden (1999) in secondary vocational education, only the meaning-directed and reproduction-directed patterns were found. Moreover, Vermunt's framework does not map well onto the categories empirically established in Canadian adult education settings by Kolody, Conti and Lockwood (1997). Cross-cultural differences in the factor structure of the ILS were reported by Ajisuksmo and Vermunt (1999).

The structure of the framework consists of Entwistle-like learning styles on the horizontal axis (which represent different levels of understanding) and a mixture of content and process categories on the vertical axis. This is clearly a framework rather than a taxonomy, as the vertical axis cannot be said to represent a dimension.

Table 37
Exemplar vignettes of
Vermunt's four learning
styles using ILS items

Meaning-directed exemplar

What I do	I try to combine the subjects that are dealt with separately in a course into one whole.
	I compare my view of a course topic with the views of the authors of the textbook used in that course.
	I use what I learn from a course in my activities outside my studies.
Why I do it	I do these studies out of sheer interest in the topics that are dealt with.
How I see learning	To me, learning means trying to approach a problem from many different angles, including aspects that were previously unknown to me.
How I plan and monitor my learning	To test my learning progress when I have studied a textbook, I try to formulate the main points in my own words.
	In addition to the syllabus, I study other literature related to the content of the course.

Application-directed exemplar

What I do	I use what I learn from a course in my activities outside my studies.
Why I do it	I do not do these studies out of sheer interest in the topics that are dealt with.
	I aim at attaining high levels of study achievement.
	When I have a choice, I opt for courses that seem useful to me for my present or future profession.
How I see learning	The things I learn have to be useful for solving practical problems.
How I plan and monitor my learning	

Reproduction-directed exemplar

What I do	I repeat the main parts of the subject matter until I know them by heart.
	I work through a chapter in a textbook item by item and I study each part separately.
Why I do it	I aim at attaining high levels of study achievement.
How I see learning	I like to be given precise instructions as to how to go about solving a task or doing an assignment.
How I plan and monitor my learning	If a textbook contains questions or assignments, I work them out completely as soon as I come across them while studying.
	I experience the introductions, objectives, instructions, assignments and test items given by the teacher as indispensable guidelines for my studies.

Undirected exemplar

What I do	
Why I do it	I doubt whether this is the right subject area for me.
How I see learning	I like to be given precise instructions as to how to go about solving a task or doing an assignment.
	The teacher should motivate and encourage me.
	When I prepare myself for an examination, I prefer to do so together with other students.
How I plan and monitor my learning	I realise that it is not clear to me what I have to remember and what I do not have to remember.

Definitions of the four styles are reasonably clear. Meaning-directed cognitive processing has an emphasis on synthesis and critical thinking, whereas reproduction-directed processing emphasises analysis and to some extent, the unthinking studying of parts. However, this contrast is not without problems, as it can be argued that mastery of a subject requires both synthesis and analysis – in other words, a full and detailed understanding of whole-part relationships. Vermunt acknowledges that learning styles can overlap and one example of this is that an interest in practical applications can be found alongside an interest in abstract ideas and subject mastery. Indeed Vermunt himself found that meaning-directed learners tended to give themselves higher ratings for concrete processing than did application-directed learners (Vermunt 1998). The 'undirected style' seems to apply to less successful learners. These may be people who study in haphazard or inconsistent ways or who simply do not study at all.

In two studies where cluster analysis rather than factor analysis was used (Wierstra and Beerends 1996; Vermetten, Lodewijks and Vermunt 2002), three, rather than four, groups were identified. In both cases, groups were found in which meaning-oriented deep processing was associated with self-regulation and in which reproduction-oriented surface processing was associated with external regulation. The studies differed, however, in finding rather different third clusters, called 'flexible learners' in one case and 'inactive learners' in the other. This may reflect the fact that students in different faculties differ in learning style and clearly illustrates the context dependency of the framework.

In some ways, Vermunt's treatment of regulation resembles the model of cognitive engagement put forward by Corno and Mandinach (1983). Self-regulation appears in both models and Vermunt's concept of external regulation (meaning relying on externally imposed learning objectives, questions and tests) resembles Corno and Mandinach's concept of passive learning or 'recipience'. However, unlike Corno and Mandinach, Vermunt does not make full use of Kuhl's theory of action control (1983), since in the ILS, he emphasises the cognitive rather than the affective aspects of metacognitive control. There are no items in the ILS relating to the control of motivation, emotions or even attention. This may well limit the predictive power of the instrument.

Vermunt's framework is compatible with more than one theory of learning, as one would expect from an approach which seeks to integrate cognitive, affective and metacognitive processes. His valuing of meaning-directed and application-directed ways of learning as well as process-based instruction (Vermunt 1995) reflects mainly cognitive and metacognitive theorising. He accepts that learners construct meanings, but has de-emphasised the interpersonal context of learning, as only undirected (largely unsuccessful) students tend to see learning in terms of opportunities for social stimulation/entertainment and cooperation (possibly in order to compensate for their fear of failure). He makes use of behavioural discourse when he speaks of the need for teachers to model, provide feedback and test. However, as argued above, his treatment of the affective domain and of personality factors is rather incomplete. So far as *conation* is concerned, this is not neglected, as the word 'try' appears in 20 different ILS items.

The empirical basis for the framework as presented in 1998 is very much stronger than in the 1996 paper. The 1996 qualitative data was based on interviews with only 24 first-year Open University students taking different courses and 11 psychology students at a traditional university; nor did the paper include a full audit trail for the categorisation of statements. However, the psychometric support for the ILS is reasonably robust, even though we are not told exactly how the choice of items for the sub-scales was made. A number of researchers have found test–retest correlations for each of the four areas in the range 0.4 to 0.8 over periods of between 3 and 6 months. This suggests that there can be as much variability and change as stability in approaches to study. Indeed, Vermetten, Lodewijks and Vermunt (1999) found that law students were using different learning strategies at the same time on four different courses.

It would be inappropriate to regard Vermunt's framework as definitive. It may not be applicable to all types and stages of learning. If it is to be used in post-16 contexts outside higher education, further theory development and validation will be needed, possibly allowing personality, affective, social-collaborative and study-skill components to feature more prominently. The well-supported theoretical models of Demetriou (Demetriou and Kazi 2001) and Marzano (1998) suggest promising ways forward. At the same time, it will be important to evaluate and seek to improve teaching and study environments as much as learning styles, since learning takes place where person and situation interact. In recent work, Vermunt has addressed this area using the ILS and the Inventory of Perceived Study Environments (IPSE) (Wierstra *et al.* 2002).

Implications for pedagogy

Vermunt developed his framework for use with post-16 learners and although its main use has been as a research tool, it is likely to be seen as meaningful and helpful by both learners and teachers. Technical terms such as *metacognition*, *regulation* and *affective* do not appear in the ILS itself, but will need clear definition and explanation for teachers who use it. The vocabulary demand of the ILS is around 12–13 years according to the Flesch-Kincaid readability index. The framework is not too complex for everyday use and its emphasis on the importance of motivation and metacognition during adolescence and beyond is well supported by research (Marzano 1998; Demetriou and Kazi 2001). It certainly provides a common language for teachers and learners to discuss how people try to learn, why they do it, how different people see learning, how they plan and monitor it and how teachers can facilitate it.

Vermunt believes that meaning-directed approaches will prove superior the more courses move away from traditional teaching programmes (with a high focus on teacher control and the transmission of knowledge) towards process-oriented study programmes – which focus on knowledge construction and utilisation by learners and are 'characterised by a gradual and systematic transfer of control over learning processes from instruction to learners' (Vermunt 1996, 49). He believes that this process will be facilitated if teachers become more aware of individual differences in learning style and address weaknesses by teaching domain-specific thinking and learning strategies. Research by Schatteman *et al.* (1997) into the effect of interactive working groups is consistent with these ideas, but is far from definitive, as the groups were not well attended and data was available for only 15 participants.

In addition to this, Vermunt sees considerable potential in the use of the ILS to reveal 'dissonant' approaches to learning; for example, by students who combine external regulation with deep processing or self-regulation with stepwise processing. So far, there are a few studies which suggest that such combinations are maladaptive (eg Beishuizen, Stoutjesdijk and Van Putten 1994).

Recognising that teachers themselves have learning styles which may well affect their practice, Vermunt has been involved in a number of studies in which his model has been applied in work with teachers and student teachers (eg Zanting, Verloop and Vermunt 2001; Oosterheert, Vermunt and Denissen 2002). In these contexts, he has again used qualitative approaches to assessing learning orientation, affective processes, mental models of learning and self-regulation as a basis for developing more objective, contextually appropriate methods. This work shows great promise for teacher education and professional development in all sectors, including post-16 education and training.

In a theoretical paper on congruence and friction between learning and teaching, Vermunt and Verloop (1999) suggest that both 'congruence' and 'constructive friction' between student and teacher regulation of learning are likely to prove beneficial. They claim that 'congruence' is to be found:

- when teacher regulation is high and student regulation is low
- when student regulation is high and teacher regulation is low.

Constructive friction occurs in situations where the teacher expects students to perform with greater self-regulation, whereas destructive friction is experienced when students are capable of more autonomy than their teachers allow or when they are incapable of taking responsibility for their own learning in a loosely structured learning environment. These ideas imply that teachers need to understand their students better than at present and to become more versatile in the roles they adopt. Common sense would support these notions, at least on the basis of extreme case scenarios, but their practical utility across higher education and for lifelong learning is as yet largely untested.

Vermunt's research into the learning of undergraduate students and others has had significant impact in northern Europe. Its main thrust has been to encourage learners to undertake voluntarily very demanding activities such as relating and structuring ideas, critical processing, reading outside the syllabus, summarising and answering self-generated questions. This kind of approach requires strong motivation, intellectual openness, a conscientious attitude, a sense of self-efficacy and self-confidence plus well-established and efficient metacognitive and cognitive strategies. These qualities have for many years been seen as desirable outcomes of higher education. However, although they can be acquired and developed, there is no easy way in which this can be achieved in the diverse areas of post-16 lifelong learning.

Vermunt has performed a valuable service in showing that, if progress is to be made, attention needs to be given not only to individual differences in learners, but to the whole teaching–learning environment. While the motivations, self-representations, metacognitive and cognitive strengths and weaknesses of learners are of concern to all involved in education, it is clear that these are also a function of the systems in which learners find themselves. Vermunt's conceptual framework and the ILS can usefully help to develop a better understanding of these complexities. His approach can certainly be adapted for use in all contexts of lifelong learning.

Empirical evidence of pedagogical impact

As yet, there is little evidence of this kind, apart from the studies mentioned in the previous sub-section. The ILS has not been widely used in post-16 intervention studies.

Table 38

Vermunt's Inventory of
Learning Styles (ILS)

	Strengths	Weaknesses
General	■ It applies to the thinking and learning of university students. ■ New versions in preparation for 16–18 age group and for learning at work. ■ Used for studying the learning styles of teachers and student teachers.	It has little to say about how personality interacts with learning style.
Design of the model	■ It is experientially grounded in interviews with students. ■ It seeks to integrate cognitive, affective, metacognitive and conative processes. ■ It includes learning strategies, motivation for learning and preferences for organising information.	■ It excludes preferences for representing information. ■ It is not comprehensive: there are no items on the control of motivation, emotions or attention. ■ The interpersonal context of learning is underemphasised. ■ Not applicable to all types and stages of learning. ■ Notions of 'constructive' and 'destructive' friction are largely untested.
Reliability and validity	It can be used to assess approaches to learning reliably and validly.	
Implications for pedagogy	■ It is dependent on context, ie a learning style is the interplay between personal and contextual influences. ■ It provides a common language for teachers and learners to discuss and promote changes in learning and teaching. ■ Emphasis not on individual differences, but on the whole teaching–learning environment.	
Evidence of pedagogical impact		■ Little evidence so far of impact on pedagogy. ■ It is not a strong predictor of learning outcomes.
Overall assessment	A rich model, validated for use in UK HE contexts, with potential for more general use in post-16 education where text-based learning is important. Reflective use of the ILS may help learners and teachers develop more productive approaches to learning.	
Key source	Vermunt 1998	

7.3
Sternberg's theory of thinking styles and his Thinking Styles Inventory (TSI)

Introduction

Robert Sternberg is a major figure in cognitive psychology; he is IBM professor of psychology and education at Yale University and was president of the American Psychological Association in 2003/04. His theory of mental self-government and model of thinking styles (1999) are becoming well known and are highly developed into functions, forms, levels, scope and leanings. He deals explicitly with the relationship between thinking styles and methods of instruction, as well as the relationship between thinking styles and methods of assessment. He also makes major claims for improving student performance via improved pedagogy.

Definition, description and scope of the model

Sternberg is keen to distinguish between style and ability. An ability 'refers to how well someone can do something'. A style 'refers to how someone likes to do something'. A style therefore is 'a preferred way of using the abilities one has' (1999, 8). 'We do not have a style, but rather a *profile* of styles' (1999, 19; original emphasis).

In his book on *Thinking styles* (1999), Sternberg used the two terms 'thinking styles' and 'learning styles' as synonyms; for example (1999, 17): 'Teachers fail to recognise the variety of thinking and learning styles that students bring to the classroom and so teach them in ways that do not fit these styles well.' However, by 2001, Sternberg was making clear distinctions between learning, thinking and cognitive styles. In more detail, he conceptualised 'learning styles' as how an individual prefers to learn by reading, for instance, or by attending lectures. 'Thinking styles' are characterised as 'how one prefers to think about material as one is learning it or after one already knows it' (Sternberg and Zhang 2001, vii). 'Cognitive styles' are described as the 'ways of cognizing (sic) the information' (Sternberg and Zhang 2001, vii) by being impulsive and jumping to conclusions, or by being reflective. Cognitive styles are considered by Sternberg to be closer to personality than either thinking or learning styles.

Sternberg's theory of thinking/learning styles is derived from his theory of mental self-government, which is based on the metaphorical assumption (for which no evidence is offered) that the kinds of government we have in the world are not merely arbitrary or random constructions, but rather 'in a certain sense are mirrors of the mind ... on this view, then, governments are very much extensions of individuals' (1999, 148). Sternberg chooses four forms of government: monarchic, hierarchic, oligarchic and anarchic, but not democratic or dictatorial. No explanation is given as to why these four forms of government have been chosen and others excluded.

Table 39
Summary of styles of thinking
Source: Sternberg (1999)

Functions	Forms
Legislative	Monarchic
Executive	Hierarchic
Judicial	Oligarchic
	Anarchic

Levels	Scope	Leanings
Global	Internal	Liberal
Local	External	Conservative

His theory is constructed from three functions of government (legislative, executive and judicial); four forms (monarchical, hierarchical, oligarchic and anarchic); two levels (global and local); the scope of government which is divided into internal and external; and leanings (liberal and conservative). Each of these aspects of government is considered necessary for the management of the self in everyday life. Sternberg provides a diagrammatic summary of his styles; he does not call it a taxonomy, but that is what it amounts to (see Table 39).

A brief description of the 13 styles is given below.

1
Legislative people like to come up with their own ways of doing things and prefer to decide for themselves what they will do and how they will do it. This style is particularly conducive to creativity: 'In schools as well as at work, legislative people are often viewed as not fitting in, or perhaps as annoying.' (1999, 33)

2
Executive people 'like to follow rules and prefer problems that are pre-structured or prefabricated ... executive stylists do what they are told and often do it cheerfully' (1999, 21). They are implementers who like to follow as well as to enforce rules. They can often 'tolerate the kinds of bureaucracies that drive more legislative people batty' (1999, 35).

3

Judicial people 'like activities such as writing critiques, giving opinions, judging people and their work, and evaluating programs' (1999, 21). They like to evaluate rules and procedures; they prefer 'problems in which they can analyse and evaluate things and ideas' (1999, 39).

Sternberg makes three general points about this style.

■ 'every organisation needs judicial people as well as legislative and executive ones' (1999, 40).

■ 'the same person can and typically will perform all three of these functions in greater or lesser degree. But people often feel more comfortable in one role or another' (1999, 40).

■ 'Any number of people who might be legislative in school might be executive in their choice of clothing or vice-versa. We thus need to understand styles in the contexts in which they are expressed' (1999, 43). The significance of context is explicitly acknowledged, but not explored in any detail.

4

Monarchic people are single-minded and driven by whatever they are single-minded about, and do not let anything get in the way of them solving a problem. They tend to be 'motivated by a single goal or need at a time' (1999, 46).

5

Hierarchic people recognise the need to set priorities, accept complexity and 'tend to fit well into organisations because they recognise the need for priorities' (1999, 23). 'They tend to be systematic and organised in their solutions to problems and in their decision making' (1999, 51).

6

Oligarchic people 'tend to be motivated by several, often competing goals of equal perceived importance' (1999, 23). 'The oligarchic person is a cross between a monarchic person and a hierarchic one' (1999, 54).

7

Anarchic people seem to be motivated by 'a potpourri of needs and goals that can be difficult for them, as well as for others, to sort out' (1999, 23). 'They are at risk for anti-social behaviour … they are the students who challenge teachers, not necessarily on principled grounds, but rather for the sake of challenging the teachers or any other authority figures' (1999, 58). They can challenge the system and have a potential for creativity.

Sternberg argues appropriately that these 'styles are not in and of themselves good or bad' (1999, 51), but it is important to point out that the titles (eg monarchic, anarchic) he employs are evaluative and normative.

8

Global individuals 'prefer to deal with relatively large and abstract issues. They ignore or don't like details, and prefer to see the forest rather than the trees' (1999, 24).

9

Local individuals 'like concrete problems requiring working with details. The danger is they may lose the forest for the trees' (1999, 24).

Sternberg argues that: 'Most people tend to be either more global or more local: they focus more on the big picture or more on the small details. But some people are both: they are equally attentive to the big picture and to the little details' (1999, 64).

10

Internal individuals 'tend to be introverted, task-oriented, aloof and sometimes socially less aware. They like to work alone' (1999, 25).

11

External individuals 'tend to be extroverted, outgoing and people-oriented. Often, they are socially sensitive and … like working with other people wherever possible' (1999, 25). According to Sternberg, 'In management, a distinction is sometimes made between task-oriented and people-oriented managers. This distinction is roughly comparable to that between internalists and externalists' (1999, 70).

12

Liberal individuals 'like to go beyond existing rules and procedures, to maximise change, and to seek situations that are somewhat ambiguous' (1999, 26).

13

Conservative individuals 'like to adhere to existing rules and procedures, minimise change, avoid ambiguous situations where possible, and stick with familiar situations in work and professional life' (1999, 26).

In general, Sternberg wishes 'to distinguish between stylistic leanings and political ones' (1999, 75). Sternberg argues that the two are probably only weakly correlated, if at all, and he gives the example of the US politician, Newt Gingrich, who has a conservative political philosophy, but a decidedly liberal personal style.

The 15 principles of thinking styles

Sternberg makes 15 general points about this theory which he feels are essential to its understanding and these are listed briefly below.

1

Styles are preferences in the use of abilities, not abilities themselves.

2

A match between styles and abilities creates a synergy that is more than the sum of its parts.

3

Life choices need to fit styles as well as abilities; for example, careers and choice of spouse.

4

People have profiles (or patterns) of styles, not just a single style.

5

Styles are variable across tasks and situations; for example, influence of weather, company, etc.

6

People differ in the strength of their preferences.

7

People differ in their stylistic flexibility.

8

Styles are socialised – that is, they are learned; for instance, by children observing role models.

9

Styles can vary across the lifespan – that is, styles, like abilities, are fluid rather than fixed, and dynamic rather than static entities; for example, the style needed by a new recruit is very different from that needed by a senior partner in a law firm.

10

Styles are measurable.

11

Styles are teachable.

12

Styles valued at one time may not be valued at another. (His claim is that different styles are required for different levels or kinds of responsibility in an organisation, which seems remarkably similar to the ninth principle.)

13

Styles valued in one place may not be valued in another.

14

Styles are not, on average, good or bad – it is a question of fit. A style may fit well in one context, but poorly or not at all in another.

15

We confuse stylistic fit with levels of ability. The consequence is that people and institutions tend to value other people and institutions that are like themselves. (But the question needs to be asked: do we not at times also value people precisely because their style is very different from our own?)

Origins and influence

One of the attractions of Sternberg's approach is that he ends his book (1999) by raising 10 of the most frequently mentioned problems with theories of learning styles and claims to deal with them all satisfactorily. As will become clear, however, some of the problems are just as applicable to Sternberg's own work as they are to the research of those he criticises. He begins by asking: Why do we need another theory? What are the problems with theories of learning styles? The 10 problems he tackles are listed below, together with a brief account of his response, plus some comment from this research team (material in brackets), where appropriate.

1

There is no unifying model or metaphor that integrates the various styles, not only between theories, but even within theories. Sternberg's contention is that his theory of mental self-government provides a clear organising metaphor, namely that of government.

2

Some of the styles seem too much like abilities; for example, the field dependence/independence theory of Witkin.

3

Some of the learning styles seem too much like personality traits; for example, Myers-Briggs. Sternberg argues that styles differ from personality traits in being more cognitive.

4

There is no compelling demonstration of the relevance of the styles in 'real world' settings. (This is so, but it is also true of Sternberg's own theory.)

5

There is insufficient connection between the theories of styles and psychological theory in general. Sternberg argues that styles cannot be considered independently of the environment in which they occur. People actively respond in varied ways to the environment, depending in large part upon their styles of responding.

6

The styles specified by the theories are sometimes simply not compelling. Sternberg lists five criteria for a successful theory – is it elegant, reasonably parsimonious, internally coherent, empirically valid and heuristically useful? He then claims that his theory meets all five criteria. (We would argue that there are serious questions to be asked about the validity and reliability of his theory.)

7

There is insufficient use of converging operations or multiple methods of measurement.

8

There is little or no serious research to show the usefulness of the styles. In Sternberg's own words (1999, 155): 'Theories and research on styles are at the fringes of the psychological world'. In this area of psychology, '*there is a high ratio of theory to data – in everyday terms, that means "big talk, no show"* ... Many schools are buying into systems for assessing students' learning styles and for teaching the students that have no solid research base at all' (1999, 155). (This is our central criticism of Sternberg's own work.)

9

The theories do not seem to be theories of styles at all, but rather of the variables that affect styles. Sternberg is right to claim that this criticism applies most clearly to the theory of Dunn and Dunn, who concentrate on environmental variables which may affect learning styles.

10

The styles specified by the theories do not satisfy some or even most of the 15 principles listed above.

Measurement by the author

Description

Sternberg has administered his inventory of thinking/learning styles in schools and elsewhere. In all, four measures have been used and these are described briefly below.

1

The Thinking Styles Inventory: 13 inventories with eight statements rated on a 1–7 scale.

2

The Thinking Styles Tasks for Students which, Sternberg claims, measure styles via performance rather than via an inventory; for example, 'When I'm studying literature, I prefer...'. The student chooses from a legislative, executive or judicial response or some other response. (The response, however, does not comprise observed performance, but self-reports of likely performance.)

3

The Thinking Styles Questionnaire for Teachers which assesses 'the styles teachers use when they teach' (1999, 124) or rather the styles which teachers report that they use.

4

Students' Thinking Styles Evaluated by Teachers.

Very little information is provided on the second, third or fourth of these instruments and yet Sternberg claims that these four measures 'meet the criteria for being good tests' (1999, 125).

Reliability and validity

There are few details given about the reliability and validity of these inventories. What data is provided is summarised below. In *The MSG Thinking Styles Inventory* by Sternberg and Wagner (1991), which is unpublished; the learner completes each of the 13 inventories on a 7-point scale from the statement '...fits me not at all well' to 'fits me extremely well'. Each style may vary' across tasks, situations and your time of life' (1999, 30).

With regard to the TSI, Sternberg (1999, 125) claims that the 13 scales had 'internal-consistency reliabilities ranging from .57 to .88 with a median of .82'. Factor analysis was employed and identified five factors, three of which were predicted and consistent with the theory; one was not predicted, but was consistent; while the last was neither predicted nor consistent. Sternberg concludes: 'Thus the statistical analysis generally supported the theory, although the second factor remains unexplained' (1999, 126).

Sternberg also claims that his scales correlate with scores on other tests, thus demonstrating good *external validity*. With the Myers-Briggs Type Indicator, for example, 30 out of 128 correlations were statistically significant; and 22 correlations out of 52 were significant with the Gregorc Style Delineator (see Zhang and Sternberg 2001 for further details). In general, the position of Sternberg and his associates is that 'The TSI has been shown to be reliable and valid for US samples' (Zhang and Sternberg 2001, 204).

External evaluation

Reliability and validity

Porter (2003) tested the reliability and validity of the TSI in a study of 150 first-year psychology undergraduates at Westminster University. According to Porter, the theory of mental self-government (MSG) and the TSI instrument 'have been presented in the literature as potentially powerful tools for use in higher education' (2002, 296) and so need to be independently evaluated. Porter describes other studies (eg Zhang and Sternberg 2001), which concluded that thinking styles contribute to academic achievement and that this contribution is differentially related to culture and gender. Porter's study, however, offers 'only limited support for the theory of MSG and the reliability and validity of the TSI' (2002, 301); he argues, therefore, that both will have to be improved before the TSI can be used in educational practice. Porter's students found the MSG theory both plausible and interesting, but they considered the 13 inventories to be both too long and boring. Porter also questioned whether first-year students understand their own learning well enough to complete the inventories satisfactorily.

Sternberg's theory and the TSI were part of the battery of tests used by Demetriou and Kazi (2001) in their attempt to build and test a theory of the mind and its development from childhood to adolescence. The scale of the project is impressive, with a sample of 840 participants from 10 to 15 years of age in Thessaloniki, Greece and a follow-up study of 322 students from the University of Cyprus. It is, however, important to realise that only the first two of the five dimensions of Sternberg's theory were tested (ie *function* and *form* were tested, but not *level*, *scope* and *learning*). Moreover, the test of thinking styles constituted only a very small part of the data collection which involved three testing periods of 2 hours; the battery consisted of six tests of cognitive ability (quantitative, causal, spatial, social understanding, drawing and creativity) and self-evaluation questionnaires on cognitive ability, personality, cognitive and problem-solving strategies and occupational preferences, as well as thinking styles. It is, nevertheless, important to note that the alphas for the three styles: executive (0.56), legislative (0.51), and evaluative (0.59) were considerably lower than those which Sternberg claimed for them.

Demetriou and Kazi (2001, 196) conclude that Sternberg's thinking styles

are derivatives of the more fundamental dimensions involved in the realms of personality and cognition. In a sense, this finding is in line with Sternberg's conception of thinking styles as the interface between personality, intelligence and actual performance. One can live without them

No conclusions were drawn by these authors in relation to thinking styles and pedagogy.

General

Each of the 13 styles is based on a short self-assessment inventory of no more than eight questions, some of which may strike some respondents as unanswerable; for example, Question 1 in the External Style Inventory reads: 'When starting a task, I like to brainstorm ideas with friends or peers'.

This statement is likely to raise the following questions in the minds of respondents: does this refer to every task? Is brainstorming appropriate for all tasks? Without a detailed description of the *kind* of task the psychologist has in mind, some respondents may find themselves unable and unwilling to answer this question. It does not matter how sophisticated the statistical analysis of responses to such questions is, if the responses do not accurately reflect the behaviour of the respondents. Each of the 13 inventories has a similar vague statement; for example, the Monarchic Style Inventory contains the following statement: 'When trying to finish a task, I tend to ignore problems that come up.' We argue that it depends on the task and on the type of problem that comes up.

The statements in the 13 inventories are rather obvious, so it is relatively easy to guess the intentions of the psychologist who wrote the item. It would therefore be simple to fake a response, for instance, to a Conservative Style statement such as 'When faced with a problem, I like to solve it in a traditional way'. Respondents could decide whether they wish to appear as left- or right-wing or somewhere in between.

Implications for pedagogy

The significance for pedagogy of Sternberg's research on thinking styles can be summarised in five brief propositions which are of a very general nature.

- Teachers should use a variety of teaching methods (eg lectures, group discussions).

- Teachers should use a variety of assessment methods (eg multiple-choice questions, essays, projects).

- Teachers should provide students with an understanding of different thinking styles and should themselves be aware of the styles they either encourage or punish.

- Teachers should know about gender and cross-cultural differences in thinking styles.

- Teachers should use extracurricular activities to enhance the quality of teaching and learning (see Zhang and Sternberg 2001).

The fifth recommendation does not appear to stem from Sternberg's own research, but from the work of others on creative thinking.

Sternberg is convinced that his theory is important for pedagogy and has carried out a series of studies of thinking/learning styles in both secondary and higher education, and cross-cultural studies in China, Hong Kong and the US. In his own words (1999, 115): 'The key principle [of the theory] is that in order for students to benefit maximally from instruction and assessment, at least some of each should match their styles of thinking'. He is convinced that different methods of instruction work best for different styles of thought and produces a table (reproduced here as Table 40) to show the various types of compatibility.

His argument is that teachers need the flexibility to vary their teaching style to suit students' different styles of thought and that few methods of instruction are likely to be optimal for everyone.

Again, Sternberg argues, without any supporting evidence, that different methods of assessment tend to benefit different thinking styles and produces a table to exemplify the connections (see Table 41).

Table 40
Thinking styles and methods of instruction

Source: Sternberg (1999)

Method of instruction	Style(s) most compatible with method of instruction
Lecture	Executive, hierarchical
Thought-based questioning	Judicial, legislative
Cooperative (group) learning	External
Problem solving of given problems	Executive
Projects	Legislative
Small group: students answering factual questions	External, executive
Small group: students discussing ideas	External, judicial
Reading	Internal, hierarchical

Table 41
Thinking styles and methods of assessment

Source: Sternberg (1999)

Method of assessment	Main skills tapped	Most compatible styles
Short-answer and multiple-choice tests	Memory	Executive, local
	Analysis	Judicial, local
	Time allocation	Hierarchical
	Working by self	Internal
Essay tests	Memory	Executive, local
	Macro analysis	Judicial, global
	Micro analysis	Judicial, global
	Creativity	Legislative
	Organisation	Hierarchical
	Time allocation	Hierarchical
	Acceptance of teacher viewpoint	Conservative
	Working by self	Internal
Projects and portfolios	Analysis	Judicial
	Creativity	Legislative
	Teamwork	External
	Working by self	Internal
	Organisation	Hierarchical
	High commitment	Monarchic
Interview	Social ease	External

Empirical evidence for impact on pedagogy

Sternberg and his associates (eg Grigorenko and Zhang) have carried out many studies exploring particular aspects of the theory of mental self-government and the TSI: for instance, the ability of thinking styles to predict academic achievement over and above ability; the relationships between thinking styles and learning approaches, student characteristics (such as age, gender and socio-economic status) and self-esteem. The significance for pedagogy of the findings of these studies tends to be inferred by the authors rather than directly studied. The results most relevant to pedagogy include the findings from a study of four US schools that 'students performed better when they were more like their teachers stylistically, independent of actual level of achievement' and that 'different school[s] rewarded different styles' (Sternberg 1999, 130). In general, it can be said that the earlier studies with Grigorenko were carried out with relatively small samples (eg 124 students from four schools), but the later cross-cultural studies with Zhang involve substantial numbers of participants (eg 646 students from Hong Kong, 215 from China and 67 from the US): see Zhang and Sternberg (2001) for more details.

Conclusions

Sternberg has produced an original theory of mental self-government (MSG) and has derived his TSI from it; this is beginning to be used and tested, particularly in China. It is important to realise that this new theory has not been developed from the thinking or empirical studies of other researchers, so it may be better to consider it not as a theory of learning or thinking styles, but as an intriguing metaphor which may or may not prove to be productive in stimulating research and in changing practice. It is, at present, too early to offer a comprehensive evaluation.

A series of research projects in universities and secondary schools in the US, Hong Kong and mainland China are now enhancing our understanding of thinking styles. The claims made for the implications of the theory for pedagogy are extensive, but the number of empirical studies which have tested these claims remains low. Moreover, the implications for pedagogy that Sternberg lists are of a very general nature and some of them have only a tenuous connection with his research.

One possible (but highly unrealistic) outcome from this theory, which describes no less than 13 different thinking styles, is that teachers and tutors could be invited to produce lessons which cater for all 13 styles. Sternberg avoids such difficulties by couching his advice in very general terms; for example, that teachers should use a variety of teaching and assessment methods and should provide their students with an understanding of different styles. In other words, the implications for pedagogy are based on common-sense inferences from the theory rather than on the findings of any experimental studies.

Grigorenko and Sternberg (1995) have suggested two main reasons for the sudden flowering of research interest in learning styles in the late 1960s and early 1970s. First, the notion was attractive to many theorists 'because of their disappointment with intelligence tests and the need for new measures of individual differences' (1995, 218). Second, researchers from psychology and business studies began to explore the concept of learning styles because it was so flexible and ill defined.

More recently, Sternberg has assessed the learning/thinking/cognitive styles field and addressed the mystery of why such research, 'so active and unified under the cognitive styles banner in the middle of the [20th] century, seems to be so much less unified and active by the end of the century' (2001, 249). He attributed the current lack of unity and activity to four main reasons: the early theories were not distinguishable from abilities or personality traits; the main theorists remained isolated from each other and from the psychological literature more generally; the quality of early empirical research was poor; and no common conceptual framework or language has emerged – in its place, different languages and labels have proliferated. Sternberg concluded (2001, 250) as follows: 'The result is a kind of balkanisation of research groups, and balkanisation has always led to division and, arguably, death by a thousand cuts'. It is also arguable that Sternberg has himself contributed to such balkanisation and that the answer to his own question – do we need another theory of learning styles? – is probably best answered in the negative.

Table 42

Sternberg's Thinking
Styles Inventory (TSI)

	Strengths	Weaknesses
General	13 thinking styles are proposed, based on the functions, forms, levels, scope and leanings of government.	■ Why these 13? 13 are too many. ■ Learners self-assess their likely behaviour by responding to statements which are context-free.
Design of the model	Based on a new theory of 'mental self-government'.	■ Sternberg offers a metaphor rather than a theory. ■ No explanation is given as to why some forms of government (eg monarchic) are chosen and not others (eg democratic).
Reliability and validity	Claimed by author to be both reliable and valid.	■ Only limited empirical support for the reliability and validity of the TSI. ■ Scores for reliability considerably lower than those found by author. ■ Little or no support for validity of the TSI.
Implications for pedagogy	■ Teachers to use a variety of teaching and assessment methods. ■ Teachers to be aware of the learning styles they encourage or punish. ■ Teachers to let students know about the range of styles. ■ Teachers to know about gender and cross-cultural differences in styles. ■ Teachers to use extra-curricular activities to enhance quality of teaching and learning.	■ No solid research base for these suggestions, which are logical deductions from the theory. ■ Fifth suggestion stems from research on creativity, rather than learning styles. The advice is of a very general, common-sense nature, most of it known to teachers before any research done on learning styles.
Evidence of pedagogical impact	A series of studies in the US and China have so far produced mixed results.	There is a need for independent evaluation.
Overall assessment	An unnecessary addition to the proliferation of learning styles models.	
Key source	Sternberg 1999	

Section 8

Implications for pedagogy

This section begins by discussing the various teaching strategies that the developers and advocates of learning style instruments have suggested, with a brief evaluation of the strengths and weaknesses of each. This entry into the world of course developers, institutional managers and front-line practitioners necessarily involves us in a much wider literature than that consulted for the 13 major models evaluated earlier in this report.

The sub-sections which follow attempt to answer two questions which are crucial for educational practice.

- Why do some people find learning styles so appealing?

- Why do others find them unacceptable?

We then discuss the lack of research into pedagogy in the UK, particularly compared with Germany; and we offer a brief overview of the different definitions of, and approaches to, pedagogy which have been taken by psychologists, sociologists and adult educators. This section ends with the crucial distinction, drawn by Alexander (2000), between 'teaching' and 'pedagogy'; we argue that the learning styles literature is in the main concerned with the former rather than the latter.

What advice for practitioners?

In the current state of research-based knowledge about learning styles, there are real dangers in commending detailed strategies to practitioners, because the theories and instruments are not equally useful and because there is no consensus about the recommendations for practice. There is a need to be highly selective. As we have seen, for example, with regard to Dunn and Dunn (Section 3.2), Gregorc (Section 3.1) and Riding (Section 4.1), our examination of the reliability and validity of their learning style instruments strongly suggests that they should not be used in education or business. On the other hand, the research of Entwistle (Section 7.1) and Vermunt (Section 7.2), which is both more guarded in its claims and built on more solid theoretical foundations, offers thoughtful advice that might, after careful trials and revisions, be extended to post-16 learning outside higher education.

A significant proportion of the literature on the practical uses of learning styles is not, however, so circumspect. Fielding, for instance, goes so far as to argue that an understanding of learning styles should be 'a student entitlement and an institutional necessity' (1994, 393). A thriving commercial industry has also been built to offer advice to teachers, tutors and managers on learning styles, and much of it consists of inflated claims and sweeping conclusions which go beyond the current knowledge base and the specific recommendations of particular theorists. For example, McCarthy (1990) developed what she calls the 4MAT cycle of learning from Kolb's model, and a US website (www.volcano.und.nodak.edu/vwdocs/msh/llc/is/4mat.html) devoted to her approach claims that 'It represents graphically the teacher behaviors appropriate to each stage and style, and provides a framework for planning any lesson or unit, for any age level or content area'.

Some of the leading learning theorists, moreover, make extravagant claims for their model, which reflect badly on the whole field of learning styles research. Rita Dunn, for example, whose approach was evaluated in Section 3.2, is quoted by O'Neil (1990, 7) as claiming that 'Within six weeks, I promise you, kids who you think can't learn will be learning well and easily … The research shows that every single time you use learning styles, children learn better, they achieve better, they like school better'.

In a similar vein, Felder has written articles on the relevance of learning styles to the teaching of science to adults. After examining four different models – the Myers-Briggs Type Indicator, Kolb's Learning Style Inventory, Herrmann's Brain Dominance Instrument and his own Felder-Silverman instrument – he concludes (1996, 23): 'Which model educators choose is almost immaterial, since the instructional approaches that teach around the cycle for each of the models are essentially identical'. We disagree strongly: it matters which model is used and we have serious reservations about the learning cycle.

For other commentators, the absence of sound evidence provides no barrier to basing their arguments on either anecdotal evidence or 'implicit' suggestions in the research. Lawrence (1997, 161), for instance, does exactly that when discussing the 'detrimental' effects of mismatching teaching and learning styles. More generally, the advice offered to practitioners is too vague and unspecific to be helpful; for example, 'restructure the classroom environment to make it more inclusive rather than exclusive'. The quality of advice given to new post-16 teachers can be gauged by examining one of the leading textbooks (Gray, Griffin and Nasta 2000), where the topic of learning styles is dealt with in three pages. The authors advocate, without justification, Honey and Mumford's four learning styles (see Section 6.2) and then refer their readers to the practical manual on learning styles produced by the Further Education Development Agency (FEDA 1995). Typical of their unproblematic approach to learning styles is the claim that 'a critical part of a carefully-planned induction … is to make an accurate assessment of each student's unique learning styles' (Gray, Griffin and Nasta 2000, 197). In sum, clear, simple, but unfounded messages for practitioners and managers have too often been distilled from a highly contested field of research.

Yet even among critics of research on learning styles, there is a tendency to write as if there was only one monolithic movement which was united in its thinking; in contradistinction, this review has presented a wide spectrum of theoretical and practical positions on a continuum, consisting of five main 'families' or schools of thought (see Figure 4, Section 2). Bloomer and Hodkinson (2000, 584), for instance, argue that 'this literature proposes that learners possess relatively fixed preferences and capacities for learning [and] it seldom explores the extent to which, and the conditions under which, preferences change'. This criticism applies only to those theorists who emphasise deep-seated personal traits at the extreme left-hand side of the continuum, but is not relevant to the clear majority of learning style theorists who are concerned to improve styles of both learning and teaching. Bloomer and Hodkinson are simply wrong in claiming that most theorists treat learning styles as fixed.

Bloomer and Hodkinson (2000) make, however, a more serious criticism of the learning styles literature to the effect that, even if they are prepared to accept that learning styles exist, they constitute only a minor part of individual dispositions which influence the reactions of learners to their learning opportunities, which include the teaching style of their teachers. Are these 'dispositions' anything more than Entwistle's (1998) 'orientations and approaches to learning'; or are they a broader concept? To Bloomer and Hodkinson, dispositions are both psychological and social; by the latter term, they mean that dispositions are constructed by the contexts in which people live and are not simply personal reactions to those contexts. Moreover, these dispositions are said to be wide-ranging in coverage, interrelated in scope and help to explain the strong reactions which many students have to the culture of different educational institutions. (See Ball, Reay and David 2002 for more research on this issue.) Dispositions would appear to be tapping contextual, cultural and relational issues which are not picked up by the learning style instruments of Entwistle (1998) or Vermunt (1998).

The strategies which follow are treated separately, but in practice, they tend to overlap and theorists often advocate a judicious selection of approaches rather than an exclusive focus on just one. Furthermore, because we have adopted the stance of treating teaching, learning and assessment as one interactive system, we avoid the temptation to deal with strategies for students separately from strategies for teachers, tutors or managers.

Increase self-awareness and metacognition

A knowledge of learning styles can be used to increase the self-awareness of students and tutors about their strengths and weaknesses as learners. In other words, all the advantages claimed for metacognition (ie being aware of one's own thought and learning processes) can be gained by encouraging all learners to become knowledgeable about their own learning and that of others. According to Sadler-Smith (2001, 300), the potential of such awareness lies in 'enabling individuals to see and to question their long-held habitual behaviours'; individuals can be taught to monitor their selection and use of various learning styles and strategies.

Moreover, as Apter (2001, 306) suggests, an understanding of the various elements which produce different states of motivation in different contexts can 'allow people to come more in control' of their motivation and hence of their learning. Learners can become more effective as learners if they are made aware of the important qualities which they and other learners possess. Such knowledge is likely to improve their self-confidence, to give them more control over their learning, and to prevent them attributing learning difficulties to their own inadequacies. The upshot could be that students and teachers choose the strategy most appropriate for the task from a 'toolbox of strategies' (Adey, Fairbrother and Wiliam 1999, 30). Kolb (1999, 5) neatly summarises the advantages of this first strategy as follows: 'Understanding your learning style type, and the strengths and weaknesses inherent in that type, is a major step toward increasing your learning power and getting the most from your learning experiences'.

One option is to leave students to diagnose their own learning style so that the responsibility for learning is passed to the learner. But Merrill (2000) argues that most students are unaware of their learning styles and so, if they are left to their own devices, they are most unlikely to start learning in new ways. Herrmann (1989) places some emphasis on the understanding of individual learning styles as a starting place for development, and as a flexible response to life changes and needs, but the popularity of a model can lead to oversimplistic generalisations. For example, the Myers-Briggs Type Indicator, which was intended to enable individuals to explore the interactions of the elements which make up personality – 'type dynamics' – has so far entered popular consciousness that sites exist on the internet advising (for example) ENTP (extrovert, intuitive, thinking and perceptive) individuals as to which other 'types' would make their ideal marriage partners. Hence, the need for dialogue with a knowledgeable tutor who understands the learning styles literature as a whole and has a critical feel for its potential and pitfalls. Such a tutor is likely to pour cold water on, for example, the extravagant claims made by Gregorc (1985) that serious, individual study of learning styles 'will reduce naivete [sic], increase personal responsibility for thoughts and actions, and improve your relationships'.

Serious in-depth study of such matters is not advocated in guidance for new teachers. For example, Huddleston and Unwin (1997, 72) define learning styles as 'study skills and transition from one style of teaching/learning to another'; and advocate, without any explicit rationale (like Gray cited earlier), the use of both Kolb's LSI (Section 6.1) and Honey and Mumford's LSQ (Section 6.2), neither of which are unproblematic, as our earlier evaluations showed.

In these debates, the research of Entwistle (Section 7.1) and Vermunt (Section 7.2) is valuable because, as discussed earlier, they have shown that attention needs to be given not only to individual differences in learners, but to the whole teaching–learning environment. Both have demonstrated that while the motivations, self-representations, metacognitive and cognitive strengths and weaknesses of learners are all key features of their learning style, these are also a function of the systems in which learners operate. A central goal of their research is to ensure that lecturers can relate concepts of learning to the specific conditions in which they and their students work – that is, it is the whole learning milieu that needs to be changed and not just the learning preferences of individuals.

A lexicon of learning for dialogue

Learning styles can provide learners with a much needed 'lexicon of learning' – a language with which to discuss, for instance, their own learning preferences and those of others, how people learn and fail to learn, why they try to learn, how different people see learning, how they plan and monitor it, and how teachers can facilitate or hinder these processes. Through dialogue with a tutor knowledgeable about the relevant literature, the students' repertoire of learning styles can be enhanced in the hope of raising their expectations and aspirations.

Students can be taught, for instance, which of the 71 learning styles are well founded and which are not, and when and how to choose the most appropriate style. Similarly, tutors can be helped to understand that what they may have been categorising as lazy, unmotivated or truculent behaviour may be caused by a clash in learning styles between themselves and students/colleagues. Even some of the fiercest critics of learning styles concede that a particular test can be safely used 'as a means of facilitating discussion about learning' (Reynolds 1997, 126). As a result, some practitioners use the topic of learning styles simply as a motivational 'ice-breaker', as a means of 'warming up' the class, or as an activity-based introduction to the topic of learning.

For students, particularly those who are less confident about their learning, the acquisition of a new vocabulary which they can use to describe and explore their own behaviour can be an immensely motivating and positive experience and has the potential to help them to reflect and develop their critical thinking. However, this is dependent both on the quality of the experience of using the learning styles instrument and on the nature of the feedback. In this respect, Jackson's LSP (Section 5.3) emerged from our review as a particularly good example of feedback in which traits are described but individuals are not labelled, and the caveat that styles are context-dependent is frequently repeated. Respondents are given areas of strength and weakness to focus on, but are urged overall to consider the goal of the task to be accomplished and to be strategic in their use of their talents.

One of the values of Honey and Mumford's work is that it is primarily aimed not so much at students in education as at managers and trainers who wish to improve the learning of their staff by means of learning styles. Their *Learning styles helper's guide* (2000) offers a number of suggestions on how to use their LSQ before, during and after training programmes; for example, to identify training needs, to predict learning difficulties, to constitute groups or teams and to devise and monitor personal development plans. Details are given of the kind of support that managers with predominantly activist, reflective, theorist or pragmatist learning styles can offer their colleagues and staff. Unfortunately, Honey and Mumford (2000) provide no empirical evidence of the effectiveness of these strategies, and we have not found any in the literature.

The recommendation for dialogue, although appealing at first hearing, is not without its difficulties. First, as has become abundantly clear already in this review, there is not one language of learning styles, but a variety of competing vocabularies, with overlapping categories all vying for attention and all dealing with different aspects of teaching; for example, mode of representation, the learning cycle, personality and cognitive processing. So it becomes important to ask: which theorists and which vocabulary are to be chosen and why? Second, the tutors who are to engage in dialogue are very unlikely to be knowledgeable about the vast research literature on learning styles: they may be responsible for hundreds of students whom they meet infrequently and they may use their professional judgement to concentrate on, say, an initiative which sponsors formative assessment, learning identities or thinking skills, rather than one on learning styles.

Third, Roberts and Newton (2001) point to those studies which have shown how difficult, if not impossible, it is at times to teach people to use non-preferred styles or strategies; indeed, many students show considerable resistance to change and their reasons for refusing to change need to be treated with respect. Fourth, problems also arise from the large number of dichotomies (eg verbalisers versus imagers) in the literature. Some theorists do not use these dichotomies as labels of people; for example, Entwistle (Section 7.1) talks about 'strategic approaches' and not about 'strategic learners'; others, however, are less circumspect (eg Gregorc and Dunn and Dunn; see Sections 3.1 and 3.2 respectively). The tendency to label people is rife in the field, but the dialogue we recommend should be based on reason, logic and evidence and on respect for the other in argument.

Career counselling

Theorists of learning style are themselves divided over the issue as to whether their instruments should be used for recruitment, selection and promotion at work, and career counselling more generally. Kolb is very much in favour, Honey and Mumford counsel against the practice, and Allinson and Hayes recommend that companies should select staff for international work according to their learning style. The Myers-Briggs Type Indicator is used extensively in the medical profession to help advanced students to decide on specialist areas of surgery, general practice or research. Kolb (2000, 41) refers to 'strong evidence that certain learning styles characterize certain occupations and groups'; for instance, he claims that teachers have a high orientation towards concrete experience. This finding is explained by Kolb both in terms of people choosing careers congruent with their learning style and then by being shaped by the careers they enter. If there is a mismatch, Kolb predicts that the individual 'will either change or leave the field' (2000, 41).

To help individuals choose an appropriate career, Kolb presents the strengths and weaknesses of each learning style, together with the means of strengthening a style which may not be well developed. So, for example, those who are good at assimilating 'disparate observations into an integrated, rational explanation' are said to be attracted into careers in the physical sciences, biology and mathematics, and in educational research, sociology, law and theology (2000, 43). Kolb also claims that their assimilating skills can be developed by practice in: organising information; building conceptual models; testing theories and ideas; designing experiments; and analysing quantitative data. No empirical data is offered to support these very detailed claims and no explanation is given of how, say, someone with a diverging style who is interested in people and creativity can add the assimilating style to their repertoire by being presented with a list of the skills associated with that style and being invited to practise them.

Matching

One of the most popular recommendations is that the learning styles of students should be linked to the teaching style of their tutor, the so-called 'matching hypothesis'. Much has been written on this topic by learning styles theorists as diverse as Riding, Dunn, Gregorc, Witkin and Myers-Briggs, but the evidence from the empirical studies is equivocal at best and deeply contradictory at worst. Smith, Sekar and Townsend (2002) recently reviewed the evidence and found nine studies which showed that learning is more effective where there is a match and nine showing it to be more effective where there is a mismatch. They concluded (2002, 411): 'For each research study supporting the principle of matching instructional style and learning style, there is a study rejecting the matching hypothesis'. Similarly, Reynolds (1997) marshalled a further five empirical studies in favour of matching and three against, but the matter cannot be settled by a head count.

For instance, Ford conducted three relatively small but rigorous empirical studies of matching and mismatching (1985, 1995; Ford and Chen 2001) and concluded on each occasion that matching was linked with improved performance. His most recent study, however, suggests that the effects of matching and mismatching 'may not be simple, and may entail complex interactions with other factors such as gender, and different forms of learning' (Ford and Chen 2001, 21). We would add another factor which is frequently neglected by the learning theorists: subject matter.

Roberts and Newton (2001) added to this debate by arguing that learning is so complex that it is unlikely to be captured by any set of learning style dichotomies. In particular, they contend that we still do not know how adults discover new learning strategies or how they choose between strategies. Hayes and Allinson also make the point that, even if matching is improving performance, 'it will do nothing to help prepare the learner for subsequent learning tasks where the activity does not match the individual's preferred style' (quoted by Sadler-Smith 2001, 299). One possible conclusion is that it is simply premature (and perhaps unethical) to be drawing simple implications for practice when there is so much complexity and so many gaps in knowledge.

The most telling argument, however, against any large-scale adoption of matching is that it is simply 'unrealistic, given the demands for flexibility it would make on teachers and trainers' (Reynolds 1997, 121). It is hard to imagine teachers routinely changing their teaching style to accommodate up to 30 different learning styles in each class, or even to accommodate four (see the sub-section below on teaching around the learning cycle); or responding to the interactions among the 22 elements in the learning style make-up of each student in the Dunn and Dunn approach (see Section 3.2). Four learning styles per class may not be too difficult to achieve during a course of study and the variety would help to provide students with an enjoyable experience; on the other hand, the constant repetition of the learning cycle – for example, beginning every new task with concrete experience – could quickly become tiresome. It must be emphasised that this review has failed to find substantial, uncontested and hard empirical evidence that matching the styles of learner and tutor improves the attainment of the learner significantly.

That finding does not prevent some of the leading developers making extravagant claims for the benefits of matching instruction and the environment with students' learning preferences. Rita Dunn, for instance, claims (1990b, 15) that when students have had their learning strengths identified by the Dunn, Dunn and Price LSI:

many researchers have repeatedly documented that, when students are taught with approaches that match their preferences ... they demonstrate statistically higher achievement and attitude test scores – even on standardized tests – than when they are taught with approaches that mismatch their preferences.

Yet, as our review of their model showed (see Section 3.2), the research she refers to is highly controversial, and much of it has been sharply criticised for its poor scholarship and for the possible influence of vested interests, because the Dunn centre conducts research into the instrument which it sells (see Kavale and Forness 1990).

One of the few studies outside higher education about the value of matching learner and teacher preferences in instructional style was conducted by Spoon and Schell (1998). It involved 12 teachers and 189 basic skills learners who were working towards a national education diploma. No significant difference in test outcomes was found between congruent groups (where both teachers and learners favoured the same instructional approach) and incongruent groups. As noted elsewhere in this report (Sections 6.1 and 6.4), the 'matching' hypothesis has not been clearly supported. Where positive results are claimed – for example, by Rita Dunn – there are frequently unresolved methodological issues with the studies cited. For example, the training provided by the Dunns goes far beyond the idea of matching instruction to learning style and introduces other systematic and generic pedagogical changes; for example, in lesson structure and in the nature of homework.

Deliberate mismatching

Grasha (1984, 51) asked a pertinent question of matching: 'How long can people tolerate environments that match their preferred learning style before they become bored?' Vermunt (1998) favours what he terms 'constructive friction', where the teacher pushes students to take more responsibility for the content, process and outcomes of their learning. Apter's research (2001) suggests that frustration or satiation is likely to cause a student to switch between motivational styles and disengage from learning. Grasha's argument is that people need to be 'stretched' to learn and stretching may mean deliberately creating a mismatch between their learning style and the teaching methods. So Grasha's aim (1984, 51) would be 'to teach people new learning styles or at least let them sample unfamiliar ones'. Gregorc's (1984) research supports Grasha's argument in that even those individuals with strong preferences for particular learning styles preferred a variety of teaching approaches to avoid boredom, although this must be set against Gregorc's other assertion (2002) that mismatched learning styles can 'harm' the student. Exhortations to match or mismatch tend to be based on different ideas about the fundamental purposes of education. For Kolb (1984, 203), the educational objectives of mismatching are personal growth and creativity:

the goal is something more than making students' learning styles adaptive for their particular career entry job. The aim is to make the student self-renewing and self-directed; to focus on integrative development where the person is highly developed in each of the four learning modes: active, reflective, abstract, and concrete. Here, the student is taught to experience the tension and conflict among these orientations, for it is from the resolution of these tensions that creativity springs.

The conflict, however, within the literature over mismatching is marked, as can be gauged from the comments of Felder (1993, 289), who drew on empirical studies of college science education in the US:

The mismatching between the prevailing teaching style in most science courses and the learning styles of most of the students have [sic] several serious consequences. Students who experience them [sic] feel as though they are being addressed in an unfamiliar foreign language: they tend to get lower grades than students whose learning styles are better matched to the instructor's teaching style and are less likely to develop an interest in the course material. If the mismatches are extreme, the students are apt to lose interest in science altogether and be among the more than 200,000 who switch to other fields each year after their first college science courses.

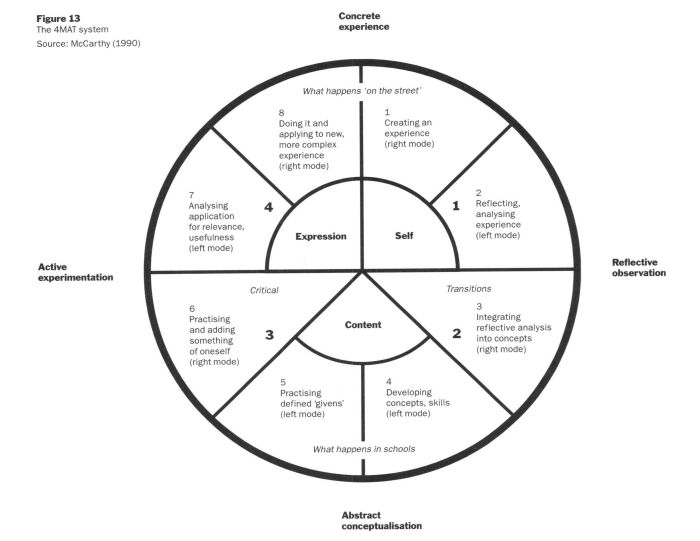

Figure 13
The 4MAT system
Source: McCarthy (1990)

Concrete experience

What happens 'on the street'

8
Doing it and applying to new, more complex experience (right mode)

1
Creating an experience (right mode)

7
Analysing application for relevance, usefulness (left mode)

4

2
Reflecting, analysing experience (left mode)

Expression

Self

1

Active experimentation

Reflective observation

Critical

Transitions

6
Practising and adding something of oneself (right mode)

3

Content

2

3
Integrating reflective analysis into concepts (right mode)

5
Practising defined 'givens' (left mode)

4
Developing concepts, skills (left mode)

What happens in schools

Abstract conceptualisation

Felder is complaining here about the negative outcomes of unintentional mismatching where, for instance, teachers are unaware of their own learning style and may, as a result, teach only in that style, thus favouring certain students and disadvantaging others. The response to such difficulties, according to Felder (1993, 289), is 'not to determine each student's learning style and then teach to it exclusively', but to 'teach around the learning cycle'. Before turning to that strategy, we wish to stress that deliberate mismatching has the status of an intuitively appealing argument which awaits empirical verification or refutation.

'Teach around the learning cycle' or the 4MAT system

This phrase refers to an eight-step instructional sequence created by McCarthy (1990) which seeks to accommodate both preferences for using the two hemispheres of the brain in learning and what she considers to be the four main learning styles. Each of these styles asks a different question and displays different strengths.

- Imaginative learners who demand to know 'why'? This type of learner likes to listen, speak, interact and brainstorm.

- Analytic learners who want to know 'what' to learn. These learners are most comfortable observing, analysing, classifying and theorising.

- Common-sense learners who want to know 'how' to apply the new learning. These learners are happiest when experimenting, manipulating, improving and tinkering.

- Dynamic learners who ask 'what if?' This type of learner enjoys modifying, adapting, taking risks and creating.

Her 4MAT system uses alternate right- and left-mode techniques of brain processing at all four stages of the learning cycle in order to engage the 'whole brain'. The 4MAT system was designed to help teachers improve their teaching by using eight strategies in a cycle of learning (see Figure 13).

According to McCarthy, 'this cycle appeals to each learner's most comfortable style in turn, while stretching her or him to function in less comfortable modes. The movement around this circle is a natural learning progression' (1990, 33). The latter is simply asserted without evidence. The roles of teachers and students change as they move round the four quadrants. In the first quadrant, the emphasis is on meaning and making connections with the new material to be learned. In the second, the focus is on content and curriculum. The third quadrant is devoted to the practical application and usefulness of the new knowledge; and the final quadrant encourages students to find creative ways of integrating the new knowledge into their lives.

McCarthy claims that when teachers begin to use the 4MAT system, it becomes an agent of change. First, teachers change their attitudes towards diversity among students and see it as a means of enhancing the learning of all types of student and not just the analytic learners who are said to thrive in traditional classrooms. Teachers then begin to realise that teaching involves more than the mere imparting of information and so they begin to use more dialogue and less monologue. Finally, teachers begin to talk to their peers about their teaching and start coaching and mentoring each other.

By 1990, McCarthy had experimented with the 4MAT system in 17 school districts in the US and had come to some wide-ranging conclusions about it. First, her initial plan to focus only on 'instruction', as she calls it, did not work. Paying attention to learning styles led directly to their implications for pedagogy, which immediately raised the question of the curriculum and then the nature of assessment. In these practical applications, McCarthy recognised the potential of the 4MAT process to act as a systems approach to change, not only for learning styles, but also for the curriculum, assessment and staff development more generally.

Advertisements for the 4MAT system are not, however, reserved about its benefits; for example: 'By teaching to all types of learners with each lesson, teachers can reach learning potentials in their students never before realized'. The developers of such systems should take some responsibility for the advertisements which promote their wares, but they cannot be held responsible for the excesses of some of their supporters. For example, Kelley, a director of human resources, chose to use the 4MAT system to integrate innovations in teaching and curriculum in public schools in Colorado; she predicted (1990, 39) that 'learning styles knowledge will enable us to make a major paradigm shift in assessment'. She also used McCarthy's work to label students, categorising work as that which is 'easy for a Quadrant Four learner, but harder for the Quadrant Two and Quadrant Three learners' (1990, 38). In the US, you can, for a fee, be helped to design and produce your own learning style instrument.

The 4MAT system has been extensively used, particularly in the US, with a wide variety of students from pre-school children to adults attending evening classes, and with a broad range of subject matter from elementary music to college courses in psychology. The approach is now generating its own literature, with the 4MAT website (www.aboutlearning.com) listing, in 2002, 43 articles and 38 doctoral theses exploring the use of the model with students or in staff development. McCarthy, St Germain and Lippitt (2001) conclude that most of these studies report positive experiences in applying 4MAT; that a few are less enthusiastic because of the low tolerance of tutors for change; and that teachers 'often have great difficulty in implementing change because the old ways are so comfortable and teachers tend to feel guilty if they are not at the front of the classroom giving information' (2001, 5).

The theoretical base for the 4MAT system is the work of Kolb. For Kolb, the learning cycle is a diagrammatic representation of his experiential learning model – how experience is translated into concepts which are then used to guide the choice of new experiences. Kolb (1999, 3) is adamant that all four phases of the cycle are necessary for effective learning, but concedes that 'different learners start at difference places in this cycle'. It needs to be remembered, however, that the statistical analyses of Wierstra and de Jong (2002) have seriously questioned the structure of Kolb's model on which the learning cycle is based (see Section 6.1 for evaluation).

In a recent article, Honey (2002) has explained why he too is 'besotted' with the learning cycle. He gives three main reasons. First, Honey argues, without producing any evidence, that the cycle describes the essential ingredients of the process of learning so that it can be analysed and improved. Second, the cycle, it is asserted, helps people to identify where their learning weaknesses lie and so encourages them to move outside their 'preference zone'. Finally, 'the learning cycle is a vehicle for making learning explicit and therefore communicable' (2002, 115). In other words, Honey always uses the learning cycle to stimulate discussion about learning. These claims have an intuitive appeal, but await empirical verification.

Logical deductions from theories of learning style

One characteristic of most of the advice offered to practitioners is that it consists of logical deductions from the various theories of learning style rather than conclusions drawn from the findings of empirical research. Such advice tends either to be of a very general nature – for example, Sternberg (1999) urges teachers to use a variety of teaching and assessment methods; or to be rather specific tips for particular types of teacher – for example, Felder (1996, 22) encourages science teachers to 'use physical analogies and demonstrations to illustrate the magnitudes of calculated quantities'. Another type of detailed advice is offered by advocates of the Dunn and Dunn model, who prescribe not only techniques for imparting information, but also the design of learning environments, including furniture, lighting, temperature, food and drink, sound, etc.

The one implication for practice which is repeated throughout the literature on learning styles is that it is the responsibility of teachers, tutors and managers to adapt their teaching style to accommodate the learning style of their students or staff members. But such an unqualified exhortation is both unhelpful and unrealistic, because it could be interpreted as meaning that the teacher/tutor/manager is obliged to respond appropriately to visual and verbal learners (and perhaps **haptic** learners also); to **inductive** and **deductive**, reflective and active, sequential and global, conceptual and concrete learners; and to those who like working in groups as well as those who prefer learning individually. Despite the strong convictions with which these ideas are promoted, we failed to find a substantial body of empirical evidence that such strategies have been tried and found successful. Advice of this type strikes practitioners as unworkable and so it tends to remain untested.

There has been some focus on the idea that some 'types' make more successful teachers or managers, though some of these measures – eg field independence – tend to be correlated to ability (Tinajero and Paramo 1997) and for others, evidence regarding the connection between the construct (intuition in entrepreneurs) and career advancement is contradictory (Armstrong 2000). Moreover, those theorists who tend to favour the idea that learning styles are fixed rather than flexible should concede that the styles of the teachers may also be resistant to change and that the styles adopted by powerful figures at work may be shaped by social, cultural and political factors which go beyond individual differences.

Change teaching styles

The topic of teaching styles has its own literature, theorists and controversies, but it is beyond the remit of this review and so will not be explored. It is sufficient here to refer to the myriad interactions between the learning style of the student and the objectives, content, sequence, teaching methods and social context of the lesson. Merrill (2000) proposed that these more fundamental teaching strategies should take precedence over learning styles, which should then be used to 'fine-tune' the teacher's plans. The metaphor of slightly adjusting an engine to make it run more efficiently seems singularly inappropriate to the current state of knowledge of learning styles.

To borrow a metaphor from the Roman poet Horace, has the mountain of research on learning styles gone into labour and produced a ridiculous mouse, or has it brought forth new ideas for a more professional practice based on learning styles? In our opinion, the critics who dismiss all the practical consequences of learning styles research as either trivial or 'old hat' are missing opportunities for professional growth and institutional change, but we leave it to the reader to judge whether all the resources and energies which have been invested in learning styles have produced an adequate return.

The appeal of learning styles

For some, learning styles have become an unquestioned minor part of their professional thinking and practice, which allows them to differentiate students quickly and simply; for others, the same instruments are considered both unreliable and invalid and so they do not use them in practice; for others still, learning styles are the central doctrine in a quasi-evangelical crusade to transform all levels of education. Such a broad range of responses to and uses of learning styles is only to be expected. What we attempt to do now is to summarise the reasons why so many practitioners have become 'converted' to their use.

■ Some of the learning style literature promises practitioners a simple solution to the complex problems of improving the attainment, motivation, attitudes and attendance of students. In an audit culture where professionals and institutions are held responsible for the attainment and behaviour of their students, it is little wonder that teachers and managers are prepared to try new techniques which claim to help them meet their targets more easily. It is probably not an exaggeration to say that much of the development and marketing of learning style instruments has been driven by the needs of practitioners in education and business, rather than by the needs of learning theorists (see Cassidy 2003).

■ Many practitioners have long since discovered for themselves that traditional methods (of transmission by teacher and assimilation by student) fail many students, and the learning style literature provides a plausible explanation for such failure. The modern cliché is that the teacher may be teaching, but no one – not even the teacher – may be learning. The argument of many learning style developers is that traditional, formal schooling (and higher education even more so) are too biased towards students who are analytic in their approach, that teachers themselves tend to be analytic learners, and that the longer people stay in the education system, the more analytic they become. They argue further that learning styles provide a means whereby the diverse learning needs of a much broader range of students can be addressed. In other words, many teachers tend to respond well to the invitation to examine their own teaching and learning style; and the hope of the theorists is that by doing so, they will become more sensitive to those whose learning style is different.

■ Because of a growing interest in learning styles, teachers and managers begin, perhaps for the first time, to explore the highly complex nature of teaching and learning. In the pedagogical triangle of teacher, students and subject, the learning styles approach trains professionals to focus on how students learn or fail to learn. When, or if, this happens, what some now see as the overemphasis on providing, for example, student teachers with an understanding of how particular subjects (English, mathematics, science, etc) are most appropriately taught may begin to be corrected. The corrective may, however, create its own imbalances: what is needed is equal attention to all parts of the triangle and their interactions. The danger is that we end up with content-free pedagogy, where process is celebrated at the expense of content.

■ For some learning style developers, there is no special category of students with learning difficulties, only teachers who have not learned that their teaching style is appropriate for perhaps a quarter of their students and seriously inappropriate for the remainder. Those teachers who have incorporated the Dunn and Dunn model into their practice speak movingly at conferences of how this re-categorisation of the problem (where students' failure to learn is reformulated as teachers' failure to teach appropriately) has transformed their attitude to students they previously dismissed as stupid, slow, unmotivated, lazy or ineducable. This is not an inconsiderable achievement.

■ It is not only front-line practitioners and middle managers who have been persuaded of the benefits of introducing learning styles. For some senior managers, for inspectors, for government agencies, policy-makers and politicians, the appeal of learning styles may prove convenient, because it shifts the responsibility for enhancing the quality of learning *from* management *to* the individual learning styles of teachers and learners. Learning styles enable the more managerialist and cynical to argue as follows: 'There's no longer any need to discuss resources, financial incentives, pay and conditions, the culture of institutions, the curriculum, the assessment regime or the quality of senior management: the researchers now tell us that failure can be laid at the door of those narrow, analytic teachers who've never heard of learning styles.'

The objections to learning styles

The critics of learning styles can be divided into two main camps. First, there are those who accept the basic assumptions of the discipline (eg the positivist methodology and the individualistic approach), but who nevertheless claim that certain models or certain features within a particular model do not meet the criteria of that discipline. A second group of critics, however, adopts an altogether more oppositional stand: it does not accept the basic premises on which this body of research, its theories, findings and implications for teaching have been built. As all the other sections of this report are devoted to a rigorous examination of 13 models of learning styles within the parameters set by the discipline itself, this sub-section will briefly explain the central objections raised by those hostile to the learning styles camp, who mutter at conferences in the informal breaks between presentations, who confide their reservations in private, but who rarely publish their disagreement. We wish to bring this semi-public critique out into the open.

■ The opponents, who are mainly those who espouse qualitative rather than quantitative research methods, dispute the objectivity of the test scores derived from the instruments. They argue, for example, that the learning style theorists claim to 'measure' the learning preferences of students. But these 'measurements' are derived from the subjective judgements which students make about themselves in response to the test items when they 'report on themselves'. These are not objective measurements to be compared with, say, those which can be made of the height or weight of students, and yet the statistics treat both sets of measures as if they were identical. In other words, no matter how sophisticated the subsequent statistical treatments of these subjective scores are, they rest on shaky and insecure foundations. No wonder, say the sceptics, that learning style researchers, even within the criteria laid down by their discipline, have difficulty establishing reliability, never mind validity.

Respondents are also encouraged to give the first answer which occurs to them. But the first response may not be the most accurate and is unlikely to be the most considered; evidence is needed to back the contention that the first response is always the one with which psychologists and practitioners should work.

■ The detractors also have reservations about some test items and cannot take others seriously. They point, for example, to item 65 in Vermunt's ILS (see Section 7.2) which reads: 'The only aim of my studies is to enrich myself.' The problem may be one of translation from the Dutch, but in English, the item could refer to either intellectual or financial enrichment and it is therefore ambiguous. Or they single out the item in Entwistle's ASSIST (see Section 7.1) which reads: 'When I look back, I sometimes wonder why I ever decided to come here.' Doesn't everyone think this at some stage in an undergraduate course?

Others quote from the Dunn, Dunn and Price PEPS instrument (see Section 3.2), the final item of which is 'I often wear a sweater or jacket indoors'. The answers from middle-class aesthetes in London, who prefer to keep their air-conditioning low to save energy, are treated in exactly the same way as those from the poor in Surgut in Siberia, who need to wear both sweaters and jackets indoors to keep themselves from freezing to death. What, ask the critics, has this got to do with learning and what sense does it make to ignore the socio-economic, cultural and even geographic context of the learner?

Those who simply wish to send up the Dunn, Dunn and Price LSI for 6–18 year olds reveal that it contains such items as: 'I like to do things with adults'; 'I like to feel what I learn inside of me'; and 'It is easy for me to remember what I learn when I feel it inside me.' It is no surprise that some psychologists argue that criticism should not be directed at individual items and that one or two poor items out of 100 do not vitiate the whole instrument. Our response is that if a few items are risible, then the instrument may be treated with scorn.

■ Other opponents object to the commercialisation of some of the leading tests, whose authors, when refuting criticism, are protecting more than their academic reputations. Rita Dunn, for example, insists that it is easy to implement her 22-element model, but that it is also necessary to be trained by her and her husband in a New York hotel. The training course in July 2003 cost $950 per person and lasted for 7 days at a further outlay of $1384 for accommodation. The cost of training all 400,000 teachers in England in the Dunn methodology would clearly be expensive for the government, but lucrative for the Dunns.

■ Some opponents question what they judge to be the unjustified prominence which is now accorded to learning styles by many practitioners. Surely, these academics argue, learning styles are only one of a host of influences on learning and are unlikely to be the most significant? They go further by requesting an answer to a question which they pose in the terms used by the learning style developers, namely: 'What percentage of the variance in test scores is attributable to learning styles?' The only direct answer to that question which we have found in the literature comes from Furnham, Jackson and Miller (1999), who study the relationship between, on the one hand, personality (Eysenck's Personality Inventory) and learning style (Honey and Mumford's LSQ); and on the other, ratings of the actual performance and development potential of 200+ telephone sales staff: 'the percentage of variance explained by personality and learning styles together was only about 8%' (1999, 1120). The critics suggest that it is perhaps time that the learning style experts paid some attention to those factors responsible for the other 92%.[12]

12
It has not been possible to answer the question 'What proportion of the variance in achievement outcomes is attributable to learning style?' because we only found one reasonably relevant study – Furnham, Jackson and Miller (1999). There is a considerable body of research in which measures of prior achievement, ability, motivation and personality have been evaluated as predictors of university first-degree performance, but we have found none in which learning styles have been considered as well. Information about the prediction of learning outcomes in post-16 education and training outside higher education is relatively sparse, but again, there is no work in which learning styles have been compared with ability measures as predictors.

In general, it can be said that no powerful predictors of learning in higher education have been identified by any researchers, since the proportion of variance accounted for in large-scale studies rarely exceeds 16%, no matter how many characteristics of learners are considered.

There is one apparent exception to the above generalisation. Drysdale, Ross and Schulz (2001) carried out one of the largest predictive studies we have found in a university context, but in that study, only learning style was used as a predictor of first-year academic performance. The effect sizes were substantial for mathematics, science and technology subjects, with Gregorc's 'sequential style' students outperforming those with a 'random' style. The reverse was true in fine arts, but no differences were found in the liberal arts or in nursing. This result is hard to understand, in view of the problems we have identified with Gregorc's Style Delineator (see Section 3.1). We recommend that similar studies be carried out with a variety of learning style instruments, but adding in other predictors. The Herrmann and Jackson instruments (see Sections 6.3 and 5.3 respectively) would be suitable for this purpose.

■ Others seek to disparage the achievements of research into learning styles by belittling what they call the rather simple conclusions which emanate from the increasingly elaborate statistical treatment of the test scores. Their argument can be summarised and presented as follows:

For more than 40 years, hundreds of thousands of students, managers and employees have filled in learning style inventories, their scores have been subjected to factor analyses of increasing complexity, numerous learning styles have been identified, and what are the conclusions that stem from such intensive labour? We are informed that the same teaching method does not work for all learners, that learners learn in different ways and that teachers should employ a variety of methods of teaching and assessment. Comenius knew that and more in seventeenth century Prague and he did not need a series of large research grants to help him find it out.

This is, of course, high-flying hyperbole, but we leave our readers to judge the accuracy of this assessment after they have read the following section.

Still no pedagogy in the UK

According to Dewey (1916, 170), pedagogy is often dismissed as futile because: 'Nothing has brought pedagogical theory into greater dispute than the belief that it is identified with handing out to teachers recipes and models to be followed in teaching'. Earlier, in 1897, while working in the University of Chicago in a combined department of philosophy, psychology and pedagogy, Dewey had issued *My pedagogic creed* in which he expressed his belief that 'education must be conceived as a continuing reconstruction of experience' (1897, 53) and that 'the teacher is engaged, not simply in the training of individuals, but in the formation of the proper social life' (1897, 59). Dewey's famous essay proved to be an inspiration to Kolb; it can also be read as a hymn to the dignity of the teacher's calling and to the importance of education as 'the fundamental method of social progress and reform' (1897, 57).

In the century that has passed since these stirring words were written, it is surprising how the concept of pedagogy has remained relatively unexplored and untheorised in the English-speaking world. In the 1980s, Simon felt obliged to ask the very pertinent question: 'Why no pedagogy in England?' According to Simon, 'the most striking aspect of current thinking and discussion about education is its eclectic character, reflecting deep confusion of thought, and of aims and purposes, relating to learning and teaching – to pedagogy' (reprinted 1999, 34).

The truth is that the widespread eclecticism and deep confusion which Simon complained of continue to dog pedagogical practice in England and elsewhere in the English-speaking world. As recently as 1996, Anthea Millett, then chief executive of the Teacher Training Agency (TTA), was making the charge that pedagogy was 'the last corner of the secret garden' and continued to be neglected; but as Alexander has pointed out, 'her real message was not about pedagogy at all: it was about performance management and teachers' need to comply with government thinking' (2000, 542).

The history of pedagogy in the UK is bedevilled by the fact that practitioners and researchers work with markedly different definitions and models of pedagogy from within the separate disciplinary perspectives of adult education, psychology and sociology. In addition, there are substantial differences in the pedagogical language and theories used in further and adult education, in higher education and in work-based training; and there is very little interaction between these differing approaches. In short, as Zukas and Malcolm argue: 'Lifelong learning pedagogies do not, as yet, exist in the UK' (2002, 203).

Into the theoretical and moral vacuum created by the lack of one generally accepted theory of pedagogy in the post-16 sector (or any other sector, for that matter) have moved official models of pedagogy of a particularly instrumental kind. The DfES Standards Unit, the inspectorates and the curriculum and awarding bodies all, in their different ways, interpret pedagogy as the unproblematical application of apparently neutral, value-free techniques, which they have accorded the status of 'best practice', without always making clear the evidential basis for their claims. In such a climate, the use of learning styles as a diagnostic assessment or as a means of differentiating students is presented to practitioners or student teachers as the uncomplicated equivalent of other injunctions about what constitutes 'best practice', such as 'facilitate learning in groups' or 'set precise targets with individual learners'.

Differing definitions and models of pedagogy

Within the general literature of education, definitions of pedagogy abound, but they can be placed on a continuum, from definitions which concentrate narrowly on teaching techniques to those which deal with broader issues such as the significance of culture, power, social structure and identity. The treatment of pedagogy in the learning styles literature leans heavily towards psychological rather than sociological definitions of the term. For example, when Kolb, a psychologist, is discussing the implications of his research for 'training design', he envisages the following four roles for the teacher, whom he prefers to call the 'facilitator' – communicator of information, guide or taskmaster, coach or helper, and role model (2000, 17). Zukas and Malcolm (2002), who are both adult educators working within a different paradigm, identified in the literature the five pedagogic roles of assurer of quality and efficiency, facilitator of learning, reflective practitioner, critical practitioner and situated learner within a community of practice. It is fascinating that, when both are discussing the main identities of the teacher, the two approaches have only one role in common, namely, the facilitation of learning.

Rather surprisingly, Simon was content to use *The Oxford English Dictionary*'s definition of pedagogy as 'the science of teaching' (1999, 39), which suggests a concern to establish the general principles of teaching and learning. But for adult educators such as Zukas and Malcolm (2002, 215), pedagogy is not primarily concerned with a well-developed repertoire of teaching skills, but with:

a critical understanding of the social, policy and institutional context, as well as a critical approach to the content and process of the educational/training transaction ... the most important elements of pedagogy are the relations between educator, student and institution, the social context, purpose and ethical implications of educational work, and the nature and social role of educational knowledge

Leach and Moon (1999, 268), clearly influenced by Lave and Wenger (1991), go further in arguing that pedagogy should be concerned with the construction and practice of learning communities:

Pedagogy is more than the accumulation of techniques and strategies: arranging a classroom, formulating questions, developing explanations, creating a curriculum. It is informed by a view of mind, of learning and learners, of the kind of knowledge that is valued and above all by the educational outcomes that are desired.

The literature is replete, however, not only with different definitions, but also with a variety of models of pedagogy and approaches to it. The range extends from those adopted by cognitive psychology (eg Eggen and Kauchak 2001), to sociology (Bernstein 1996), workplace learning (Fuller and Unwin 2002) and adult education (Boud 1989). Teachers, tutors and managers working in the post-16 sector are likely to have been influenced to varying degrees by these different traditions, research interests, theoretical frameworks and languages; and yet these are the groups which remain to be convinced that learning styles have important implications for their pedagogy. In the absence of an explicit, coherent and agreed theory of pedagogy, any attempt to convince practitioners of the usefulness of learning styles will have to take account of these conflicting and implicit traditions in different sectors within post-16 learning.

This report is not, however, the place to provide *either* an introduction to the vast literature on teaching and learning in the post-16 sector *or* a detailed explanation of all the various traditions within pedagogy in the UK which have relevance for post-16 learning. That would amount to another research project, which would examine the history, the theory, the practice and the current status of humanistic pedagogy, critical pedagogy and andragogy (the teaching of adults), to mention but three. Instead, we outline briefly two significant contributions: one from psychology (that of Jerome Bruner) and one from sociology (that of Basil Bernstein), which have yet to be integrated into one comprehensive socio-psychological theory of pedagogy.

Bruner's (1996) main argument is that educational reform necessarily involves changing the folk pedagogical theories of not just teachers, but also of students. The significance of Bruner's contribution is that he shifts the focus from different types of learning style to four alternative models of the minds of learners. To Bruner, it matters profoundly whether teachers see students as *either* empty receptacles to be filled with propositional knowledge; *or* as apprentices in thinking who acquire 'know-how' through imitation; *or* as sophisticated knowers who grasp the distinction between personal and objective knowledge; *or* as collaborative thinkers who can learn through participation how their own and other people's minds work. Bruner wants all 'four perspectives to be fused into some congruent unity' and wants all teachers and students to become more metacognitive, to be as aware of how they go about teaching and learning as they are about the subject matter. In his own words, improvements in pedagogy are predicated on teachers and students understanding the minds of learners and on 'getting teachers (and students) to think *explicitly* about their folk psychological assumptions, in order to bring them out of the shadows of tacit knowledge' (1996, 47; original emphasis). A pressing issue for this review is whether it would be more beneficial for the quality of learning in the post-compulsory sector to recommend that Bruner's advice be followed rather than administering a learning styles instrument to a group of students and then discussing the outcomes with them.

In contrast to the work of, for example, so many learning style theorists who are concerned with the implications of the various styles for methods of instruction, Bernstein (1996) sought to make connections between the macro structures of power and control within society and the micro processes within schools that generate practices of inclusion and exclusion. In Bernstein's quest to create a new sociology of pedagogy, he showed how different types of knowledge are differentially distributed to different social groups and how, within educational institutions, some students are valued, while the 'voices' of others remain unheard.

According to Edwards (2002, 530), Bernstein was particularly critical of:

[the] *classroom researchers' habit of detaching teacher-pupil interactions from structures of power and control in which they are embedded. In his model, pedagogy was much more than the transmission of a curriculum. It covered the structure and categories of school knowledge, what can be said and written 'legitimately' under its various headings, how specifically or diffusely the required learning outcomes are assessed, and how different education codes relate to modes of production and to pupils' anticipated occupational futures.*

A striking feature of the British research on learning styles is its lack of engagement both with structures of power and with deeper structural inequalities. There exists, for example, no extensive research in the UK on learning styles and social class, or on learning styles and ethnicity. One of the few learning styles researchers to take account of contextual influences is Entwistle (see Section 7.1), but even he limits his coverage to the immediate influences of course design and neglects the problems of unequal access to the knowledge and skills needed to become a successful learner.

While we await a fusion of these two approaches to pedagogy in psychology and sociology, the comparative studies of Alexander (2000) constitute, in our opinion, the most compelling explanation of how, in different countries and within any one country, history, culture and teaching come together to create very different pedagogies.

So, for example, in Germany, staff in education departments, when teaching pedagogy, draw on the historical, theoretical contributions of Kant, Herbart, Froebel and Pestalozzi, as well as such modern theorists as Harmut von Hentig, Dietrich Benner and Elmar Tanorth. In other words, German pedagogy is a well-established and respected intellectual tradition which is divided into nine sub-disciplines (eg *Schulpädagogik*, *Sonderpädagogik* or pedagogy of special education, *Berufs/Wirscharftspädagogik* or pedagogy of vocational education), 10 subject specialisms (eg *Sexualpädagogik*, *Umweltpädagogik* or environmental pedagogy, and *Interkulturelle Pädagogik*), and seven practical areas (eg management education, *Gesundheitserziehung* or health education, and *Friedenserziehung* or peace education) – see Lenzen (1989) for a full explanation of the *Struktur der Pädagogik*. Beneath all of these come the *Fachdidaktiken* – that is, the teaching methods for all the subject disciplines of mathematics, history, chemistry and so on, which German students of education study in the relevant university department.

The contrast with the UK, where there is still no reputable and honoured tradition of pedagogical research and thinking, could hardly be more marked. Recently, however, a start has been made by Alexander who concluded his monumental study (2000) by proposing a useful distinction between teaching and pedagogy and, in doing so, pressed into service the sociological term 'discourse', which Ball (1994, 21) defined as follows: 'Discourses are about what can be said, and thought, but also about who can speak, when, where and with what authority'. Alexander is keen to differentiate the two terms 'teaching' and 'pedagogy' in order to discourage their interchangeable usage in the UK:

teaching is an act *while pedagogy is both act and discourse. Pedagogy encompasses the performance of teaching together with the theories, beliefs, policies and controversies that inform and shape it ... Pedagogy connects the apparently self-contained act of teaching with culture, structure and mechanisms of social control.*
(2000, 540; original emphasis)

It is our contention that most of the models of learning styles have so far confined themselves to teaching and only a few of the best have even begun to address pedagogy.

Section 9

Recommendations and conclusions

This report began with an overview of the challenges presented by the nature of the research into learning styles. These challenges meant that this report had to:

- evaluate the main theories about learning styles for academic, policy-making and practitioner audiences

- select the most important studies from an extensive literature

- assess the theoretical robustness of each model and the psychometric quality of the accompanying instrument used to measure learning styles

- evaluate the implications of these models for pedagogy in different post-16 contexts.

In addressing these challenges, the research team combined expertise in cognitive psychology, education, the professional development of post-16 practitioners, sociology and policy studies. The team approach has enabled us to produce a report based on robust internal critique of draft sections and regular discussions of our different perspectives on the main issues raised by the review. An important aim from the outset was to extend debate about learning styles from the specialist discipline of cognitive psychology and to locate claims for learning styles in the social and political context of the learning and skills sector. A concomitant aim was to go beyond a merely technical discussion of teaching and learning styles as a set of unproblematic techniques for teachers to apply and to show that pedagogy itself is a much broader, complex and contested notion.

This final section draws directly on the evidence and arguments presented earlier in this review. Here we:

- present nine problems which continue to beset the research field of learning styles

- indicate the major gaps in the current state of knowledge which could form the basis of future research projects

- make some final comments about the prospects for learning styles.

First, though, we want to begin by stressing the valuable features which have emerged from our close reading of the literature. We wish to offer some positive recommendations for the LSDA and other agencies to consider.

Positive recommendations

We wish to start this section by acknowledging the beneficial uses of those models which have proved to be the most psychometrically sound and ecologically valid. We agree with Entwistle (1990, 676) that the primary professional responsibility of teachers and trainers is to maximise the learning opportunities of their students or staff and that 'We should surely not leave effective study strategies to evolve through trial and error when we are now in a position to offer coherent advice'.

Self-awareness and metacognition

A reliable and valid instrument which measures learning styles and approaches could be used as a tool to encourage self-development, not only by diagnosing how people learn, but by showing them how to *enhance* their learning. As Garner (2000) has argued, self-development is more likely to result from increasing learners' knowledge of the relative advantages and weaknesses of different models, than from learners being assigned a particular learning style. One of the main aims of encouraging a metacognitive approach is to enable learners to choose the most appropriate learning strategy from a wide range of options to fit the particular task in hand; but it remains an unanswered question as to how far learning styles need to be incorporated into metacognitive approaches.

Desmedt *et al.* (2003, 147–148) have begun to question why and how an awareness of one's learning style should be thought to have a positive effect on the quality of one's learning. They conclude that learning style awareness is only a 'cog in the wheel of the learning process' and that 'it is not very likely that the self-concept of a student, once he or she has reached a certain age, will drastically develop by learning about his or her personal style'.

Despite reservations about their model and questionnaire (see Section 6.2), we recognise that Honey and Mumford have been prolific in showing how individuals can be helped to play to their strengths or to develop as all-round learners (or both) by means, for example, of keeping a learning log or of devising personal development plans; they also show how managers can help their staff to learn more effectively. *We wish to recommend that consideration be given to developing for schools, colleges, universities and firms new programmes of study focused on human learning and how it can be fostered.*

Our recommendation in favour of increased self-awareness should not, however, be interpreted as support for more individualised instruction, as Kolb (1984) has argued. The benefits of individualised teaching are often greatly exaggerated, although many teachers will admit that it is extremely difficult to ensure that learners are benefiting from specially tailored approaches when there is a large class to manage. In a synthesis of 630 studies, Hattie (1992) found an average effect size of only 0.14 for individualised teaching in schools. This trivial result strongly suggests that in general, it is not a good use of teacher time to try to set up, monitor and support individual learning programmes where there are large groups to deal with. It should be noted that the potential of ICT to support individualised instruction has not been fully evaluated. However, the key point is that individualised instruction is not likely to work if it means more unsupported individual learning. Whether or not skilled individual or small-group teaching support can improve the situation is an unanswered question, but the near zero mean effect size for team teaching (also reported by Hattie) does not provide grounds for optimism. Within post-16 learning, the extent to which tutors can offer individualised programmes varies considerably. Individualisation is both more appropriate and easier to organise, for example, in an evening class on tailoring than in an A-level history class.

A lexicon of learning for dialogue

On the grounds of robustness and ecological validity, we recommend that the concepts, developed by Entwistle (Section 7.1) and others, of deep, surface and strategic approaches to learning, and by Vermunt (Section 7.2) of meaning-directed, application-directed and reproduction-directed learning styles, be adopted for general use in post-16 learning rather than any of the other competing languages. It needs to be remembered, however, that the instruments were designed for university students and need to be redesigned to fit the extremely wide range of contexts within post-16 learning. The potential and pitfalls of creating a dialogue with students about, say, the implications of adopting a surface approach to learning have been discussed in detail in Section 8. Here we simply want to reiterate that the tutors/trainers who involve their students/staff in dialogue need to be knowledgeable about the strengths and limitations of the model they are using; to be aware of the dangers of labelling and discrimination; and to be prepared to respect the views of students who may well resist any attempts to change their preferred learning style. In a project designed to put the concepts of 'teaching thinking' and 'metacognitive awareness' into practice, Leat and Lin (2003) found that having a language to describe the new pedagogy and specific roles for teachers to experiment with were critical to success.

If this recommendation is adopted, some formidable barriers will need to be overcome; for example, ACE tutors, work-based trainers and college lecturers will need a different form of initial teacher training and staff development to enable them to explore critically the more promising models and instruments. Similarly, middle and senior managers throughout the learning and skills sector will need a critical understanding of learning styles and how dialogue about learning between tutors and students can lead to wider institutional change. Management skills need to be expanded from an understandable concentration on finance and accountability to embrace a critical understanding of the central role of teaching and learning in the reform of post-16 education and training.

Pedagogy on its own is not enough

Both McCarthy (1990) and Entwistle and Walker (2000) have spotted the potential of learning styles to act as an agent for broader change. Open-ended dialogue between tutor and students may begin by identifying forms of support such as courses on study skills and, with a tutor alive to the possibilities of growth, it should lead on to a discussion of the curriculum and assessment. If this in turn encourages tutors to discuss among themselves how they can improve students' approaches to learning, then the door is open for course teams, initial teacher trainers and continuing professional developers to use the topic of learning as a springboard for broader cultural change within the organisation. What may begin as a concern to respond more appropriately to variation in patterns of students' learning may provoke a re-assessment of the goals of education or training, the purposes of assessment and the relevance of certain aspects of the curriculum. If learning styles are to be used to improve practice, we recommend that they are employed in the hope that an exploration of pedagogy may well usher in far-reaching change. As Leat and Lin comment (2003, 410): 'as teachers become more confident in their practice so they are more likely to demand access to school policies and procedures'.

The positive recommendation we are making is that a discussion of learning styles may prove to be the catalyst for individual, organisational or even systemic change. We also want, however, to stress the limitations of an approach which may restrict itself to changes in teaching techniques; for, as Lave and Wenger (1991, 100) have argued, the most fundamental problems of education are not pedagogical:

Above all, they have to do with the ways in which the community of adults reproduces itself, with the places that newcomers can or cannot find in such communities, and with relations that can or cannot be established between these newcomers and the cultural and political life of the community.

Professional choice – which intervention to choose?

Before making any change in practice, professionals are duty-bound to consider two possibilities: first, that the proposed change may make matters worse; and second, that some alternative change may be more beneficial than their preferred option. Moreover, professionals need to operate with an explicit and tested model of change before they introduce any innovation. We have discussed at length the potential for the allocation of a learning style to turn into a learning handicap. We also wish to discuss the range of options currently open to tutors and trainers in the post-compulsory sector because these professionals are not faced with the simple choice of accepting or rejecting learning styles. On the contrary, they are faced with a panoply of possible interventions, all with their supporters and attendant evidence.

As Hattie (1999) has argued, most innovations have positive effects on students' achievement, so we need estimates of the magnitude of the impact – namely, effect sizes as well as statistical significance. Post-16 learning is currently subjected to a series of pressures from policy initiatives, financial directives, institutional change strategies, qualifications and awarding bodies, the inspectorate, CPD, and student demands. Into this highly stressful environment, the case for responding to the different learning styles of students is already being pushed by managers in further education under the need for 'differentiation'. According to one FE lecturer, the new buzzword of 'differentiation' is being used 'to maintain pressure and perpetuate the feeling that things are not being done properly: that teachers are inadequate' (Everest 2003, 49).

The *meta-analysis* of educational interventions conducted by Hattie (1999) can help us form a judgement on what to do next. His painstaking research indicates that the effect sizes for different types of intervention are as shown in Table 43 (extracted from Hattie 1999).

It seems sensible to concentrate limited resources and staff efforts on those interventions that have the largest effect sizes.

The case for learning styles will also have to compete with arguments in favour of, say, thinking skills, or peer tutoring, or learning identities, or formative assessment, or critical intelligence or any one of a host of options. We willl explore briefly the claims which could be made for two approaches which are competing with learning styles for research funds – namely, metacognition and formative assessment. With regard to the first competitor, we refer in Section 8 to Bruner's (1996) advice to introduce tutors, trainers and students to different conceptions of learners' minds. His advice could perhaps be accommodated by including it in the standard definition of metacognition – that is, the ability to set explicit, challenging goals; to identify strategies to reach those goals; and to monitor progress towards them.

Table 43
Effect sizes for different types of intervention

Intervention	Effect size
Reinforcement	1.13
Student's prior cognitive ability	1.00
Instructional quality	1.04
Direct instruction	0.82
Student's disposition to learn	0.61
Class environment	0.56
Peer tutoring	0.50
Parental involvement	0.46
Teacher style	0.42
Affective attributes of students	0.24
Individualisation	0.14
Behavioural objectives	0.12
Team teaching	0.06

As for the research evidence in favour of metacognition, Marzano (1998) reported on the largest meta-analysis of research on instruction ever undertaken. He found that approaches which were directed at the metacognitive level of setting goals, choosing appropriate strategies and monitoring progress are more effective in improving knowledge outcomes than those which simply aim to engage learners at the level of presenting information for understanding and use. Interventions targeted at improving metacognition produced an average gain of 26 percentile points (across 556 studies). This is about 5 points higher than the mean gain calculated for the 1772 studies in which attempts were made to improve cognition without an explicit metacognitive component.

As to the second competitor, the decision as to what innovation to introduce is made all the keener by reference to the proposals of Black and Wiliam (1998a), who conducted an extensive survey of the research literature on assessment, comparable in size to this review on learning styles. They concluded from their study of the most carefully conducted quantitative experiments that:

innovations which include strengthening the practice of formative assessment produce significant, and often substantial, learning gains. These studies range over ages (from five-year olds to university undergraduates), across several school subjects, and over several countries … The formative assessment experiments produce typical effect sizes *of between 0.4 and 0.7: such effect sizes are larger than most of those found for educational interventions*
(Black and Wiliam 1998b, 3–4; original emphasis)

Policy-makers and politicians also have important choices to make; for example, do they spend scarce resources on training all new and in-service teachers and tutors in learning styles; or would they better serve the cause of post-16 learning by using the same money to increase the new adult learning grants from the low figure of £30 per week?

Influencing the attitude of official agencies to learning styles

It is not our job, however, to make the final decision on behalf of politicians, course leaders, institutional managers or those engaged in initial teacher training: it is our task to sharpen up those decisions. Our role is to point out that the research evidence in favour of introducing either metacognition or assessment for learning is more robust and extensive than the evidence we have reviewed here on learning styles, regardless of whether they emerged poorly or relatively unscathed from our evaluation. Given the effects claimed for improving formative assessment in the school sector, a productive avenue for research and development may be to extend this research into post-16 education. The Assessment Reform Group, for example, has been extremely influential in promoting Black and Wiliam's ideas (1998a, 1998b) and is about to extend its work into post-16 assessment.

Other organisations, such as the QCA, awarding bodies, the post-16 inspectorates, NIACE, the teaching unions, the Association of Colleges (AoC), the Universities Council for the Education of Teachers' (UCET) post-16 committee and the DfES Standards Unit already have their own list of priorities for research, and we hope to engage them critically with the conclusions of our report. In addition, any further research in response to our report would benefit strongly from being connected closely to other high-profile research into post-16 learning and pedagogy such as the Economic and Social Research Council's (ESRC) Teaching and Learning Research Programme (TLRP).

For convenience, we list here some *specific recommendations* for some of the main institutional players.

- *DfES* – different branches of the DfES are currently engaged in initiatives that draw on learning styles research; they need to reflect on our report before deciding to fund any research or practice using the inventories we review here and before issuing guidelines about 'best practice' in teaching or learning styles.

- *QCA and awarding bodies* – assessment specifications and guidance to teachers (eg about differentiation) reveal explicit and implicit assumptions about learning styles; officials therefore need to review these assumptions, particularly in relation to qualifications for post-16 teacher training.

- *FENTO, the UCET's post-16 committee and the Centre for Excellence in Leadership* – the national standards of competence for teacher training in further education contain uncritical and unsustainable attitudes towards learning styles, while standards for management training contain no references to learning at all; FENTO officials and providers of initial teacher education for the learning and skills sector need to assess the implications of our report for these qualifications and for training teachers and managers.

- *Ofsted and ALI* – although neither inspectorate appears to have an official view on learning styles, reports on particular institutions reveal simplistic assumptions about learning styles as the basis for judgements about 'good practice'; these assumptions need to be re-assessed in the light of our report.

Continuing problems within the research field of learning styles

Theoretical incoherence and conceptual confusion

The field of learning styles consists of a wide variety of approaches that stem from different perspectives which have some underlying similarities and some conceptual overlap. There are numerous groups working in isolation from each other and, with few exceptions, from mainstream research in psychology. Research into learning styles can, in the main, be characterised as small-scale, non-cumulative, uncritical and inward-looking. It has been carried out largely by cognitive and educational psychologists, and by researchers in business schools and has not benefited from much interdisciplinary research.

As a result, as Sternberg has argued: 'the literature has failed to provide any common conceptual framework and language for researchers to communicate with each other or with psychologists at large' (2001, 250). The previous sections of this review have provided detailed evidence of a proliferation of concepts, instruments and pedagogical strategies, together with a 'bedlam of contradictory claims' (Reynolds 1997, 116). The sheer number of dichotomies in the literature conveys something of the current conceptual confusion. We have, in this review, for instance, referred to:

- convergers versus divergers
- verbalisers versus imagers
- holists versus serialists
- deep versus surface learning
- activists versus reflectors
- pragmatists versus theorists
- adaptors versus innovators
- assimilators versus explorers
- field dependent versus field independent
- globalists versus analysts
- assimilators versus accommodators
- imaginative versus analytic learners
- non-committers versus plungers
- common-sense versus dynamic learners
- concrete versus abstract learners
- random versus sequential learners
- initiators versus reasoners
- intuitionists versus analysts
- extroverts versus introverts
- sensing versus intuition
- thinking versus feeling
- judging versus perceiving
- left brainers versus right brainers
- meaning-directed versus undirected
- theorists versus humanitarians
- activists versus theorists
- pragmatists versus reflectors
- organisers versus innovators
- lefts/analytics/inductives/successive processors versus rights/globals/deductives/ simultaneous processors
- executive, hierarchic, conservative versus legislative, anarchic, liberal.

The sheer number of dichotomies betokens a serious failure of accumulated theoretical coherence and an absence of well-grounded findings, tested through replication. Or to put the point differently: there is some overlap among the concepts used, but no direct or easy comparability between approaches; there is no agreed 'core' technical vocabulary. The outcome – the constant generation of new approaches, each with its own language – is both bewildering and off-putting to practitioners and to other academics who do not specialise in this field.

In addition, the complexity of the learning styles field and the lack of an overarching synthesis of the main models, or of dialogue between the leading proponents of individual models, lead to the impression of a research area that has become fragmented, isolated and ineffective. In the last 20 years, there has been only a single use of the term 'learning styles' and three uses of the term 'cognitive styles' in the *Annual Review of Psychology*. We have also noted that these terms are not included in the indexes in four widely used textbooks on cognitive and educational psychology. Instead, psychometric specialists speak mainly to each other about the merits or otherwise of particular instruments. Even the proponents of the more credible models, namely those offered by Allinson and Hayes (see Section 6.4) or Vermunt (Section 7.2), tend not to engage with each other's models or those from other families.

Although the theorists tend to claim routinely that all learning styles within a particular model are equally viable, the terminology that they have chosen is neither neutral nor value-free. It is clearly preferable, for instance, to use a *deep* rather than *surface* learning approach, to be *field independent* rather than *field dependent*, and to exhibit the *hierarchic* rather than the *anarchic* thinking style. Yet, as our review of Entwistle's model (Section 7.1) showed, sometimes a strategic approach is effective and students need to be able to judge when different approaches to learning are appropriate. The value judgements evident in various models need to be made more explicit if students are independently to evaluate the different approaches to learning styles.

Learning styles in practice: labelling, vested interests and overblown claims

The theorists warn of the dangers of labelling, whereby teachers come to view their students as being a certain type of learner, but despite this warning, many practitioners who use their instruments think in stereotypes and treat, for instance, vocational students as if they were all non-reflective activists. The literature is full of examples of practitioners and some theorists themselves referring to 'globals and analytics' (Brunner and Majewski 1990, 22), or 'Quadrant Four learners' (Kelley 1990, 38), or 'integrated hemisphere thinkers' (Toth and Farmer 2000, 6). In a similar vein, Rita Dunn writes as follows: 'It is fascinating that analytic and global youngsters appear to have different environmental and physiological needs' (1990c, 226). Similarly, students begin to label themselves; for example, at a conference attended by one of the reviewers, an able student reflected – perhaps somewhat ironically – on using the Dunn and Dunn Productivity Environmental Preference Survey (PEPS): 'I learned that I was a low auditory, kinaesthetic learner. So there's no point in me reading a book or listening to anyone for more than a few minutes'. The temptation to classify, label and stereotype is clearly difficult to resist. Entwistle has repeatedly warned against describing students as 'deep' or 'surface' learners, but these warnings tend to be ignored when instruments move into mainstream use.

Another tendency among some of the researchers whose work was reviewed earlier in this report has been 'to rush prematurely into print and marketing with very early and preliminary indications of factor loadings based on one dataset' (Curry 1990, 51). The field is bedevilled by vested interests because some of the leading developers of learning style instruments have themselves conducted the research into the psychometric properties of their own tests, which they are simultaneously offering for sale in the marketplace. We shall return later in this section to the need for critical, independent research which is insulated from the market.

Moreover, the status of research in this field is not helped by the overblown claims of some of the developers and their enthusiastic devotees. For example, Carbo, the director of the National Reading Styles Institute in the US, claimed that when staff were trained for 4 or 5 days in 'matching' techniques, 'very often the results have been phenomenal, not just significant. We've had some gains of 10 times as high as students were achieving before' (quoted by O'Neil 1990, 7). Rigorously conducted research, as we saw earlier, has experienced difficulty in establishing that matching produced significant, never mind phenomenal, gains. The commercial industry that has grown around particular models makes independent researchers think twice before publicly criticising either the shortcomings of the models or the hyperbolic claims made for them.

These central features of the research field – the isolated research groups, the lack of theoretical coherence and of a common conceptual framework, the proliferating models and dichotomies, the dangers of labelling, the influence of vested interests and the disproportionate claims of supporters – have created conflict, complexity and confusion. They have also produced wariness and a growing disquiet among those academics and researchers who are interested in learning, but who have no direct personal or institutional interest in learning styles. After more than 30 years of research, no consensus has been reached about the most effective instrument for measuring learning styles and no agreement about the most appropriate pedagogical interventions.

Nor are there any signs of the leading theorists coming together to address the central problems of their field. If left to itself, research into learning styles looks as if it will continue to produce more disorganised proliferation. A psychological version of Gresham's Law is already in operation in that the bad publicity caused by unreliable and invalid instruments is turning those interested in improving the quality of learning away from the achievements of the more careful scholars in the field. As we argued in Section 8, the vacuum created by the absence of an agreed theory (or theories) of post-16 pedagogy, and by the lack of widespread understanding about learning has enabled those versions of 'best practice' produced by the DfES to gain prominence.

The variable quality of learning style models

This review (this report and Coffield *et al.* 2004) examined in considerable detail 13 models of learning style and one of the most obvious conclusions is the marked variability in quality among them; they are not all alike nor of equal worth and it matters fundamentally which instrument is chosen. The evaluation, which is reported in Sections 3–7, showed that some of the best known and widely used instruments have such serious weaknesses (eg low reliability, poor validity and negligible impact on pedagogy) that we recommend that their use in research and in practice should be discontinued. On the other hand, other approaches emerged from our rigorous evaluation with fewer defects and, with certain reservations detailed below, we suggest that they deserve to be researched further. A brief summarising comment is added about each of the models that we appraised as promising.

Allinson and Hayes: of all the instruments we have evaluated, the Cognitive Style Index (CSI) of Allinson and Hayes has the best psychometric credentials, despite the debate about whether it should be scored to yield one or two measures of intuition and analysis. It was designed to be used in organisational and business contexts, and is less relevant for use with students than by teachers and managers. It was designed as a simple instrument and its items are focused very transparently on decision making and other procedures at work. Although there is already some evidence of predictive validity, the authors acknowledge that relatively little is known about how the interplay of cognitive styles in different situations relates to work outcomes such as performance, absenteeism, professional development and attitudes. It is a suitable research instrument for studying educational management as well as for more specific applications – for example, seeking to identify the characteristics of successful entrepreneurs.

Apter: reversal theory is a theory of personality, not of learning style. It was included because the concepts of motivation and reversal (eg change from work to play) are important for understanding learning styles. Reversal theory is relevant to groups and organisations as well as to individuals, who are not pigeon-holed as having fixed characteristics. Apter's Motivational Style Profile (MSP) is a useful addition to learning style instruments.

Entwistle: his Approaches and Study Skills Inventory for Students (ASSIST) is useful as a sound basis for discussing effective and ineffective strategies for learning and for diagnosing students' existing approaches, orientations and strategies. It is an important aid for course, curriculum and assessment design, including study skills support. It is widely used in universities for staff development and discussion about learning and course design. It could perhaps be used for higher education taught in FE colleges, but would need to be redesigned and revalidated for use in other post-16 contexts such as adult education, work-based training and 14–19 provision. It is crucial, however, that the model is not divorced from the inventory, that its complexity and limitations are understood by users, and that students are not labelled as 'deep' or 'surface' learners.

Herrmann: his 'whole brain' model is suitable for use with learners as well as with teachers and managers, since it is intended to throw light on group dynamics as well as to encourage awareness and understanding of self and others. Herrmann and others have devised well-tried procedures for facilitating personal and organisational change. In completing Herrmann's Brain Dominance Instrument (HBDI), respondents draw on their experience of life outside working contexts as well as within them. Herrmann's model may prove especially valuable in education and training, since its raison d'être is to foster creative thinking and problem solving. It is unlikely that productive change will occur nationally in the area of lifelong learning until it is widely recognised that only a certain percentage of people function best when given a precise set of rules to follow. Although the Herrmann 'whole brain' approach to teaching and learning needs further research, development and independent evaluation within education, it is grounded in values which are inclusive, open, optimistic and systematic. More than any other model we have reviewed, it encourages flexibility, adaptation and change, rather than an avoidance of less preferred activities.

Jackson: the Learning Styles Profiler (LSP) is a relatively new, but sophisticated, instrument which has yet to be tested by independent researchers. Jackson acknowledges that learning styles are influenced by biology, experience and conscious control. It deserves to be widely studied.

Vermunt: his Inventory of Learning Styles (ILS) can be safely used in higher education, both to assess approaches to learning reliably and validly, and to discuss with students changes in learning and teaching. It is already being used widely in northern Europe to research the learning of undergraduates and so may be relevant for those settings in post-16 learning which are closest to higher education. It will need, however, to be completely revalidated for the wide range of learning contexts in post-16 learning which have little in common with higher education.

Table 44
13 learning-styles models matched against minimal criteria

✓
criterion met

×
criterion not met

—
no evidence either way or issue still to be settled

Note
The evaluation is in all cases 'external', meaning an evaluation which explored the theory or instruments associated with a model and which was not managed or supervised by the originator(s) of that model.

		Internal consistency	Test–retest reliability	Construct validity	Predictive validity
1	**Jackson**	—	—	—	—
2	**Riding**	×	×	×	×
3	**Sternberg**	×	×	×	×
4	**Dunn and Dunn**	×	×	×	✓
5	**Gregorc**	×	×	×	✓
6	**Honey and Mumford**	×	✓	×	×
7	**Kolb**	—	✓	×	×
8	**Entwistle**	✓	—	✓	×
9	**Herrmann**	—	✓	✓	—
10	**Myers-Briggs**	✓	✓	×	×
11	**Apter**	✓	✓	—	✓
12	**Vermunt**	✓	✓	✓	×
13	**Allinson and Hayes**	✓	✓	✓	✓

Psychometric weaknesses

This review (see also Coffield *et al.* 2004) selected for detailed study 13 of the most influential and potentially influential models of learning styles from a total of 71 which we identified in the literature. [Mitchell (1994) claimed that there were over 100 models, but we have found 71 worthy of consideration.] Each model was examined for evidence, provided by independent researchers, that the instrument could demonstrate both internal consistency and test–retest reliability and construct and predictive validity. These are the minimum standards for any instrument which is to be used to redesign pedagogy. Only three of the 13 models – those of Allinson and Hayes, Apter and Vermunt – could be said to have come close to meeting these criteria. A further three – those of Entwistle, Herrmann and Myers-Briggs met two of the four criteria. The Jackson model is in a different category, being so new that no independent evaluations have been carried out so far. The remaining six models, despite in some cases having been revised and refined over 30 years, failed to meet the criteria and so, in our opinion, should not be used as the theoretical justification for changing practice.

Table 44 presents our psychometric findings diagrammatically. It can be seen that only Allinson and Hayes met all four of the minimal criteria and that Riding and Sternberg failed to meet any of them. Jackson's model has still to be evaluated. In more detail, the 13 instruments can be grouped as follows.

- Those meeting none of the four criteria: Jackson; Riding; Sternberg.
- Those meeting one criterion: Dunn and Dunn; Gregorc; Honey and Mumford; Kolb.
- Those meeting two criteria: Entwistle; Herrmann; Myers-Briggs.
- Those meeting three criteria: Apter, Vermunt.
- Those meeting all four criteria: Allinson and Hayes.

There are other limitations to psychometric measures of approaches to learning, highlighted in our review of Entwistle's model above (Section 7.1). For example, apparently robust classifications of students' orientations to learning derived from a questionnaire are shown to be unreliable when the same students are interviewed. Moreover, self-report inventories 'are not sampling learning behaviour but learners' impressions' (Mitchell 1994, 18) of how they learn, impressions which may be inaccurate, self-deluding or influenced by what the respondent thinks the psychologist wants to hear. As Price and Richardson (2003, 287) argue: 'the validity of these learning style inventories is based on the assumption that learners can accurately and consistently reflect:

- how they process external stimuli
- what their internal cognitive processes are'.

The unwarranted faith placed in simple inventories

A recurrent criticism we made of the 13 models studied in detail in Sections 3–7 was that too much is being expected of relatively simple self-report tests. Kolb's LSI, it may be recalled, now consists of no more than 12 sets of four words to choose from. Even if all the difficulties associated with self-report (ie the inability to categorise one's own behaviour accurately or objectively, giving socially desirable responses, etc; see Riding and Rayner 1998) are put to one side, other problems remain. For example, some of the questionnaires, such as Honey and Mumford's, force respondents to agree or disagree with 80 items such as 'People often find me insensitive to their feelings'. Richardson (2000, 185) has pointed to a number of problems with this approach:

the respondents are highly constrained by the predetermined format of any particular questionnaire and this means that they are unable to calibrate their understanding of the individual items against the meanings that were intended by the person who originally devised the questionnaire or by the person who actually administers it to them

We therefore advise against pedagogical intervention based solely on any of the learning style instruments. One of the strengths of the models developed by Entwistle and Vermunt (see Sections 7.1 and 7.2) is that concern for ecological validity has led them to adopt a broader methodology, where in-depth qualitative studies are used in conjunction with an inventory to capture a more rounded picture of students' approaches to learning.

As Curry (1987) points out, definitions of learning style and underlying concepts and theories are so disparate between types and cultures (eg US and European) that each model and instrument has to be evaluated in its own terms. One problem is that 'differences in research approaches continue and make difficult the resolution of acceptable definitions of validity' (1987, 2). In addition, she argues that a great deal of research and practice has proceeded 'in the face of significant difficulties in the bewildering confusion of definitions surrounding cognitive style and learning style conceptualisations…' (1987, 3). Her evaluation, in 1987, was that researchers in the field had not yet established unequivocally the reality, utility, reliability and validity of these concepts. Our review of 2003 shows that these problems still bedevil the field.

Curry's evaluation (1987, 16) also offers another important caveat for policy-makers, researchers and practitioners that is relevant 16 years later:

The poor general quality of available instruments (makes it) unwise to use any one instrument as a true indicator of learning styles … using only one measure assumes [that] *that measure is more correct than the others. At this time (1987) the evidence cannot support that assumption.*

There is also a marked disparity between the sophisticated, statistical treatment of the scores that emanate from these inventories (and the treatment is becoming ever more sophisticated), and the simplicity – some would say the banality – of many of the questionnaire items. However, it can be argued that the items need to be obvious rather than recondite if they are to be valid.

There is also an inbuilt pressure on all test developers to resist suggestions for change because, if even just a few words are altered in a questionnaire, the situation facing the respondent has been changed and so all the data collected about the test's reliability and validity is rendered redundant.

No clear implications for pedagogy

There are two separate problems here. First, learning style researchers do not speak with one voice; there is widespread disagreement about the advice that should be offered to teachers, tutors or managers. For instance, should the style of teaching be consonant with the style of learning or not? At present, there is no definitive answer to that question, because – and this brings us to the second problem – there is a dearth of rigorously controlled experiments and of longitudinal studies to test the claims of the main advocates. A move towards more controlled experiments, however, would entail a loss of ecological validity and of the opportunity to study complex learning in authentic, everyday educational settings. Curry (1990, 52) summarised the situation neatly:

Some learning style theorists have conducted repeated small studies that tend to validate the hypotheses derived from their own conceptualizations. However, in general, these studies have not been designed to disconfirm hypotheses, are open to expectation and participation effects, and do not involve wide enough samples to constitute valid tests in educational settings. Even with these built-in biases, no single learner preference pattern unambiguously indicates a specific instructional design.

An additional problem with such small-scale studies is that they are often carried out by the higher-degree students of the test developers, with all the attendant dangers of the 'Hawthorne Effect' – namely, that the enthusiasm of the researchers themselves may be unwittingly influencing the outcomes. The main questions still to be resolved – for example, whether to match or not – will only be settled by large-scale, randomly controlled studies using experimental and control groups.

It may be argued that it is important to provide for all types of learning style in a balanced way during a course of study in order to improve the learning outcomes of all students. Yet the problem remains: which model of learning styles to choose? Many courses in further and adult education are short or part-time, making the choice more difficult still.

This particular example reinforces our argument about the need for any pedagogical innovation to take account of the very different contexts of post-16 learning. These contextual factors include resources for staff development and the need for high levels of professional competence if teachers are to respond to individual learning styles. Other pressures arise from narrow ideas about 'best practice', the nature of the teaching profession (so many part-timers) and the limited opportunities for discussing learning in post-16 initial teacher education programmes.

We also wish to stress that pedagogy should not be separated from a deeper understanding of motivation and from the differing values and beliefs about learning held by staff within the various traditions in further and adult education and work-based learning. For example, if teachers and students regard education as being primarily about the accumulation of human capital and the gaining of qualifications, they are more likely to employ surface learning as a way of getting through the assessment requirements as painlessly as possible. Moreover, the way that staff in schools, further education and higher education teach and assess the curriculum may be encouraging 'surface' or 'strategic' rather than 'deep' learning.

The tentative conclusion from some researchers (eg Boyle *et al.* 2003; Desmedt *et al.* 2003) is that while the dominant pedagogy in higher education with its emphasis on analytic processes is encouraging 'surface' or 'strategic' learning, and while tutors commend 'deep learning' but at the same time spoon-feed their students, the world of work claims that it is crying out for creative, 'rule-bending' and original graduates who can think for themselves. In particular, Desmedt *et al.* (2003) in a study of both medical and education students concluded that, because of the curriculum, students are not interested in learning, but in assessment.

Decontextualised and depoliticised views of learning and learners

The importance of context serves to introduce a further problem, which is best illustrated with an example. One of the items from the Sternberg–Wagner Self-Assessment Inventory on the Conservative Style reads as follows: 'When faced with a problem, I like to solve it in a traditional way' (Sternberg 1999, 73). Without a detailed description of the *kind* of problem the psychologist has in mind, the respondent is left to supply a context of his or her choosing, because methods of solving a problem depend crucially on the character of that problem. The Palestinian–Israeli conflict, the fall in the value of stocks and shares, teenage pregnancies and the square root of –1 are all problems, some of which may be solved in a traditional way, some of which may need new types of solution, while others still may not be amenable to solution at all. Crucially, some problems can only be resolved collectively. Nothing is gained by suggesting that all problems are similar or that the appropriate reaction of a respondent would be to treat them all in a similar fashion.

Reynolds, in a fierce attack on the research tradition into learning styles, has criticised it not only for producing an individualised, decontextualised concept of learning, but also for a depoliticised treatment of the differences between learners which stem from social class, race and gender. In his own words, 'the very concept of learning style obscures the social bases of difference expressed in the way people approach learning … labelling is not a disinterested process, even though social differences are made to seem reducible to psychometric technicalities' (1997, 122, 127). He goes on to quote other critics who claim that in the US, Black culture has been transformed into the concrete, as opposed to the abstract, learning style. His most troubling charge is that the learning style approach contributes 'the basic vocabulary of discrimination to the workplace through its incorporation into educational practice' (1997, 125).

There is indeed a worrying lack of research in the UK into learning styles and social class, or learning styles and ethnicity, although more of the latter have been carried out in the US. It is worth pointing out that when Sadler-Smith (2001) published his reply to Reynold's wide-ranging critique, he did not deal with the most serious charge of all, namely that of discrimination, apart from advising practitioners and researchers to be alert to the possible dangers.

The main charge here is that the socio-economic and the cultural context of students' lives and of the institutions where they seek to learn tend to be omitted from the learning styles literature. Learners are not all alike, nor are they all suspended in cyberspace via distance learning, nor do they live out their lives in psychological laboratories. Instead, they live in particular socio-economic settings where age, gender, race and class all interact to influence their attitudes to learning. Moreover, their social lives with their partners and friends, their family lives with their parents and siblings, and their economic lives with their employers and fellow workers influence their learning in significant ways. All these factors tend to be played down or simply ignored in most of the learning styles literature.

Lack of communication between different research perspectives on pedagogy

What is needed in the UK now is a theory (or set of theories) of pedagogy for post-16 learning, but this does not exist. What we have instead is a number of different research schools, each with its own language, theories, methods, literature, journals, conferences and advice to practitioners; and these traditions do not so much argue with as ignore each other. We have, for example, on the one hand those researchers who empirically test the theories of Basil Bernstein and who seem almost totally unaware of – or at least appear unwilling to engage with – the large body of researchers who study learning styles and pedagogy and whose models we review in this report. For example, the recent collection of articles devoted to exploring Bernstein's contribution to developing a sociology of pedagogy (Morais *et al.* 2001) contains only two references by one out of 15 contributors to the work of 'Entwhistle' (sic). The learning style researchers, for their part, continue to write and argue among themselves, either as if Bernstein's theorising on pedagogy had never been published or as if it had nothing important to say about their central research interests. For instance, Entwistle's publications contain neither a detailed discussion of Bernstein's thinking nor even a reference to it.

Similarly, there are other groups of researchers who explore the ideas of Bourdieu or Engeström or Knowles and are content to remain within their preferred paradigm, choosing to ignore significant and relevant research in cognate areas. There are, however, honourable exceptions which prove the rule: Daniels (2001), for example, has contrasted the two theoretical traditions of Engeström (activity theory) and Bernstein (pedagogy); and his book *Vygotsky and pedagogy* shows how Bernstein's contribution may lead to a generative model of pedagogy 'which connects a macro level of institutional analysis with the micro level of interpersonal analysis' (2001, 175). The rhetoric of the universities' funding councils attempts to counteract such compartmentalisation and fragmentation by extolling the virtues of interdisciplinary research, but their current reward structures [eg the Research Assessment Exercise (RAE)] continue to remunerate those who develop narrow specialisations.

Within the subject discipline of education, one of the most unhelpful divisions is that between sociologists and psychologists, who too often hold each other's research in mutual suspicion, if not contempt. For example, at psychological conferences, many psychologists, when talking to each other, use the adjective 'sociological' as a pejorative term, which they place, as it were, within inverted commas to indicate their distaste, if not fear; sociology for them is neither history nor politics nor a discipline in its own right. Similarly, at their conferences, sociologists too readily dismiss the work of psychologists by hinting that the latter choose their discipline in the hope of finding some insight into, and some alleviation of, their personal problems.

The practical consequence of this divide is two separate literatures on pedagogy which rarely interact with each other. Typically, sociologists and psychologists pass each other by in silence, for all the world like two sets of engineers drilling two parallel tunnels towards the same objective in total ignorance of each other.

One of the values of the concept of lifelong learning is that it should make us re-examine the major stratifications within the education system because the very notion implies continuity and progression. Zukas and Malcolm, however, point out that instead of conceptual bridges, we run into pedagogical walls 'between those sectors that might be regarded as contributing to the virtual concept of lifelong learning. There is little conceptual connection between adult and further education, higher education, training and professional development' (2002, 203).

What national policy and local practice need, however, is for these unconnected literatures to be brought together, and for the main protagonists to be actively encouraged to use each other's findings, *not* to poke fun at their opponents, but to test and improve their own ideas. Such a rapprochement is one of the biggest challenges facing the ESRC's programme of research into teaching and learning in the post-compulsory phase (see www.tlrp.org) and could become one of its most significant achievements. It would be a fitting tribute to Bernstein's memory if there were to be wider recognition of his argument that what is required is less allegiance to an approach but more dedication to a problem.

The comparative neglect of knowledge

At the eighth annual conference of the European Learning Styles Information Network (ELSIN) at the University of Hull in July 2003, an advocate of the Dunn and Dunn model announced: 'In the past, we taught students knowledge, skills and attitudes. We must now reverse the order. We should now be teaching attitudes, skills and knowledge.' This has become a fashionable platitude which, if put into operation, would result in the modish but vacuous notion of a content-free curriculum, all learning styles and little or no subject knowledge. This downgrading of knowledge is, irony of ironies, to be implemented in the interests of creating a knowledge-based economy. It is also worth pointing out that the greater emphasis on process, which Klein *et al.* (2003) employed when introducing the Dunn and Dunn model to FE colleges, did *not* lead to higher attainment by the students in the experimental group.

The more sophisticated learning style models appreciate that different disciplines require different teaching, learning and assessment methods. Entwistle, McCune and Walker (2001, 108), for example, are clear on this point: 'The processes involved in a deep approach ... have to be refined within each discipline or professional area to ensure they include the learning processes necessary for conceptual understanding in that area of study'.

Alexander (2000, 561) knew he was adopting an unfashionable standpoint when he argued that it was:

a fact that different ways of knowing and understanding demand different ways of learning and teaching. Mathematical, linguistic, literary, historical, scientific, artistic, technological, economic, religious and civic understanding are not all the same. Some demand much more than others by way of a grounding in skill and propositional knowledge, and all advance the faster on the basis of engagement with existing knowledge, understanding and insight.

Gaps in knowledge and possible future research projects

Our review shows that, above all, the research field of learning styles needs independent, critical, longitudinal and large-scale studies with experimental and control groups to test the claims for pedagogy made by the test developers. The investigators need to be independent – that is, without any commitment to a particular approach – so that they can test, for instance, the magnitude of the impact made by the innovation, how long the purported gains last, and employ a research design which controls for the Hawthorne Effect. Also, given the potential of Apter's Motivational Styles Profiler (MSP), Herrmann's Brain Dominance Instrument (HBDI) and Jackson's Learning Styles Profiler (LSP), they should now be tested by other researchers.

It would also be very useful to find out what learning style instruments are currently being used in FE colleges, in ACE and WBL and for what purposes. A number of research questions could be addressed, as follows.

- Do students/employees receive an overview of the whole field with an assessment of its strengths and weaknesses?

- Are they introduced to one model and if so, on what grounds?

- How knowledgeable are the tutors about the research field on learning styles?

- What impacts are learning styles having on methods of teaching and learning?

- How well do learning style instruments predict attainment in post-16 learning?

- Are students being labelled by tutors, or are they labelling themselves, or do they develop a broader repertoire of learning styles?

- Do students and staff know how to monitor and improve their own learning via metacognition?

- How far do different types of motivation affect students' and teachers' responses to knowledge about their learning styles?

- How adequate is the training that teachers and tutors receive on learning styles?

- Given a free choice, would tutors and managers choose to introduce learning styles or some other intervention?

- What is the impact of individualised instruction on attainment within the different contexts of post-16 learning?

Only empirical research can answer these questions.

We still do not know, as Grasha pointed out (1984, 51) 'the costs and benefits of designing classroom methods and procedures based on learning styles versus continuing to do what is already done'. That type of knowledge is essential before any large-scale reforms of pedagogy on the basis of learning styles are contemplated. Grasha's question, however, prompts another, more fundamental one: should research into learning styles be discontinued, as Reynolds has argued? In his own words: 'Even using learning style instruments as a convenient way of introducing the subject [of learning] generally is hazardous because of the superficial attractions of labelling and categorizing in a world suffused with uncertainties' (1997, 128). Our view is that a policy of using learning styles instruments to introduce the topic of learning is too undiscriminating and our review of the leading models (Sections 3–7) counsels the need to be highly selective.

The suggestions made here for further research would necessitate the investment of considerable financial and human resources over a long period of time in order to make learning styles relevant to a diverse post-16 sector. But would such investment pay real dividends and is it the highest priority for research funding in the sector?

Final comments

This report has sought to sift the wheat from the chaff among the leading models and inventories of learning styles and among their implications for pedagogy: we have based our conclusions on the evidence, on reasoned argument and on healthy scepticism. For 16 months, we immersed ourselves in the world of learning styles and learned to respect the enthusiasm and the dedication of those theorists, test developers and practitioners who are working to improve the quality of teaching and learning. We ourselves have been reminded yet again how complex and varied that simple-sounding task is and we have learned that we are still some considerable way from an overarching and agreed theory of pedagogy. In the meantime, we agree with Curry's summation (1990, 54) of the state of play of research into learning styles: 'researchers and users alike will continue groping like the five blind men in the fable about the elephant, each with a part of the whole but none with full understanding'.

Our penultimate question is: what are the prospects for the future of learning styles? From within the discipline, commentators like Cassidy (2003) are calling for rationalisation, consolidation and integration of the more psychometrically robust instruments and models. Is such integration a likely outcome, however? We wish it were, but some internal characteristics of the field militate against rationalisation.

First, learning styles models and instruments are being simultaneously developed in the relatively autonomous university departments of business studies, education, law, medicine and psychology. No one person or organisation has the responsibility to overview these sprawling fields of endeavour and to recommend changes; in the UK, the academic panels for the RAE are subject-based and the area of learning styles straddles three, if not more, of the existing units of assessment.

Second, fortunes are being made as instruments, manuals, videotapes, in-service packages, overhead transparencies, publications and workshops are all commercially advertised and promoted vigorously by *some* of the leading figures in the field. In short, the financial incentives are more likely to encourage further proliferation than sensible integration. It also needs to be said that there are other, distinguished contributors to research on learning styles who work in order to enhance the learning capabilities of individuals and firms and not in order to make money.

Third, now that most of the instruments can be administered, completed and scored online, it has become a relatively simple matter to give one's favourite learning styles inventory (no matter how invalid or unreliable) to a few hundred university students who complete the forms as part of their course; in this way, some trivial hypothesis can be quickly confirmed or refuted. The danger here is of mindless and atheoretical empiricism. We conclude that some order will, sooner or later, have to be imposed on the learning styles field from outside.

Finally, we want to ask: why should politicians, policy-makers, senior managers and practitioners in post-16 learning concern themselves with learning styles, when the really big issues concern the large percentages of students within the sector who either drop out or end up without any qualifications? Should not the focus of our collective attention be on asking and answering the following questions?

- Are the institutions in further, adult and community education in reality centres of learning for *all* their staff and students?

- Do some institutions constitute in themselves barriers to learning for certain groups of staff and students?

References

Abramson N, Lane H, Nagai H and Takagi H (1993).
A comparison of Canadian and Japanese cognitive styles – implications for management interaction. *Journal of International Business Studies*, 24(3), 575–587.

Adey P, Fairbrother R and Wiliam D (1999).
Learning styles and strategies: a review of research. Report for Ofsted. London: King's College, School of Education.

Ajisuksmo CRP and Vermunt JD (1999).
Learning styles and self-regulation of learning at university: an Indonesian study. *Asia Pacific Journal of Education*, 19(2), 45–49.

Alexander R (2000).
Culture and pedagogy: international comparisons in primary education. Oxford: Blackwell.

Allinson CW, Armstrong SJ and Hayes J (2001).
The effect of cognitive style on leader-member exchange: a study of manager-subordinate dyads. *Journal of Occupational and Organizational Psychology*, 74, 201–220.

Allinson CW, Chell E and Hayes J (2000).
Intuition and entrepreneurial performance. *European Journal of Work and Organizational Psychology*, 9(1), 31–43.

Allinson CW and Hayes J (1988).
The Learning Styles Questionnaire: an alternative to Kolb's Inventory. *Journal of Management Studies*, 25(3), 269–281

Allinson CW and Hayes J (1990).
Validity of the Learning Styles Questionnaire. *Psychological Reports*, 67, 859–866.

Allinson C and Hayes J (1996).
The Cognitive Style Index. *Journal of Management Studies*, 33, 119–135.

Allinson CW and Hayes CJ (2000).
Cross-national differences in cognitive style: implications for management. *International Journal of Human Resource Management*, 11(1), 161–170.

Antonietti A (1999).
Can students predict when imagery will allow them to discover the problem solution? *European Journal of Cognitive Psychology*, 11(3), 407–428.

Apter MJ (1976).
Some data inconsistent with the optimal arousal theory of motivation. *Perceptual and Motor Skills*, 43, 1209–1210.

Apter MJ (2001).
Motivational styles in everyday life: a guide to reversal theory. Washington DC: American Psychological Association.

Apter MJ and Heskin K (2001).
Basic research on reversal theory. In MJ Apter (ed.) *Motivational styles in everyday life: a guide to reversal theory.* Washington DC: American Psychological Association.

Apter M, Mallows R and Williams S (1998).
The development of the Motivational Style Profile. *Personality and Individual Differences*, 24(1), 7–18.

Archer SN, Robilliard DL, Skene DJ, Smits M, Williams A, Arendt J and von Schantz M (2003).
A length polymorphism in the Circadian clock gene Per3 is linked to delayed sleep phase syndrome and extreme diurnal preference. *Sleep*, 26(4), 413–415.

Armstrong SJ (2000).
The influence of individual cognitive style on performance in management education. *Educational Psychology*, 20(3), 323–339.

Armstrong SJ (2002).
Effects of cognitive style on the quality of research supervision. In M Valcke and D Gombeir (eds) *Learning styles: reliability and validity*, 431–440. Proceedings of the 7th Annual European Learning Styles Information Network Conference, 26–28 June, Ghent. Ghent: University of Ghent.

Armstrong SJ, Allinson CW and Hayes C (2002).
Formal mentoring systems: an examination of the effects of mentor/protégé cognitive styles on the mentoring process. *Journal of Management Studies*, 39(8), 1111–1137.

Atkinson S (1998).
Cognitive style in the context of design and technology project work. *Educational Psychology*, 18(2), 183–192.

Ball AL (1982).
The secrets of learning styles: your child's and your own. *Redbook*, 160(1), 73–76.

Ball SJ (1994).
Education reform: a critical and post-structural approach. Buckingham: Open University Press.

Ball SJ, Reay D and David M (2002).
Ethnic choosing: minority ethnic students, social class and higher education choice. *Race, Ethnicity and Education*, 5(4), 333–357.

Baron-Cohen S (2003).
Essential difference: men, women and the extreme male brain. London: Allen Lane.

Bates M and Keirsey D (1978).
Please understand me: character and temperament types. Del Mar, CA: Prometheus Nemesis.

Bayne R (1994).
The 'Big Five' versus the Myers-Briggs. *The Psychologist*, 7(1), 1.

Beishuizen J, Stoutjesdijk E and Van Putten K (1994).
Studying textbooks: effects of learning styles, study task and instruction. *Learning and Instruction*, 4, 151–174.

Bernstein B (1996).
Pedagogy, symbolic control and identity. London: Taylor & Francis.

Bess TL and Harvey RJ (2002).
Bimodal score distributions and the Myers-Briggs
Type Indicator: fact or artifact? *Journal of Personality
Assessment*, 78(1), 176–186.

Biggers JL (1980).
Body rhythms, the school day, and academic
achievement. *Journal of Experimental Education*,
49(1), 45–47.

Biggs J (1993).
What do inventories of students' learning processes
really measure? A theoretical view and clarification.
British Journal of Educational Psychology, 63, 9–19.

Biggs JB (1978).
Individual and group differences in study processes.
British Journal of Educational Psychology, 48, 266–279.

Black PJ and Wiliam D (1998a).
Assessment and classroom learning.
Assessment in Education, 5(1), 7–73.

Black PJ and Wiliam D (1998b).
*Inside the black box: raising standards through
classroom attainment.* London: King's College London.

Bloom BS (ed.) (1956).
*Taxonomy of educational objectives.
Handbook 1: cognitive domain.* New York: Longman.

Bloomer M and Hodkinson P (2000).
Learning careers: continuing and change
in young people's dispositions to learning.
British Educational Research Journal, 26, 583–597.

Bokoros MA, Goldstein MB and Sweeney MM (1992).
Common factors in five measures of cognitive style.
Current Psychology: Research & Reviews,
11(2), 99–109.

Bosacki S, Innerd W and Towson S (1997).
Field independence-dependence and self-esteem
in preadolescents: does gender make a difference?
Journal of Youth and Adolescence, 26(6), 691–715.

Bouchard TJ and Hur Y-M (1998).
Genetic and environmental influences on
the continuous scales of the Myers-Briggs Type
Indicator: an analysis based on twins reared apart.
Journal of Personality, 66(2), 135–149.

Boud D (1989).
Some competing traditions in experiential learning.
In *Making sense of experiential learning*, (eds)
SW Weil and I McGill. Milton Keynes: Society for
Research into Higher Education/Open University Press.

Boyle E, Duffy T and Dunleavy K (2003).
Learning styles and academic outcome: the validity
and utility of Vermunt's Inventory of Learning Styles
in a British higher education setting. *British Journal
of Educational Psychology*, 73, 267–290.

Boyle E, MacDonald J, Aked J, Main D and
Dunleavy K (2003).
Thinking styles and social problem solving.
In S Armstrong, M Graff, C Lashley, E Peterson,
S Raynor, E Sadler-Smith, M Schiering and D Spicer
(eds) *Bridging theory and practice*, 67–79. Proceedings
of the Eighth Annual European Learning Styles
Information Network Conference, University of Hull.
Hull: University of Hull.

Boyle GJ (1995).
Myers-Briggs Type Indicator (MBTI): some psychometric
limitations. *Australian Psychologist*, 30(1), 71–74.

Brady F (1995).
Sports skill classification, gender and perceptual style.
Perceptual and Motor Skills, 81, 611–620.

Breaugh JA (2003).
Effect size estimation: factors to consider and mistakes
to avoid. *Journal of Management*, 29(1), 79–97.

Brew CR (2002).
Kolb's Learning Style Instrument: sensitive to gender.
Educational and Psychological Measurement, 62(2),
373–390.

Broverman DM (1960a).
Cognitive style and intra-individual variation in abilities.
Journal of Personality, 28, 240–256.

Broverman DM (1960b).
Dimensions of cognitive style.
Journal of Personality, 28, 167–185.

Bruer JT (1998).
The brain and child development: time for
some critical thinking. *Public Health Reports*,
113 (September/October), 388–397.

Buch K and Bartley S (2002).
Learning style and training delivery mode preference.
The Journal of Workplace Learning, 14(1).

Burke, K (2003).
Impact of learning-style strategies on mathematics.
In R Dunn and S Griggs (eds) *Synthesis of the Dunn
and Dunn learning styles model research: who,
what, when, where and so what – the Dunn and Dunn
learning styles model and its theoretical cornerstone.*
New York: St John's University.

Burnand G (2002).
Hemisphere specialization as an aid in early infancy.
Neuropsychology Review, 12(4), 233–251.

Burns DE, Johnson SE and Gable RK (1998).
Can we generalize about the learning style
characteristics of high academic achievers?
Roeper Review, 20(4), 278–281.

Busato VV, Prins FJ, Elshout JJ and Hamaker C (2000).
Intellectual ability, learning style, personality,
achievement motivation and academic success
of psychology students in higher education.
Personality and Individual Differences,
29(6), 1057–1068.

Butler KA (1988).
Learning styles. *Learning*, 88, 30–34.

LSRC reference   **References**   page 148/149

Callan R (1999).
Effects of matching and mismatching students'
time-of-day preferences. *Journal of Educational
Research and Extension*, 92(5), 295–299.

Capraro RM and Capraro MM (2002).
Myers-Briggs Type Indicator score reliability across
studies: a meta-analytic reliability generalization study.
Educational and Psychological Measurement,
62(4), 590–602.

Carbo ML (1983).
Research in reading and learning style: implications
for exceptional children. *Exceptional Children*,
49(6), 486–493.

Carey JC, Stanley DA and Biggers JL (1988).
A peak alert time and rapport between residence hall
roommates. *Journal of College Student Development*,
29, 239–243.

Carlson R (1980).
Studies of Jungian typology. *Journal of Personality
and Social Psychology*, 38, 801–810.

Carroll JB (1993).
*Human cognitive abilities: a survey of factor-analytic
studies*. Cambridge: Cambridge University Press.

Cassidy S (2003).
Learning styles: an overview of theories, models
and measures. In S Armstrong, M Graff, C Lashley,
E Peterson, S Raynor, E Sadler-Smith, M Schiering
and D Spicer (eds) *Bridging theory and practice*,
80–102. Proceedings of the Eighth Annual European
Learning Styles Information Network Conference,
University of Hull. Hull: University of Hull.

Cavanagh SJ and Coffin DA (1994).
Matching instructional preference and teaching
styles: a review of the literature. *Nurse Education Today*,
14, 106–110.

Chevrier J, Fortin G, Théberge M and Leblanc R (2000).
Le style d'apprentissage: une perspective historique.
Education and Francophonie, 28(1).

Claxton CS and Murrell PH (1987).
*Learning styles: implications for improving education
practices*. Higher Education Report No 4. Washington
DC: Association for the Study of Higher Education.

Claxton CS and Ralston Y (1978).
Learning styles. In CS Claxton and Y Ralston (eds)
*Learning styles: their impact on teaching and
administration*. Washington: American Association
for Higher Education.

Claxton RP and McIntyre JM (1994).
Empirical relationships between need for cognition and
cognitive style: implications for consumer psychology.
Psychological Reports, 74, 723–732.

Claxton RP, McIntyre JM, Clow KE and Zemanek JJE
(1996).
Cognitive style as a potential antecedent to values.
Journal of Social Behaviour and Personality,
11(2), 355–373.

Cloninger CR (1993).
A psychobiological model of temperament and
character. *Archives of General Psychiatry*, 50, 975–989.

CRLI (1997).
*ASSIST – Approaches and Study Skills Inventory
for Students*. Edinburgh: University of Edinburgh.

Coffield FJ, Moseley DV, Hall E and Ecclestone K (2004).
*Should we be using learning styles? What research
has to say to practice*. London: Learning and Skills
Research Centre/University of Newcastle upon Tyne.

Cohen J (1988).
Statistical power analysis for the behavioural sciences.
2nd ed. New York: Academic Press.

Coleman S and Zenhausern R (1979).
Processing speed, laterality patterns, and memory
encoding as a function of hemispheric dominance.
Bulletin of the Psychonomic Society, 14, 357–360.

Colley H, Hodkinson P and Malcolm J (2003).
*Informality and formality in learning: a report for the
Learning and Skills Research Centre*. London: Learning
and Skills Research Centre/University of Leeds.

Collinson E (2000).
A survey of elementary students' learning style
preferences and academic success. *Contemporary
Education*, 71(4), 42–49.

Constantinidou F and Baker S (2002).
Stimulus modality and verbal learning performance
in normal aging. *Brain and Language*, 82(3), 296–311.

Cooper SE and Miller JA (1991).
MBTI learning style-teaching style discongruencies.
Educational and Psychological Measurement,
51, 699–706.

Corno L and Mandinach EB (1983).
The role of cognitive engagement in classroom
learning and motivation. *Educational Psychologist*,
18(2), 88–108.

Cornwell JM, Manfredo PA and Dunlap WP (1991).
Factor analysis of the 1985 revision of Kolb's
Learning Style Inventory. *Educational and
Psychological Measurement*, 51.

Curry L (1983).
An organization of learning styles theory and constructs.
Paper presented at the Annual Meeting of the American
Educational Research Association, Montreal, Quebec.

Curry L (1987).
*Integrating concepts of cognitive learning styles:
a review with attention to psychometric standards*.
Ottawa: Canadian College of Health
Services Executives.

Curry L (1990).
A critique of the research on learning styles.
Educational Leadership, 48(2), 50–56.

Curry L (1991).
Patterns of learning style across selected medical specialities. *Educational Psychology*, 11(3 and 4), 247–277.

Daniels H (2001).
Vygotsky and pedagogy. London: RoutledgeFalmer.

Davies MF (1993).
Field-dependence and hindsight bias: output interference in the generation of reasons. *Journal of Research in Personality*, 27(3), 222–237.

De Bello TC (1990).
Comparison of eleven major learning styles models: variables, appropriate populations, validity of instrumentation, and the research behind them. *Reading, Writing, and Learning Disabilities*, 6, 203–222.

De Ciantis SM and Kirton MJ (1996).
A psychometric re-examination of Kolb's experiential learning cycle construct: a separation of level, style and process. *Educational and Psychological Measurement*, 56, 809–820.

De Gregoris CN (1986).
Reading comprehension and the interaction of individual sound preferences and varied auditory distractions. Doctoral dissertation, Hofstra University.

Delahoussaye M (2002).
Is it time to let learning styles come in? *Training and Development*, May, 28–36.

Della Valle J, Dunn K, Dunn R, Geisert G, Sinatra R and Zenhausern R (1986).
The effects of matching and mismatching students' mobility preferences on recognition and memory tasks. *Journal of Educational Research and Extension*, 79(5), 267–272.

Demetriou A and Kazi S (2001).
Unity and modularity in the mind and self. London: Routledge.

Desmedt E and Valcke M (2003).
Learning style awareness: why would it work? In S Armstrong, M Graff, C Lashley, E Peterson, S Raynor, E Sadler-Smith, M Schiering and D Spicer (eds) *Bridging theory and practice*, 139–150. Proceedings of the Eighth Annual European Learning Styles Information Network Conference, University of Hull. Hull: University of Hull.

Desmedt E, Valcke M, Carrette L and Derese A (2003).
Comparing the learning styles of medicine and pedagogical sciences students. In S Armstrong, M Graff, C Lashley, E Peterson, S Raynor, E Sadler-Smith, M Schiering and D Spicer (eds) *Bridging theory and practice*, 133–138. Proceedings of the Eighth Annual European Learning Styles Information Network Conference, University of Hull. Hull: University of Hull.

Deverensky JL (1978).
Modal preferences and strengths: implications for reading research. *Journal of Reading Behaviour*, 10(1), 7–23.

De Vito AJ (1985).
Review of Myers-Briggs Type Indicator. In JV Mitchell (ed.) *The Ninth Mental Measurements Yearbook*. Lincoln, Nebraska: University of Nebraska.

Dewey J (1897).
My pedagogical creed. *The School Journal*, IV(3), 44–59.

Dewey J (1916).
Democracy and education: an introduction to the philosophy of education. New York: Macmillan.

Diseth A (2001).
Validation of a Norwegian version of the Approaches and Study Skills Inventory for Students (ASSIST): application of structural equation modelling. *Scandinavian Journal of Educational Research*, 45(4), 381–394.

Diseth A (2002).
The relationship between intelligence, approaches to learning and academic achievement. *Scandinavian Journal of Educational Research*, 46(2), 219–230.

Di Tiberio JK (1996).
Education, learning styles and cognitive styles. In AL Hammer (ed.) *MBTI applications: a decade of research on the Myers-Briggs Type Indicator*. Palo Alto, CA: Consulting Psychologists Press.

Drummond RJ and Stoddard AH (1992).
Learning style and personality type. *Perceptual and Motor Skills*, 75, 99–104.

Drysdale MTB, Ross JL and Schulz RA (2001).
Cognitive learning styles and academic performance in 19 first-year university courses: successful students versus students at risk. *Journal of Education for Students Placed at Risk*, 6(3), 271–289.

Duff A (1997).
A note on the reliability and validity of a 30-item version of Entwistle & Tait's Revised Approaches to Studying Inventory. *British Journal of Educational Psychology*, 67, 529–539.

Duff A (2001).
Psychometric methods in accounting education: a review, some comments and implications for accounting education researchers. *Accounting Education*, 10(4), 383–401.

Duff A (2002).
Approaches to learning: factor invariance across gender. *Personality and Individual Differences*, 33, 997–1010.

Duff A and Duffy T (2002).
Psychometric properties of Honey & Mumford's Learning Styles Questionnaire (LSQ). *Personality and Individual Differences*, 33, 147–163.

Dunn R (1983).
Learning style and its relationship to exceptionality at both ends of the spectrum. *Exceptional Children*, 49(6), 496–506.

Dunn R (1990a).
Bias over substance: a critical analysis of Kavale
and Forness' report on modality-based instruction.
Exceptional Children, 56(4), 352–356.

Dunn R (1990b).
Rita Dunn answers questions on learning styles.
Educational Leadership, 48(2), 15–19.

Dunn R (1990c).
Understanding the Dunn and Dunn learning styles
model and the need for individual diagnosis and
prescription. *Reading, Writing and Learning Disabilities*,
6, 223–247.

Dunn R (2001a).
Learning style: state of the science.
Theory into Practice, 13(1), 10–19.

Dunn R (2001b).
Learning style differences of nonconforming
middle-school students. *NASSP Bulletin*,
85(626), 68–75.

Dunn R (2003a).
Response to the [LSRC] project team on the Dunn and
Dunn learning style model. Personal communication.

Dunn R (2003b).
The Dunn and Dunn learning style model and its
theoretical cornerstone. In R Dunn and S Griggs (eds)
*Synthesis of the Dunn and Dunn learning styles model
research: who, what, when, where and so what – the
Dunn and Dunn learning styles model and its theoretical
cornerstone*, 1–6. New York: St John's University.

Dunn R (2003c).
The Dunn and Dunn learning style model: theoretical
cornerstone, research and practical applications.
In S Armstrong, M Graff, C Lashley, E Peterson,
S Raynor, E Sadler-Smith, M Schiering and D Spicer
(eds) *Bridging theory and practice*. Proceedings
of the Eighth Annual European Learning Styles
Information Network Conference, University of Hull.
Hull: University of Hull.

Dunn R (2003d).
Epilogue: so what? In R Dunn and S Griggs (eds)
*Synthesis of the Dunn and Dunn learning styles
model research: who, what, when, where and
so what – the Dunn and Dunn learning styles model
and its theoretical cornerstone*, 269–270.
New York: St John's University.

Dunn R (2003e).
Practical applications of the research. In R Dunn and
S Griggs (eds) *Synthesis of the Dunn and Dunn
learning styles model research: who, what, when,
where and so what – the Dunn and Dunn learning
styles model and its theoretical cornerstone*, 7–10.
New York: St John's University.

Dunn R (2003f).
*The Dunn and Dunn learning style model: theoretical
cornerstone, research and practical applications*.
Keynote speech to the Eighth Annual European
Learning Styles Information Network Conference,
University of Hull, 30 June–2 July.

Dunn R and Dunn K (1992).
*Teaching secondary students through their individual
learning styles*. Needham Heights, MA: Allyn and Bacon.

Dunn R, Dunn K, Primavera L, Sinatra R and Virostko J
(1987).
A timely solution: a review of research on the effects of
chronobiology on children's achievement and behaviour.
The Clearing House, 61(1), 5–8.

Dunn R and Griggs SA (1988).
*Learning styles: a quiet revolution in American
secondary schools*. Reston, VA: National Association
of Secondary School Principals.

Dunn R and Griggs SA (1990).
Research on the learning style characteristics
of selected racial and ethnic groups. *Journal of Reading,
Writing, and Learning Disabilities*, 6(3), 261–280.

Dunn R and Griggs S (2003).
*Synthesis of the Dunn and Dunn learning styles model
research: who, what, when, where and so what – the
Dunn and Dunn learning styles model and its theoretical
cornerstone*. New York: St John's University.

Dunn R, Griggs SA, Gorman BS, Olson J and Beasley M
(1995).
A meta-analytic validation of the Dunn and Dunn model
of learning-style preferences. *The Journal of Educational
Research*, 88(6), 353–363.

Dunn R, Klavas A and Ingram J (1990).
Homework disc. New York: St John's University.

Dunn R, Shea TC, Evans W, MacMurren H (1991).
Learning style and equal protection: the next frontier.
The Clearing House, 65, 93–96.

Dunn R, Sklar RI, Beaudry J and Bruno J (1990).
Effects of matching and mismatching
minority developmental college students'
hemispheric preferences on mathematics scores.
Journal of Educational Research and Extension,
83(5), 283–288.

Dunn R and Stevenson JM (1997).
Teaching diverse college students to study with
a learning-styles prescription. *College Student Journal*,
31, 333–339.

Edwards JA, Lanning K and Hooker K (2002).
The MBTI and social information processing:
an incremental validity study. *Journal of Personality
Assessment*, 78(3), 432–450.

Edwards T (2002).
A remarkable sociological imagination. *British Journal
of Sociology of Education*, 23(4), 527–535.

Eggen PD and Kauchak DP (2001).
*Strategies for teachers: teaching content and
thinking skills*. Boston: Allyn and Bacon.

Ehrhard BJ (2000).
The effect of learning style self-knowledge
on student academic achievement.
Humanities and Social Sciences, 61(6-A), 2267.

Ellis MC (1996).
Field dependence-independence and
the discrimination of musical parts.
Perceptual and Motor Skills, 82(3), 947–954.

Entwistle N (1978a).
Identifying distinctive approaches to studying.
Higher Education, 8, 365–380.

Entwistle N (1978b).
Knowledge structures and styles of learning:
a summary of Pask's recent research. *British Journal
of Educational Psychology*, 48, 255–265.

Entwistle N (1988).
Styles of learning and teaching. London: David Fulton.

Entwistle N (1990).
Teaching and the quality of learning in higher education.
In N Entwistle (ed.) *Handbook of educational ideas and
practices*. London: Routledge.

Entwistle N (1997).
Contrasting perspectives on learning. In F Marton,
DJ Hounsell and N Entwistle (eds) *The Experience
of Learning*, 2nd ed. Edinburgh: Academic Press.

Entwistle NJ (1998).
Improving teaching through research on student
learning. In JJF Forrest (ed.) *University teaching:
international perspectives*. New York: Garland.

Entwistle NJ (2002).
Response to LSRC draft report on learning styles.
Personal communication.

Entwistle N, Hanley M and Hounsell D (1979).
Identifying distinctive approaches to studying.
Higher Education, 8, 365–380.

Entwistle N and McCune V (2003).
The conceptual basis of study strategy inventories
in higher education. *Educational Psychology Review*
(in press).

Entwistle N, McCune V and Walker P (2001).
Conceptions, styles and approaches within higher
education: analytic abstractions and everyday
experience. In RJ Sternberg and L-F Zhang (eds)
Perspectives on thinking, learning and cognitive styles.
Mahwah, New Jersey: Lawrence Erlbaum.

Entwistle N and Peterson E (2003).
*Conceptions of learning and knowledge in higher
education: relationships with study behaviour and
influences of learning environments*. Paper presented
to Workshop on Powerful Learning Environments,
Antwerp, May.

Entwistle N, Tait H and McCune V (2000).
Patterns of response to an approaches to studying
inventory across contrasting groups and contexts.
European Journal of the Psychology of Education,
XV(1), 38.

Entwistle N and Walker P (2000).
Strategic alertness and expanded awareness
within sophisticated conceptions of teaching.
Instructional Science, 28, 335–362.

Eraut M, Alderton J, Cole G and Senker P (1999).
The impact of the manager on learning in the workplace.
In F Coffield (ed.) *Speaking truth to power: research and
policy on lifelong learning* 19–29. Bristol: Policy Press.

Ewing NJ and Yong FL (1992).
A comparative study of the learning style preference
among gifted African-American, Mexican-American
and American-born Chinese middle-grade students.
Roeper Review, 14(3), 120–123.

Eysenck H (1997).
Can personality study ever be objective? In C Cooper
and V Varma (eds) *Processes in individual differences*.
London: Routledge.

Eysenck H and Eysenck M (1985).
Personality and individual differences.
New York: Plenum.

Eysenck HJ, Barrett P, Wilson G and Jackson CJ (1992).
Primary trait measurement of the 21 components
of the P-E-N system. *European Journal of Psychological
Assessment*, 8, 109–117.

FEDA (1995).
Learning styles. London: Further Education
Development Agency.

Federico PA and Landis DB (1984).
Cognitive styles, abilities and aptitudes: are they
dependent or independent? *Contemporary Educational
Psychology*, 9, 146–161.

Felder RM (1993).
Reaching the second tier: learning and teaching styles
in college science education. *College Science Teaching*,
23(5), 286–290.

Felder RM (1996).
Matters of style. *American Society of Electrical
Engineers: Prism*, 6(4), 18–23.

Ferrell BG (1983).
A factor analytic comparison of four learning styles
instruments. *Journal of Educational Psychology*,
75(1), 33–39.

Fielding M (1994).
Valuing differences in teachers and learners: building on
Kolb's learning styles to develop a language of teaching
and learning. *The Curriculum Journal*, 5(3).

Fitzgerald D and Hattie JA (1983).
An evaluation of the 'Your style of learning and thinking'
inventory. *British Journal of Educational Psychology*,
53, 336–346.

Flavell J (1979).
Metacognition and cognitive monitoring: a new area of
cognitive development enquiry. *American Psychologist*,
34, 906–911.

Fleenor JW (2001).
Review of the Myers-Briggs Type Indicator, Form M.
In JC Impara and BS Blake (eds) *The fourteenth mental measurements yearbook*. Lincoln, NE: Buros Institute of Mental Measurement.

Fogarty GJ and Taylor JA (1997).
Learning styles among mature age students: some comments on the ASI-S. *Higher Education Research and Development*, 16, 321–330.

Ford N (1985).
Learning styles and strategies of postgraduate students. *British Journal of Educational Technology*, 16, 65–79.

Ford N (1995).
Levels and types of mediation in instructional systems: an individual differences approach. *International Journal of Human-Computer Studies*, 43, 241–259.

Ford N and Chen SY (2001).
Matching/mismatching revisited: an empirical study of learning and teaching styles. *British Journal of Educational Technology*, 32(1), 5–22.

Forqurean JM, Meisgeier C and Swank P (1990).
The link between learning style and Jungian psychological type: a finding of two bipolar preference dimensions. *Journal of Experimental Education*, 58(3), 225–237.

Frank BM and Davis JK (1982).
Effect of field-independence match or mismatch on a communication task. *Journal of Educational Psychology*, 74(1), 23–31.

Freedman RD and Stumpf SA (1978).
What can one learn from the Learning Style Inventory? *Academy of Management Journal*, 21(2), 275–282.

Fuller A and Unwin L (2002).
Developing pedagogies for the contemporary workplace. In K Evans, P Hodkinson and L Unwin (eds) *Working to learn: transforming learning in the workplace*, 95–111. London: Kogan Page.

Fung YH, Ho ASP and Kwan KP (1993).
Reliability and validity of the Learning Styles Questionnaire. B*ritish Journal of Educational Technology*, 24, 12–21.

Furnham A (1992).
Personality and learning style: a study of three instruments. *Personality and Individual Differences*, 13(4).

Furnham A (1995).
The relationship of personality and intelligence to cognitive learning style and achievement. Thinking styles. In DH Saklofske and M Zeidner (eds.) *International Handbook of Personality and Intelligence*. New York: Plenum Press.

Furnham A (1996a).
The big five versus the big four: the relationship between the Myers-Briggs Type Indicator (MBTI) and NEO-PI Five-Factor Model of Personality. *Personality and Individual Differences*, 21(2), 303–307.

Furnham A (1996b).
The FIRO-B, the Learning Style Questionnaire, and the Five-Factor Model. *Journal of Social Behaviour and Personality*, 11(2), 285.

Furnham A, Jackson CJ and Miller T (1999).
Personality learning style and work performance. *Personality and Individual Differences*, 27, 1113–1122.

Gadt-Johnson CD and Price GE (2000).
Comparing students with high and low preferences for tactile learning. *Education and Training*, 120(3), 581–585.

Gardner H (1983).
Frames of mind, 1st ed. New York: Basic Books.

Gardner H (1993).
Frames of mind, 2nd ed. New York: Basic Books.

Gardner RW and Long RI (1962).
Cognitive controls of attention and inhibition: a study of individual consistencies. *British Journal of Psychology*, 53, 381–388.

Garlinger DK and Frank BM (1986).
Teacher-student cognitive style and academic achievement: a review and mini-meta-analysis. *Journal of Classroom Interaction*, 21(2), 2–8.

Garner I (2000).
Problems and inconsistencies with Kolb's learning styles. *Educational Psychology*, 20(3), 341–348.

Geiger MA and Pinto JK (1991).
Changes in learning style preference during a three-year longitudinal study. *Psychological Reports*, 69, 755–762.

Geiger MA and Pinto JK (1992).
Changes in learning-style preferences: a reply to Ruble and Stout. *Psychological Reports*, 70, 1072–1074.

Geller LM (1979).
Reliability of the Learning Style Inventory. *Psychological Reports*, 44, 555–561.

Geschwind N and Galaburda AM (1987).
Cerebral lateralisation: biological mechanisms, associations and pathology. Cambridge, MA: MIT Press.

Gevins A and Smith ME (2000).
Neurophysiological measures of working memory and individual differences in cognitive ability and cognitive style. *Cerebral Cortex*, 5(10), 829–839.

Girelli SA and Stake J (1993).
Bipolarity in Jungian type theory and the Myers-Briggs Type Indicator. *Journal of Personality Assessment*, 60(2), 290–301.

Glass A and Riding RJ (1999).
EEG differences and cognitive style. *Biological Psychology*, 51(1), 23–41.

Glicksohn J and Bozna M (2000).
Developing a personality profile of the bomb-disposal expert: the role of sensation seeking and field dependence-independence. *Personality and Individual Differences*, 28(1), 85.

Goldstein MB and Bokoros MA (1992).
Tilting at windmills: comparing the Learning Style Inventory and the Learning Styles Questionnaire. *Educational and Psychological Measurement*, 52(3), 701–708.

Gordon HRD and Yocke R (1999).
Relationship between personality characteristics and observable teaching effectiveness of selected beginning career and technical education teachers. *Journal of Vocational and Technical Education*, 16(1).

Grasha AF (1984).
Learning styles: the journey from Greenwich Observatory (1796) to the college classroom (1984). *Improving College and University Teaching*, 32(1), 46–53.

Gray D, Griffin C and Nasta T (2000).
Training to teach in further and adult education. Cheltenham: Stanley Thornes.

Gray JA (1973).
Causal theories of personality and how to test them. In JR Royce (ed.) *Multivariate analysis and psychological theory.* New York: Academic Press.

Gray JA (1982).
The neuropsychology of anxiety: an enquiry into the functions of the septo-hippocampus system. Oxford: Oxford University Press.

Gregorc AF (1979).
Learning/teaching styles: potent forces behind them. *Educational Leadership*, 36, 234–237.

Gregorc AF (1982a).
ORGANON: an adult's guide to style. Columbia, CT: Gregorc Associates Inc.

Gregorc AF (1982b).
Gregorc Style Delineator: development, technical and administration manual. Columbia, CT: Gregorc Associates Inc.

Gregorc AF (1984).
Style as a symptom: a phenomenological perspective. *Theory into Practice*, 23(1), 51–55.

Gregorc AF (1985).
Style Delineator: a self-assessment instrument for adults. Columbia, CT: Gregorc Associates Inc.

Gregorc AF (2002).
Frequently asked questions on style. At www.gregorc.com/faq.html

Gremli JL (2003).
Impact of learning-style strategies on music education. In R Dunn and S Griggs (eds) *Synthesis of the Dunn and Dunn learning styles model research: who, what, when, where and so what – the Dunn and Dunn learning styles model and its theoretical cornerstone.* New York: St John's University.

Grigorenko EL and Sternberg RJ (1995).
Thinking styles. In DH Saklofske and M Zeidner (eds.) *International Handbook of Personality and Intelligence.* New York: Plenum Press.

Griggs SA (1984).
Counselling the gifted and talented based on learning styles. *Exceptional Children*, 50(5), 429–432.

Guilford JP (1967).
The nature of human intelligence. New York: McGraw-Hill.

Guilford JP (1977).
Way beyond the IQ: guide to improving intelligence and creativity. Buffalo: Creative Executive Foundation.

Guilford JP (1980).
Cognitive styles: what are they? *Educational and Psychological Measurement*, 40, 715–735.

Haggis T (2003).
Constructing images of ourselves? A critical investigation into 'approaches to learning' research in higher education. *British Educational Research Journal*, 29(1), 89–104.

Hammer AL (ed.) (1996).
MBTI applications: a decade of research on the Myers-Briggs Type Indicator. Palo Alto, CA: Consulting Psychologists Press.

Hankinson C (2003).
Learning styles: a minimal intervention strategy. Available via www.learningstylesuk.com

Harasym PH, Leong EJ, Juschka BB, Lucier GE and Lorsheider FL (1995a).
Myers-Briggs psychological type and achievement in anatomy and physiology. *Advances in Physiology Education*, 13(1), 61–65.

Harasym PH, Leong EJ, Juschka BB, Lucier GE and Lorsheider FL (1995b).
Gregorc learning styles and achievement in anatomy and physiology. *Advances in Physiology Education*, 13(1), 56–60.

Harasym PH, Leong EJ, Juschka BB, Lucier GE and Lorsheider FL (1996).
Relationship between Myers-Briggs Type Indicator and Gregorc Style Delineator. *Perceptual and Motor Skills*, 82, 1203–1210.

Harrison AF and Bramson RM (1982).
Styles of thinking. New York: Doubleday.

Harrison AF and Bramson RM (1988).
InQ: Inquiry Mode Questionnaire: a measure of how you think and make decisions. Berkeley, CA: Bramson, Parlette, Harrison and Assoc.

Hartman SE, Hylton J and Sanders RF (1997).
The influence of hemispheric dominance on scores of the Myers-Briggs Type Indicator. *Educational and Psychological Measurement*, 57(2), 440–449.

Hayes J and Allinson CW (1997).
Learning styles and training and development in work settings: lessons from educational research. *Educational Psychology*, 17(1/2).

Heffler B (2001).
Individual learning style and the Learning Style
Inventory. *Educational Studies*, 27(3), 307–316.

Hergovich A (2003).
Field dependence, suggestibility and belief in
paranormal phenomena. *Personality and Individual
Differences*, 34, 195–209.

Herrmann N (1989).
The creative brain. North Carolina: Brain Books,
The Ned Hermann Group.

Herrmann N (1996).
The whole brain business book. New York: McGraw-Hill.

Hicks LE (1984).
Conceptual and empirical analysis of some
assumptions of an explicit typological theory.
Journal of Personality and Social Psychology,
46, 1118–1131.

Higgs M (2001).
Is there a relationship between the Myers-Briggs
Type Indicator and emotional intelligence?
Journal of Management Psychology, 16(7), 509–533.

Hill J, Puurula A, Sitko-Lutek A and Rokowska A (2000).
Cognitive style and socialisation: an exploration of
learned sources of style in Finland, Poland and the UK.
Educational Psychology, 20(3), 285–305.

Hlawaty H and Honigsfeld A (2002).
Commentary on reliability and validity issues on
two cross-national comparative learning styles
research studies. In M Valcke and D Gombeir (eds)
Learning styles: reliability and validity. Proceedings
of the 7th Annual European Learning Styles Information
Network Conference, 26–28 June, Ghent. Ghent:
University of Ghent.

Hodges H (1985).
*An analysis of the relationships among preferences
for a formal/informal design, one element of learning
style, academic achievement and attitudes of seventh
and eighth grade students in remedial mathematics
classes in a New York City junior high school*.
Doctoral dissertation, St John's University, New York.

Hodgkinson GP and Sadler-Smith E (2003).
Complex or unitary? A critique and empirical
re-assessment of the Allinson-Hayes Cognitive
Style Index. *Journal of Occupational and
Organisational Psychology*, 76, 243–268.

Holzman PS and Klein GS (1954).
The relation of assimilation tendencies in
visual, auditory and kinaesthetic time error to
cognitive attitudes of levelling and sharpening.
Journal of Personality, 23, 375–394.

Honey P (1994).
101 ways to develop your people, without really trying!
Maidenhead: Peter Honey Publications.

Honey P (2002a).
Why I am besotted with the learning cycle.
In P Honey (ed.) *Peter Honey's articles on learning
and this and that*, 115–116. Maidenhead: Peter Honey
Publications Ltd.

Honey P (2002b).
Personal communication.

Honey P (2002c).
Personal communication.

Honey P and Mumford A (1992).
The manual of learning styles.
Maidenhead: Peter Honey Publications.

Honey P and Mumford A (2000).
The learning styles helper's guide.
Maidenhead: Peter Honey Publications Ltd.

Honigsfeld A and Dunn R (2003).
High school male and female learning style
similarities and differences in diverse nations.
Journal of Educational Research, 96(4), 195–206.

Honigsfeld A and Schiering M (2003).
Learning styles in teacher education.
In S Armstrong, M Graff, C Lashley, E Peterson,
S Raynor, E Sadler-Smith, M Schiering and D Spicer
(eds) *Bridging theory and practice*. Proceedings
of the Eighth Annual European Learning Styles
Information Network Conference, University of Hull.
Hull: University of Hull.

Houghton A (2000).
Using the Myers-Briggs Type Indicator for career
development. *BMJ Classified*, June, 2–3.

Howes RJ and Carskadon TG (1979).
Test-retest reliabilities of the Myers-Briggs
Type Indicator as a function of mood changes.
Research in Psychological Type, 2, 67–72.

Huang J and Chao L (2000).
Field dependence versus field independence
of students with and without learning disabilities.
Perceptual and Motor Skills, 90(1), 343–347.

Huddleston P and Unwin L (1997).
Teaching and learning in further education.
London: Routledge.

Hughes JN (1992).
Review of the Learning Styles Inventory
[Price Systems, Inc.]. In JJ Kramer and JC Conoley (eds)
The eleventh mental measurements yearbook.
Lincoln, NE: Buros Institute of Mental Measurements.

Hunt D, Butler L *et al.* (1978).
*Assessing conceptual level by the paragraph
completion method*. Toronto: Ontario Institute
for Studies in Education.

Hyman R and Roscoff B (1984).
Matching learning and teaching styles: the jug and
what's in it. *Theory into Practice*, 23(1), 35–43.

Jackson C (2002).
Manual of the Learning Styles Profiler.
Available via www.psi-press.co.uk

Jackson CJ, Furnham A, Forde L and Cotter T (2000).
The structure of the Eysenck Personality Profiler.
British Journal of Psychology, 91, 223–239.

Jackson CJ and Lawty-Jones M (1996).
Explaining the overlap between personality and learning style. *Personality and Individual Differences*, 20(3), 293–300.

Jarlstrom M (2000).
Personality preferences and career expectations of Finnish business students. *Career Development International*, 5(3), 144–154.

Jaspers F (1994).
Target group characteristics: are perceptual modality preferences relevant for instructional materials design? *Educational and Training Technology International*, 31(1), 11–18.

Johnson J, Prior S and Artuso M (2000).
Field dependence as a factor in second language communicative production. *Language learning*, 50(3), 529–567.

Jonassen DH and Grabowski BL (1993).
Handbook of individual differences, learning and instruction. Hillsdale, NJ: Lawrence Erlbaum.

Joniak AJ and Isaksen SG (1988).
The Gregorc Style Delineator: internal consistency and its relationship to Kirton's adaptive-innovative distinction. *Educational and Psychological Measurement*, 48, 1043–1049.

Jung CG (1968).
Analytical psychology: its theory and practice – the Tavistock Lectures. New York: Random House.

Kagan J (1966).
Reflection-impulsivity: the generality and dynamics of conceptual tempo. *Journal of Abnormal Psychology*, 71, 17–24.

Kagan J and Kogan N (1970).
Individual variations in cognitive processes. In L Carmichael and PH Mussen (eds) *Carmichael's manual of child psychology*, vol 1, 1273–1365. New York: Wiley.

Kagan J and Krathwohl DR (1967).
Studies in human interaction. East Lansung, MI: Michigan State University.

Kaiser J (1998).
Review of the Productivity Environmental Preferences Survey. In JC Impara and BS Blake (eds), *The thirteenth mental measurements yearbook*. Lincoln, NE: Buros Institute of Mental Measurements.

Kampwirth TJ and Bates M (1980).
Modality preference and teaching method: a review of the research. *Academic Therapy*, 15(5), 597–605.

Katz N (1986).
Construct validity of Kolb's Learning Style Inventory, using factor analysis and Guttman's smallest space analysis. *Perceptual and Motor Skills*, 63, 1323–1326.

Katz N (1990).
Problem solving and time: functions of learning style and teaching methods. *The Occupational Therapy Journal of Research*, 10(4), 221–236.

Kavale KA and Forness SR (1987).
Substance over style: assessing the efficacy of modality testing and teaching. *Exceptional Children*, 54(3), 228–239.

Kavale KA and Forness SR (1990).
Substance over style: a rejoinder to Dunn's animadversions. *Exceptional Children*, 56(4), 357–361.

Kelley LS (1990).
Using 4MAT to improve staff development, curriculum assessment and planning. *Educational Leadership*, 48(2), 38–39.

Kember D and Gow L (1990).
Cultural specificity of approaches to study. *British Journal of Educational Psychology*, 60, 356–363.

Kember D and Harper G (1987).
Implications for instruction arising from the relationship between approaches to studying and academic outcomes. *Instructional Science*, 16, 35–46.

Kirby P (1979).
Cognitive styles, learning style and transfer skill acquisition. Information series No 195. Columbus, OH: Ohio State University.

Kirton MJ (1976).
Adapters and innovators: a description and measure. *Journal of Applied Psychology*, 61, 622–629.

Klein C (1998).
Learning styles: a literature review with special reference to low/under-achievers. Unpublished document. London: Qualifications and Curriculum Authority.

Klein C and Swaby A (2003).
Using a learning styles approach to improve learning, achievement and retention in further education. In S Armstrong, M Graff, C Lashley, E Peterson, S Raynor, E Sadler-Smith, M Schiering and D Spicer (eds) *Bridging theory and practice*. Proceedings of the Eighth Annual European Learning Styles Information Network Conference, University of Hull. Hull: University of Hull.

Klein C, Swaby A, Richardson G and Leung C (2003a).
Using a learning style approach to improve learning, achievement and retention in further education. *Launch of the Learning Styles Toolkit*. London: South Bank University.

Klein C, Swaby A, Richardson G and Leung C (2003b).
Using a learning styles approach to improve learning, achievement and retention in further education. Final project report. London: London Language and Literacy Unit/South Bank University.

Knapp TR (1994).
Review of the Learning Styles Inventory [Price Systems, Inc.]. In JC Impara and BS Blake (eds), *The thirteenth mental measurements yearbook*. Lincoln, NE: Buros Institute of Mental Measurements.

Kogan N (1973).
Creativity and cognitive style: a life-span
perspective. In PB Baltes and KW Shaie (eds)
*Life span developmental psychology: personality
and socialisation*. New York: Academic Press.

Kolb DA (1981).
Experiential learning theory and the Learning
Style Inventory: a reply to Freedman and Stumpf.
Academy of Management Review, 6(2), 289–296.

Kolb DA (1984).
*Experiential learning: experience as the source
of learning and development*. Englewood Cliffs,
New Jersey: Prentice Hall.

Kolb DA (1999).
The Kolb Learning Style Inventory, Version 3.
Boston: Hay Group.

Kolb DA (2000).
Facilitator's guide to learning. Boston: Hay/McBer.

Kolb D, Boyatzis RE and Mainemelis C (2001).
Experiential learning theory: previous research and
new directions. In RJ Sternberg and L-F Zhang (eds)
Perspectives on thinking, learning and cognitive styles.
Mahwah, New Jersey: Lawrence Erlbaum.

Kolb D, Lublin S, Spoth J and Baker R (1986).
Strategic management development: using experiential
learning theory to assess and develop managerial
competencies. *Journal of Management Competencies*,
5(3), 13–24.

Kolody RC, Conti GJ and Lockwood S (1997).
Identifying groups of learners through the use
of learning strategies. In Proceedings of the
27th Annual SCUTREA Conference, 1–5.

Krimsky J (1982).
*A comparative analysis of the effects of matching
and mismatching fourth grade students with
their learning style preference for the environmental
element of light and their subsequent reading
speed and accuracy scores*. Doctoral dissertation,
St John's University, New York.

Kuhl J (1983).
Volitional aspects of achievement motivation
and learned helplessness: toward a comprehensive
theory of action control. In BA Maher (ed.)
Progress in experimental personality research.
New York: Academic Press.

Lam SSK (1997).
Reliability and classification stability of Learning Style
Inventory in Hong Kong. *Perceptual and Motor Skills*,
85(1).

LaMothe J, Belcher A, Cobb K and Richardson V (1991).
Reliability and validity of the Productivity Environmental
Preference Survey (PEPS). *Nurse Educator*,
16(4), 30–35.

Laurillard D (1979).
The processes of student learning.
Higher Education, 8, 395–409.

Lave J and Wenger E (1991).
Situated learning: legitimate peripheral participation.
Cambridge: Cambridge University Press.

Lawrence MV (1997).
Secondary school teachers and learning style
preferences: action or watching in the classroom?
Educational Psychology, 17(1/2), 157–170.

Leach J and Moon B (1999).
Recreating pedagogy. In J Leach and B Moon (eds)
Learners and pedagogy, 265–276.
London: Paul Chapman/Open University.

Leat D and Lin M (2003).
Developing a pedagogy of metacognition and transfer:
some signposts for the generation and use of
knowledge and the creation of research partnerships.
British Educational Research Journal, 29(3), 383–415.

Lenehan MC, Dunn R, Ingham J, Signer B and
Murray JB (1994).
Effects of learning-style invention on college
students' achievement, anxiety, anger, and curiosity.
Journal of College Student Development, 35, 461–466.

Lenzen G (1989).
Enzyklopadie Erziehungswissenschaft, Vol 9.
Stuttgart: Klette.

Lewthwaite B (1999).
The Productivity Environmental Preference Survey
and Building Excellence: a statistical comparison
of two adult learning-style diagnostic instruments.
EdD dissertation, St John's University, New York.

Lim TK (1994).
Relationships between learning styles and
personality types. *Research in Education*, 52, 99.

Littlemore J (2001).
An empirical study of the relationship between
cognitive style and the use of communication strategy.
Applied Linguistics, 22(2), 241–265.

Livingston K, Soden R and Kirkwood M (2003).
Post-16 pedagogy and thinking skills: an evaluation.
London: Learning and Skills Research Centre/University
of Strathclyde.

Loehlin JC (1992).
Genes and environment in personality development.
London: Sage.

Löfström E (2002).
Person-situation interactions in SMEs: a study
of cognitive style and sources of job satisfaction.
In M Valcke and D Gombeir (eds) *Learning styles:
reliability and validity*. Proceedings of the
7th Annual European Learning Styles Information
Network Conference, 26–28 June, Ghent.
Ghent: University of Ghent.

Loo R (1997).
Evaluating change and stability in learning style scores:
a methodological concern. *Educational Psychology*,
17(1/2).

Loo R (1999).
Confirmatory factor analyses of Kolb's Learning Style Inventory (LSI-1985). *British Journal of Educational Psychology*, 69(2), 213–219.

Loomis M and Singer J (1980).
Testing the bipolar assumption in Jung's typology. *Journal of Analytical Psychology*, 25, 351–356.

Lovelace MK (2003).
A meta-analysis of experimental research studies based on the Dunn and Dunn learning styles model. In R Dunn and S Griggs (eds) *Synthesis of the Dunn and Dunn learning styles model research: who, what, when, where and so what – the Dunn and Dunn learning styles model and its theoretical cornerstone*, 217–224. New York: St John's University.

Lundstrom KV and Martin RE (1986).
Matching college instruction to student learning style. *College Student Journal*, 20, 270–274.

Luria AR (1996).
Human brain and psychological processes. New York: Harper and Row.

Luster T and McAdoo H (1996).
Family and child influences on educational attainment: a secondary analysis of the High/Scope Perry Pre-school data. *Developmental Psychology*, 32(1), 26–39.

MacLean PD (1952).
Some psychiatric implications of physiological studies on frontotemporal portion of limbic system (visceral brain). *Electroencephalography and Clinical Neurophysiology*, 4, 407–418.

Mainemelis C, Boyatzis RE and Kolb DA (2002).
Learning styles and adaptive flexibility: testing experiential learning theory. *Management Learning*, 33(1), 5–33.

Mangino C and Griggs S (2003).
Learning styles in higher education. In R Dunn and S Griggs (eds) *Synthesis of the Dunn and Dunn learning styles model research: who, what, when, where and so what – the Dunn and Dunn learning styles model and its theoretical cornerstone*. New York: St John's University.

Marshall JC and Merritt SL (1986).
Reliability and construct validity of the Learning Style Questionnaire. *Educational and Psychological Measurement*, 46(1), 257–262.

Martin D (1994).
Whole brain teaching and learning. *Training and Development*, August, 11–13.

Martin D (2003).
Profile patterns from local UK Ned Herrmann Group database. Personal communication.

Marton F and Säljö R (1976).
On qualitative differences in learning: 1 – outcome and process. *British Journal of Educational Psychology*, 46, 4–11.

Marzano R J (1998).
A theory-based meta-analysis of research on instruction. Aurora, CO: Mid-continent Regional Educational Laboratory.

Massarro DW and Ferguson E (1993).
Cognitive style and perception: the relationship between category width and speech perception, categorization and discrimination. *American Journal of Psychology*, 106(1), 25–40.

Mastrangelo PM (2001).
Review of the Myers-Briggs Type Indicator, Form M. In JC Impara and BS Blake (eds), *The fourteenth mental measurements yearbook*. Lincoln, NE: Buros Institute of Mental Measurements.

McCarthy B (1990).
Using the 4MAT System to bring learning styles to schools. *Educational Leadership*, 48(2), 31–37.

McCarthy B, St Germain C and Lippitt L (2001).
Synopsis of the 4MAT research guide. Available via www.aboutlearning.com

McCrae RR and Costa PT (1987).
Validation of the Five-Factor Model of Personality across instruments and observers. *Journal of Personality and Social Psychology*, 49, 710–721.

McCrae RR and Costa PT (1989).
Reinterpreting the Myers-Briggs Type Indicator from the perspective of the Five-Factor Model of Personality. *Journal of Personality*, 57(1), 17–37.

McCune V and Entwistle N (2000).
The deep approach to learning: analytic abstraction and idiosyncratic development. Paper presented at the Higher Education Conference, Helsinki, Finland, 30 August to 2 September.

McIntyre RP and Meloche MS (1995).
Cognitive style and customer orientation. *Journal of Business and Psychology*, 10(1), 75–86.

McNeal GH and Dwyer F (1999).
Effect of learning style on consistent and inconsistently designed instruction. *International Journal of Instructional Media*, 26(3), 337–347.

McNair S and Parry G (2003).
Learning together: age mixing in further education colleges. London: Learning and Skills Research Centre.

Meredith GM (1981).
Focus scan learning strategy correlates of students' appraisal of instruction. *Perceptual and Motor Skills*, 53, 620.

Meredith GM (1985).
Transmitter-facilitator teaching style and focus-scan learning style in higher education. *Perceptual and Motor Skills*, 61, 545–546.

Merrill MD (2000).
Instructional strategies and learning styles: which takes precedence? In R Reiser and J Dempsey (eds) *Trends and issues in instructional technology*. New York: Prentice Hall.

Messick S (1984).
The nature of cognitive styles: problems and promise in educational practice. *Educational Psychologist*, 19(2), 59–74.

Meyer JHF and Eley MG (1999).
The development of affective subscales to reflect variation in students' experiences of studying mathematics in higher education. *Higher Education*, 37, 197–216.

Meyer JHF and Parsons P (1989).
Approaches to studying and course perceptions using the Lancaster Inventory: a comparative study. *Studies in Higher Education*, 14, 137–153.

Miller A (1991).
Personality types, learning styles and educational goals. *Educational Psychology*, 11(3 and 4), 217–238.

Miller JA, Dunn R, Beasley M, Ostrow S, Geisert G and Nelson B (2000/01).
Effects of traditional versus learning style presentations of course content in ultrasound and anatomy on the achievement and attitude of allied college health students. *National Forum of Applied Educational Research Journal*, 13(2), 50–62.

Millett A (1996).
Pedagogy – the last corner of the secret garden. Third Annual Education Lecture. London: King's College London.

Mintzberg H (1976).
Planning on the left side and managing on the right. *Harvard Business Review*, July–August, 49–58.

Mitchell DP (1994).
Learning style: a critical analysis of the concept and its assessment. In R Hoey (ed.) *Design for learning: aspects of educational technology*. London: Kogan Page

Morais A, Neves E, Davies B and Daniels H (2001).
Towards a sociology of pedagogy: the contribution of Basil Bernstein to research. New York: Peter Lang.

Moreno R and Mayer RE (1999).
Cognitive principles of multimedia learning: the role of modality and contiguity. *Journal of Educational Psychology*, 91(2), 358–368.

Moseley D, Baumfield V, Elliott J, Gregson M, Higgins S, Lin M, Miller J, Newton D and Robson S (2003).
Thinking skill frameworks for post-16 learners: an evaluation. London: Learning and Skills Research Centre.

Mosley MGL (2001).
Relationship between major contributors of style/learning inventories and Carl Jung's original theory of personality types. At www.cgjungpage.org/articles/learningstylemosley.html

Mumford A (1987).
Helping managers learn to learn: using learning styles and learning biography. *Journal of Management Development*, 6(5), 49–60.

Mumford A (2003).
Personal communication.

Murphy HJ, Kelleher WE, Doucette PA and Young JD (1998).
Test-retest reliability and construct validity of the Cognitive Style Index for business undergraduates. *Psychological Reports*, 82, 595–600.

Murrain PG (1983).
Administrative determinations concerning facilities utilisation and instructional grouping: an analysis of the relationships between selected thermal environments and preferences for temperature, an element of learning style, as they affect word recognition scores of secondary students. Doctoral dissertation, St John's University, New York.

Murray JB (1990).
Review of research on the Myers-Briggs Type Indicator. *Perceptual and Motor Skills*, 70, 1187–1202.

Murray-Harvey R (1994).
Learning styles and approaches to learning: distinguishing between concepts and instruments. *British Journal of Educational Psychology*, 64, 373–388.

Myers IB and McCaulley MH (1985).
Manual: a guide to the development and use of the Myers-Briggs Type Indicator. Palo Alto, CA: Consulting Psychologists Press.

Myers IB and McCaulley MH (1998).
Manual: a guide to the development and use of the Myers-Briggs Type Indicator. Palo Alto, CA: Consulting Psychologists Press.

Napolitano RA (1986).
An experimental investigation of the relationships among achievement, attitude scores, and traditionally, marginally and under-prepared college students enrolled in an introductory psychology course when they are matched and mismatched with their learning style preferences for the element of structure. Doctoral dissertation, St John's University, New York.

Nelson B, Dunn R, Griggs S, Primavera L, Fitzpatrick M, Bacilious ZF and Miller R (1993).
Effects of learning-style interventions on college students' retention and achievement. *Journal of College Student Development*, 34(5), 364–380.

Newstead SE (1992).
A study of two 'quick-and-easy' methods of assessing individual differences in student learning. *British Journal of Educational Psychology*, 62, 299–312.

Nganwa-Bagumah M and Mwamenda T (1991).
Effects on reading comprehension tests of matching and mismatching students' design preferences. *Perceptual and Motor Skills*, 72(3), 947–951.

Nordvik H (1996).
Relationships between Holland's vocational typology, Schein's career anchors and Myers-Briggs' types. *Journal of Occupational and Organizational Psychology*, 69(3), 263–276.

O'Brien TP (1990).
Construct validation of the Gregorc Style Delineator: an application of LISREL 7. *Educational and Psychological Measurement*, 50, 631–636.

O'Neil J (1990).
Findings of styles research: murky at best. *Educational Leadership*, 48(2), 7.

Oosterheert IE, Vermunt JD and Denissen E (2002).
Assessing orientations to learning to teach. *British Journal of Educational Psychology*, 72, 41–64.

Oswick C and Barber P (1998).
Personality type and performance in an introductory level accounting course: a research note. *Accounting Education*, 7(3), 249–254.

Paivio A (1971).
Styles and strategies of learning. *British Journal of Educational Psychology*, 41, 128–148.

Pask G (1976).
Styles and strategies of learning. *British Journal of Educational Psychology*, 46, 128–148.

Pederson NL and Lichtenstein P (1997).
Biometric analyses of human abilities. In C Cooper and V Varma (eds) *Processes in individual differences*. London: Routledge.

Pederson NL, Plomin R and McClearn GE (1994).
Is there a G beyond g? (Is there genetic influence on specific cognitive abilities independent of genetic influence on general cognitive ability?). *Intelligence*, 18, 133–143.

Penney CG and Godsell A (1999).
Unusual modality effects in less-skilled readers. *Journal of Experimental Psychology: Learning, Memory and Cognition*, 25(1), 284–289.

Perry WGJ (1970).
Forms of intellectual and ethical development in the college years: a scheme. New York: Reihard and Wilson.

Peterson ER, Deary IJ and Austin EJ (2003a).
The reliability of Riding's Cognitive Style Analysis test. *Personality and Individual Differences*, 33.

Peterson ER, Deary IJ and Austin EJ (2003b).
On the assessment of cognitive style: four red herrings. *Personality and Individual Differences*, 34, 899–904.

Pittenger DJ (1993).
The utility of the Myers-Briggs Type Indicator. *Review of Educational Research*, 63(4), 467–488.

Pizzo J (1981).
An investigation of the relationships between selected acoustic environments and sound, an element of learning style, as they affect sixth grade students' reading achievement and attitudes. St John's University, New York.

Porter AP (2003).
An examination of the reliability and construct validity of the Thinking Styles Inventory. In M Valcke and D Gombeir (eds) *Learning styles: reliability and validity*, 295–301. Proceedings of the 7th Annual European Learning Styles Information Network Conference, 26–28 June, Ghent. Ghent: University of Ghent.

Price GE (1996).
The Productivity Environment Preference Survey: PEPS manual. Lawrence, KS: Price Systems, Inc.

Price GE and Dunn R (1997).
The Learning Style Inventory: LSI manual. Lawrence, KS: Price Systems, Inc.

Price L and Richardson JTE (2003).
Meeting the challenge of diversity: a cautionary tale about learning styles. In C Rust (ed) *Improving student learning theory and practice 10 years on*. Oxford: Oxford Centre for Staff and Learning Development, Oxford Brookes University.

Pyryt MC, Sandals LH and Begorya J (1998).
Learning style preferences of gifted, average-ability, and special needs students. A multivariate perspective. *Journal of Research in Childhood Education*, 13(1), 71–77.

Quenck NL (2003).
Personal communication.

Ramsden P (1983).
Context and strategy: situational influences on learning. In N Entwistle and P Ramsden (eds) *Understanding student learning*. London: Croom Helm.

Ramsden P and Entwistle NJ (1981).
Effects of academic departments on students' approaches to studying. *British Journal of Educational Psychology*, 51, 368–383.

Rayner S and Riding R (1997).
Towards a categorisation of cognitive styles and learning styles. *Educational Psychology*, 17(1/2).

Redmond JA, Mullally AAP and Parkinson AB (2002).
Test-retest reliability of Riding's CSA. In M Valcke and D Gombeir (eds) *Learning styles: reliability and validity*. Proceedings of the 7th Annual European Learning Styles Information Network Conference, 26–28 June, Ghent. Ghent: University of Ghent.

Reese S (2002).
Understanding our differences. *Techniques*, January, 20–23.

Reynolds M (1997).
Learning styles: a critique.
Management Learning, 28(2), 115–133.

Richardson JTE (1990).
Reliability and replicability of the Approaches
to Studying Questionnaire. *Studies in Higher Education*,
15(2), 155–168.

Richardson JTE (1992).
A critical evaluation of the short form of the ASI.
Psychology Teaching Review, 1, 34–45.

Richardson JTE (1997).
Meaning orientation and reproducing orientation:
a typology of approaches to studying in higher
education? *Educational Psychology*, 17, 301–311.

Riding R (1991a).
Cognitive Styles Analysis – CSA administration.
Birmingham: Learning and Training Technology.

Riding R (1991b).
Cognitive Styles Analysis users' manual.
Birmingham: Learning and Training Technology.

Riding R (1994).
Personal style awareness and personal development.
Birmingham: Learning and Training Technology.

Riding R (1998a).
Cognitive Styles Analysis – CSA administration.
Birmingham: Learning and Training Technology.

Riding R (1998b).
Cognitive Styles Analysis – research applications.
Birmingham: Learning and Training Technology.

Riding R (2002).
School learning and cognitive style.
London: David Fulton.

Riding R (2003a).
On the assessment of cognitive style: a commentary on
Peterson, Deary and Austin. *Personality and Individual
Differences*, 34, 893–897.

Riding R (2003b).
Personal communication.

Riding R and Agrell T (1997).
The effect of cognitive style and cognitive
skill on school subject performance.
Educational Studies, 23(2), 311–323.

Riding R and Buckle C (1990).
Learning styles and training performance.
Sheffield: Department of Employment.

Riding R and Cheema I (1991).
Cognitive styles – an overview and integration.
Educational Psychology, 11, 193–216.

Riding R and Craig O (1999).
Cognitive style and types of problem behaviour in
boys in special schools. *British Journal of Educational
Psychology*, 69(3), 307–322.

Riding R and Douglas G (1993).
The effect of cognitive style and mode of presentation
on learning performance. *British Journal of Educational
Psychology*, 63, 297–307.

Riding R and Dyer V (1983).
The nature of learning styles and their relationship
to cognitive performance in children. *Educational
Psychology*, 3, 273–279.

Riding R, Glass A, Butler S and
Pleydell-Pearce CW (1997).
Cognitive style and individual differences
in EEG Alpha during information processing.
Educational Psychology, 17(1/2).

Riding RJ, Grimley M, Dahraei H and Banner G (2003).
Cognitive styles, working memory and learning
behaviour and attainment in school subjects.
British Journal of Educational Psychology, 73, 149–169.

Riding R and Rayner S (1998).
*Cognitive styles and learning strategies:
understanding style differences in learning behaviour*.
London: David Fulton Publishers Ltd.

Riding R and Taylor EM (1976).
Imagery performance and prose comprehension in
seven-year-old children. *Educational Studies*, 2, 21–27.

Riding R and Wigley S (1997).
The relationship between cognitive style and
personality in further education students.
Personality and Individual Differences, 23(3), 379–389.

Roberts MJ and Newton EJ (2001).
Understanding strategy selection.
International Journal of Computer Studies, 54, 137–154.

Roberts PH (2003).
Multisensory resources reveal the secrets of science.
In R Dunn and S Griggs (eds) *Synthesis of the Dunn
and Dunn learning styles model research: who,
what, when, where and so what – the Dunn and Dunn
learning styles model and its theoretical cornerstone*.
New York: St John's University.

Romero JE, Tepper BJ and Tetrault LA (1992).
Development and validation of new scales to measure
Kolb's (1985) learning style dimensions. *Educational
and Psychological Measurement*, 52, 171–180.

Ross JL, Drysdale MTB and Schulz RA (2001).
Cognitive learning styles and academic performance
in two postsecondary computer application courses.
Journal of Research on Computing in Education,
33(4), 400–412.

Rourke BP, Ahmad SA, Collins DW, Hayman-Abello BA,
Hayman-Abello SE and Warriner EM (2002).
Child clinical/pediatric neuropsychology: some recent
advances. *Annual Review of Psychology*, 53, 309–339.

Rowan K (1988).
Learning styles and teacher inservice education.
Doctoral dissertation, University of Tennessee.

Ruble TL and Stout DE (1992).
Changes in learning-style preferences: comments on
Geiger and Pinto. *Psychological Reports*, 70, 697–698.

Rushton JP, Fulker DW, Neale MC, Nias DK and Eysenck HJ (1986).
Altruism and aggression: the heritability of individual differences. *Journal of Personality and Social Psychology*, 50, 1192–1198.

Sadler-Smith E (1999a).
Intuition-analysis cognitive style and learning preferences of business and management students – a UK exploratory study. *Journal of Managerial Psychology*, 14(1), 26–38.

Sadler-Smith E (1999b).
Intuition-analysis style and approaches to studying. *Educational Studies*, 25(2), 159–173.

Sadler-Smith E (2001a).
Does the Learning Styles Questionnaire measure style or process? A reply to Swailes and Senior (1999). *International Journal of Selection and Assessment*, 9(3), 207–214.

Sadler-Smith E (2001b).
The relationship between learning style and cognitive style. *Personality and Individual Differences*, 30, 609–616.

Sadler-Smith E, Allinson CW and Hayes J (2000).
Learning preferences and cognitive style: some implications for continuing professional development. *Management Learning*, 31(2), 239–256.

Sadler-Smith E and Riding R (1999).
Cognitive style and instructional preferences. *Instructional Science*, 27(5), 355–371.

Sadler-Smith E, Spicer DP and Tsang F (2000).
Validity of the Cognitive Style Index: replication and extension. *British Journal of Management*, 11, 175–181.

Sadler-Smith E and Tsang F (1998).
A comparative study of approaches to studying in Hong Kong and the United Kingdom. *British Journal of Educational Psychology*, 68, 81–93.

Saggino A, Cooper CL and Kline P (2001).
A confirmatory factor analysis of the Myers-Briggs Type Indicator. *Personality and Individual Differences*, 30, 3–9

Salter DW, Evans NJ and Forney DS (1997).
Test-retest of the Myers-Briggs Type Indicator: an examination of dominant functioning. *Educational and Psychological Measurement*, 57(3), 590–597.

Saracho ON (1998a).
Teachers' perceptions of their matched students. *International Journal of Educational Research*, 29(3), 219–225.

Saracho ON (1998b).
Research directions for cognitive style and education. *International Journal of Educational Research*, 29(3), 287–290.

Saracho ON and Dayton CM (1980).
Relationship of teachers' cognitive styles to pupils' academic achievement gains. *Journal of Educational Psychology*, 72(4), 544–549.

Schatteman A, Carette E, Couder J and Eisendrath H (1997).
Understanding the effects of a process-oriented instruction in the first year of university by investigating learning style characteristics. *Educational Psychology*, 17(1/2).

Schuller I (1988).
Category width cognitive style and decision making processes. *Studia Psychologica*, 40(4), 250–254.

Sears SJ, Kennedy JJ and Kaye GL (1997).
Myers-Briggs personality profiles of prospective educators. *The Journal of Educational Research*, 90 (March/April), 195–202.

Seidel L and England E (1999).
Gregorc's cognitive styles: college students' preferences for teaching methods and testing techniques. *Perceptual and Motor Skills*, 88(3), 859–875.

Sein MK and Robey D (1991).
Learning style and the efficacy of computer training methods. *Perceptual and Motor Skills*, 72, 243–248.

Sharp JE (1997).
Applying Kolb learning style theory in the communication classroom. *The Bulletin of the Association for Business Communication*, 60(2), 129–135.

Shaughnessy MF (1998).
An interview with Rita Dunn about learning styles. *The Clearing House*, 71(3), 141–145.

Shaver S (1985).
Effects of matching and mismatching selected elementary students with their learning style preference for light as reflected by reading achievement scores. Doctoral dissertation, Northwestern State University.

Shea TC (1983).
An investigation of the relationship among preferences for the learning style element of design, selected instructional environments and reading achievement of ninth grade students to improve administrative determinations concerning effective educational facilities. Doctoral dissertation, St John's Unversity, New York.

Shwery CS (1994).
Review of the Learning Styles Inventory [Price Systems, Inc.]. In JC Impara and BS Blake (eds), *The thirteenth mental measurements yearbook*. Lincoln, NE: Buros Institute of Mental Measurements.

Silver H, Strong R and Perini M (1997).
Integrating learning styles and multiple intelligences. *Educational Leadership*, 55(1), 22–28.

Simon B (1999).
Why no pedagogy in England? In J Leach and B Moon (eds) *Learners and pedagogy*, 34–45. London: Paul Chapman/Open University.

Sims RR (1986).
The reliability and classification stability of the
Learning Style Inventory. *Educational and Psychological
Measurement*, 46(3), 753–760.

Sims RR, Veres JG and Shake LG (1989).
An exploratory examination of the convergence
between the Learning Styles Questionnaire
and the Learning Style Inventory II. *Educational and
Psychological Measurement*, 49, 227–233.

Sims RR, Veres JG III, Watson P and Buckner KE (1986).
The reliability and classification stability of the
Learning Style Inventory. *Educational and Psychological
Measurement*, 46, 753–760.

Sinatra R, Hirshoren A and Primavera LH (1987).
Learning style, behavior ratings, and achievement
interactions for adjudicated adolescents.
Educational and Psychological Research, 7(1), 21–32.

Sinatra R, Primavera L and Waked WJ (1986).
Learning style and intelligence of reading disabled
students. *Perceptual and Motor Skills*, 63, 1243–1250.

Slaats A, Lodewijks H and Van der Sanden J (1999).
Learning styles in secondary vocational education:
disciplinary differences. *Learning and Instruction*,
9, 475–492.

Smith KCP and Apter MJ (1975).
A theory of psychological reversals.
Chippenham: Picton.

Smith W, Sekar S and Townsend K (2002).
*The impact of surface and reflective teaching and
learning on student academic success*. In M Valcke and
D Gombeir (eds) *Learning styles: reliability and validity*,
407–418. Proceedings of the 7th Annual European
Learning Styles Information Network Conference,
26–28 June, Ghent. Ghent: University of Ghent.

Spence JW and Tsai RJ (1997).
On human cognition and the design of information
systems. *Information and Management*, 32, 65–73.

Sperry RW (1964).
The great cerebral commissure.
Scientific American, 210(1), 42–52.

Spicer DP (2002).
The impact of approaches to learning and cognition
on academic performance. In M Valcke and D Gombeir
(eds) *Learning styles: reliability and validity*. Proceedings
of the 7th Annual European Learning Styles Information
Network Conference, 26–28 June, Ghent. Ghent:
University of Ghent.

Spirrison CL and Gordy CC (1994).
Nonintellective intelligence and personality: variance
shared by the Constructive Thinking Inventory and
the Myers-Briggs Type Indicator. *Journal of Personality
Assessment*, 62(2), 352–363.

Spoon JC and Schell JW (1998).
Aligning student learning styles with instructor
teaching styles. *Journal of Industrial Teacher Education*,
35(2), 41–56.

Springer SP and Deutsch G (1989).
Left brain, right brain. New York: Freeman.

Stellwagen JB (2001).
A challenge to the learning style advocates.
The Clearing House, 74(5), 265–268.

Sternberg RJ (1999).
Thinking styles.
Cambridge: Cambridge University Press.

Sternberg RJ (2001).
Epilogue: another mysterious affair at styles.
In RJ Sternberg and L-F Zhang (eds) *Perspectives
on thinking, learning and cognitive styles*.
Mahwah, New Jersey: Lawrence Erlbaum.

Sternberg RJ and Grigorenko EL (2001).
A capsule history of theory and research on styles.
In RJ Sternberg and L-F Zhang (eds) *Perspectives
on thinking, learning and cognitive styles*.
Mahwah, New Jersey: Lawrence Erlbaum.

Sternberg RJ and Wagner RK (1991).
MSG Thinking Styles Inventory. Unpublished manual.

Sternberg RJ and Zhang L-F (eds) (2001).
Perspectives on thinking, learning and cognitive styles.
Mahwah, New Jersey: Lawrence Erlbaum.

Stevenson J (1997).
The genetic basis of personality. In C Cooper and
V Varma (eds) *Processes in individual differences*.
London: Routledge.

Stiles R (1985).
*Learning style preferences for design and their
relationship to standardised test results*.
Doctoral dissertation, University of Tennessee.

Stilwell NA, Wallick MM, Thal SE and
Burleson JA (1998).
Myers-Briggs type and medical specialty choice:
a new look at an old question. *Teaching and Learning
in Medicine*, 12(1), 14–20.

Stumpf SA and Freedman RD (1981).
The Learning Style Inventory: still less than meets the
eye. *Academy of Management Review*, 6(2), 297–299.

Sugarman L (1985).
Kolb's model of experiential learning: touchstone
for trainers, students, counsellors and clients.
Journal of Counselling and Development,
64 (December), 264–268.

Swailes S and Senior B (1999).
The dimensionality of Honey and Mumford's Learning
Styles Questionnaire. *International Journal of Selection
and Assessment*, 7(1), 1–11.

Swailes S and Senior B (2001).
The Learning Styles Questionnaire: closing comments?
International Journal of Selection and Assessment,
9(3), 215–217.

Tarver SG and Dawson MM (1978).
Modality preference and the teaching of reading:
a review. *Journal of Learning Disabilities*, 11(1), 17–29.

Taylor S (2002).
*Widening adult participation: ways to extend
good practice – a research report for the Learning
and Skills Council*. London: Learning and Skills
Development Agency.

Tendy SM and Geiser WF (1998/9).
The search for style: it all depends on where you look.
National Forum of Teacher Education Journal,
9(1), 3–15.

Tennant M (1998).
Psychology and adult learning. London: Routledge.

Tepper BJ, Tetrault LA, Braun CK and Romero JE (1993).
Discriminant and convergent validity of the
Problem Solving Style Questionnaire. *Educational
and Psychological Measurement*, 53, 437–444.

Thaddeus T (1998).
Review of the Productivity Environmental Preferences
Survey. In JC Impara and BS Blake (eds), T*he thirteenth
mental measurements yearbook*. Lincoln, NE: Buros
Institute of Mental Measurements.

Thies AP (2003).
Implications of neuroscience and neuropsychology for
the Dunn and Dunn learning-style theory. In R Dunn and
S Griggs (eds) *Synthesis of the Dunn and Dunn learning
styles model research: who, what, when, where and so
what – the Dunn and Dunn learning styles model and its
theoretical cornerstone*. New York: St John's University.

Thomas P and Bain JD (1982).
Consistency in learning strategies.
Higher Education, 11, 249–259.

Thompson J and Bing-You RG (1998).
Physicians' reactions to learning style and personality
type inventories. *Medical Teacher*, 20(1), 10–14.

Thorne A and Gough H (1999).
Portraits of type: an MBTI research compendium.
2nd ed. Gainesville, FLA: Center for Applications
of Psychological Type, Inc.

Tinajero C and Paramo MF (1997).
Field dependence-independence and academic
achievement: a re-examination of their relationship.
The British Journal of Educational Psychology,
67(2), 199–213.

Tinajero C and Paramo MF (1998a).
Field dependence-independence cognitive style
and academic achievement: a review of research and
theory. *European Journal of Psychology of Education*,
13(2), 227–251.

Tinajero C and Paramo MF (1998b).
Field dependence-independence and strategic learning.
International Journal of Educational Research,
29(3), 251–262.

Tinajero C, Paramo MF, Cadaveira F and
Rodriguez-Holguin S (1993).
Field dependence-independence and brain organization:
the confluence of two different ways of describing
general forms of cognitive functioning? A theoretical
review. *Perceptual and Motor Skills*, 77, 787–802.

Torrance EP, Reynolds CR, Riegel T and Ball OE (1977).
'Your style of learning and thinking' forms A and B:
preliminary norms, abbreviated technical notes, scoring
keys and selected references. *Gifted Child Quarterly*,
21, 563–573.

Trigwell K and Prosser M (1991).
Relating learning approaches, perceptions
of context and learning outcomes.
Higher Education, 22, 251–266.

Van B (1992).
The MBTI: implications for retention.
Journal of Developmental Education, 16(1), 20–25.

Van Zwanenberg N, Wilkinson LJ and Anderson A
(2000).
Felder and Silverman's Index of Learning Styles and
Honey and Mumford's Learning Styles Questionnaire:
how do they compare and do they predict academic
performance? *Educational Psychology*, 20(3), 365–380.

Veres JG, Sims RR and Locklear TS (1991).
Improving the reliability of Kolb's
Revised Learning Style Inventory.
Educational and Psychological Measurement, 51.

Veres JG, Sims RR and Shake LG (1987).
The reliability and classification stability of the
Learning Style Inventory in corporate settings.
Educational and Psychological Measurement, 47.

Vermetten YJ, Lodewijks HG and Vermunt JD (1999).
Consistency and variability of learning strategies in
different university courses. *Higher Education*, 37, 1–21.

Vermunt JD (1992).
*Learning styles and directed learning processes in
higher education: towards a process-oriented instruction
in independent thinking*. Lisse: Swets and Zeitlinger.

Vermunt JD (1994).
Inventory of Learning Styles (ILS) in higher education.
Tilburg: University of TIburg.

Vermunt JD (1995).
Process-oriented instruction in learning and
thinking strategy. *European Journal of the
Psychology of Education*, 10(4), 325–349.

Vermunt JD (1996).
Metacognitive, cognitive and affective aspects
of learning styles and strategies: a phenomenographic
analysis. *Higher Education*, 31, 25–50.

Vermunt JD (1998).
The regulation of constructive learning processes.
British Journal of Educational Psychology, 68, 149–171.

Vermunt JD (2003).
Personal communication.

Vermunt JD and Verloop N (1999).
Congruence and friction between learning and
teaching. *Learning and Instruction*, 9, 257–280.

Ward J and Edwards J (2000).
Learning journeys: learners' voices.
London: Learning and Skills Development Agency.

Waugh RF (1999).
Approaches to studying for students in higher
education: a Rasch measurement model analysis.
British Journal of Educational Psychology, 69, 63–79.

Westman AS (1992).
Review of the Learning Styles Inventory
[Price Systems, Inc.]. In JJ Kramer and JC Conoley (eds)
The eleventh mental measurements yearbook.
Lincoln, NE: Buros Institute of Mental Measurements.

Westman AS, Alliston GR and Thierault EA (1997).
Lack of correlations of sense-modality oriented indices
of learning styles with each other and with classroom
tasks. *Perceptual and Motor Skills*, 84, 731–737.

Westman AS and Stuve M (2001).
Three exploratory studies of relations between young
adults' preference for activity involving a specific sense
modality and sensory attributes of early memories.
Perceptual and Motor Skills, 92, 435–446.

White R (1981).
*An investigation of the relationship between selected
instructional methods and selected elements
of emotional learning style upon student achievement
in seventh grade social studies.* Doctoral dissertation,
St John's University, New York.

Wierstra RFA and Beerends EPM (1996).
Leeromgeningspercepties en leerstrategieën van
eerstejaars studenten sociale wetenschappen.
[Perceptions of the learning environment and learning
strategies of first year students of social sciences].
Tijdschrift voor Onderwijsresearch, 21, 306–322.

Wierstra RFA and de Jong JA (2002).
A scaling theoretical evaluation of Kolb's Learning
Style Inventory-2. In M Valcke and D Gombeir (eds)
Learning styles: reliability and validity, 431–440.
Proceedings of the 7th Annual European Learning
Styles Information Network Conference, 26–28 June,
Ghent. Ghent: University of Ghent.

Wierstra RF, Kanselaar G, Van der Linden JL,
Lodewijks HG and Vermunt JD (2002).
The impact of the university context on European
students' learning approaches and learning
environment preferences. *Higher Education*,
45(4), 503–523.

Wilson DK (1986).
An investigation of the properties of Kolb's Learning
Style Inventory. *Leadership and Organisation
Development Journal*, 7(3), 3–15.

Witkin HA (1962).
Psychological differentiation: studies of development.
New York: Wiley.

Witkin HA and Goodenough DR (1981).
Cognitive styles: essence and origins.
New York: International Universities Press.

Witkin HA, Moore CA, Oltman PK, Goodenough DR,
Friedman F, Owen D and Raskin E (1977).
Role of field dependent and field independent cognitive
styles in academic evolution: a longitudinal study.
Journal of Educational Psychology, 69, 197–211.

Wittling W (1996).
Brain asymmetry in the control of autonomic
physiological activity. In RJ Davidson and K Hugdahl
(eds) *Brain asymmetry*. Cambridge, MA: MIT Press.

Woolhouse LS and Bayne R (2000).
Personality and the use of intuition: individual
differences in strategy and performance on an implicit
learning task. *European Journal of Personality*,
14, 157–169.

Zanting A, Verloop N and Vermunt JD (2001).
Student teachers' beliefs about mentoring and learning
to teach during teaching practice. *British Journal of
Educational Psychology*, 71, 57–80.

Zenhausern R (1979).
Differential hemispheric activation instrument.
New York: St John's University.

Zenhausern R, Dunn R, Cavanaugh DP and Eberle BM
(1981).
Do left and right 'brained' students learn differently?
The Roeper Review, 36–39.

Zenhausern R and Gebhardt M (1979).
Hemispheric dominance in recall and recognition.
Bulletin of the Psychonomic Society, 14, 71–73.

Zenhausern R and Nickel L (1979).
Hemispheric dominance and maze learning.
Bulletin of the Psychonomic Society, 14, 435–436.

Zhang L-F and Sternberg RJ (2001).
Thinking styles across cultures: their relationships with
student learning. In RJ Sternberg and L-F Zhang (eds)
Perspectives on thinking, learning and cognitive styles,
197–226. Mahwah, New Jersey: Lawrence Erlbaum.

Zukas M and Malcolm J (2002).
Pedagogies for lifelong learning: building bridges
or building walls? In R Harrison, F Reeve, A Hanson
and J Clarke (eds) *Supporting lifelong learning*.
London: Routledge/Open University.

List of learning-styles instruments and theories
(models chosen for study in bold type)

Author(s)	Measure	Key terms/descriptors	Date introduced
Allinson and Hayes	**Cognitive Style Index (CSI)**	*intuitive/analytic*	**1996**
Apter	**Motivational Style Profile (MSP)**	*telic/paratelic – negativism/conformity – autic mastery/autic sympathy – alloic mastery/alloic sympathy – arousal avoidance/arousal seeking – optimism/pessimism – arousability – effortfulness*	**1998**
Bartlett		*sensory modality preferences*	1932
Betts	Betts Inventory	*imagery*	1909
Biggs	Study Process Questionnaire	*surface/deep achieving*	1987
Broverman		*automatisation – restructuring*	1960
Cacioppo and Petty	Need for Cognition Scale	*related to field dependence/independence – articulative/global*	1982
Canfield	Canfield Learning Style Inventory (CLSI)	*conditions – content – modes – expectancy*	1980
Christensen	Lifescripts	*(social context but relevant to cognition) analyser – controller – supporter – promoter*	1980
Conti and Kolody	Self-Knowledge Inventory of Lifelong Learning Skills (SKILLS)	*metacognition – metamotivation – memory – critical thinking – resource management*	1990
Cooper	Learning Styles ID	*visual/verbal – holist/analyst, environmental preference*	1997
Curry	'Onion' model	*instructional preference – information processing style – cognitive personal style*	1983
Das		*simultaneous/successive processing and planning*	1988
Dunn and Dunn	■ **Learning Style Questionnaire (LSQ)** ■ **Learning Styles Inventory (LSI)** ■ **Productivity Environmental Preference Survey (PEPS)** ■ **Building Excellence Survey (BES)**	*environmental – emotional – sociological – physiological processing*	**1979** **1975** **1979** **2003**
Entwistle	■ **Approaches to Study Inventory (ASI)** ■ **Revised Approaches to Study Inventory (RASI)** ■ **Approaches and Study Skills Inventory for Students (ASSIST)**	■ *meaning orientation – reproducing orientation – achieving orientation – non-academic orientation – self-confidence* ■ *deep approach – surface approach – strategic approach – lack of direction – academic self-confidence – metacognitive awareness*	**1979** **1995** **2000**
Epstein and Meier	Constructive Thinking Inventory (CTI)	*emotional coping – behavioural coping – personal superstitious thinking – categorical thinking – esoteric thinking – naïve optimism – global constructive thinking*	1989
Felder and Silverman	Index of Learning Styles (ILS)	*active/reflective – sensing/intuitive – visual/verbal – sequential/global*	1996
Friedman and Stritter	Instructional Preference Questionnaire		1976
Galbraith and James		*perceptual ability*	1984
Gardner *et al.*		*tolerant/intolerant*	1959
Gordon	Scale of Imagery Control	*imagery*	1949

Author(s)	Measure	Key terms/descriptors	Date introduced
Grasha-Riechmann	Student Learning Style Scales (SLSS)	*competitive/collaborative – independent/dependent – participant/avoidant*	1974
Gregorc	**Gregorc Mind Styles Delineator (MSD)**	***concrete sequential/abstract random – abstract sequential/concrete random***	**1977**
Groner	Cognitive Style Scale	*heuristic/algorithmic*	1990
Guilford		*convergent/divergent thinking*	1950
Harrison-Branson	Revised Inquiry Mode Questionnaire	*synthesist – idealist – pragmatist – analyst – realist*	1998
Herrmann	**Brain Dominance Instrument (HBDI)**	***theorist/humanitarian – organiser/innovator***	**1995**
Hermanussen, Wierstra, de Jong and Thijssen	Questionnaire Practice-oriented Learning (QPL)	*immersion – reflection – conceptualisation – experimentation – regulation*	2000
Hill	Cognitive Style Profile	*symbol processing – modalities of inference – cultural determinants*	1976
Holzman and Klein	Schematising Test	*leveller/sharpener*	1954
Honey and Mumford	**Learning Styles Questionnaire (LSQ)**	***activist/reflector – theorist/pragmatist***	**1982**
Hudson	(following Guilford)	*diverging/converging*	1966
Hunt	Paragraph Completion Method	*need for structure: conforming – dependent*	1978
Jackson	**Learning Styles Profiler (LSP)**	***initiator – analyst – reasoner – implementer***	**2002**
Kagan	Matching Familiar Figures Test	*impulsivity/reflexivity – focus/scan*	1965 1967
Kaufmann	The A-E Inventory	*assimilator/explorer*	1989
Keefe and Monke (NASSP)	NASSP Learning Style Profile (explicit attempt at meta-taxonomy)	*physiological – environmental – cognitive – affective domains plus information processing*	1986
Kirby *et al.*	Multidimensional verbal-visual LSQ	*verbal/visual*	1988
Kirton	Kirton Adaption-Innovation inventory (KAI)	*adaptor/innovator*	1989
Kogan	Sorting styles into types	*3 types of style:* ■ *maximal performance (ability) measures* ■ *value directionality (advantageous) styles* ■ *value-differentiated measures*	1973
Kolb	**Learning Style Inventory (LSI) Revised Learning Style Inventory (R-LSI) LSI Version 3**	***accommodating – diverging – converging – assimilating styles***	**1976 1985 1999**
Letteri	Cognitive Style Delineators	*analytic/global*	1980
Marks	Marks Vividness of Visual Imagery Questionnaire	*imagery*	1973
Marton and Säljö		*deep/surface processing*	1976

Author(s)	Measure	Key terms/descriptors	Date introduced
McCarthy	4MAT	*innovative – analytic – common-sense – dynamic*	1987
McKenney and Keen	Model of cognitive style	*perceptive/receptive – systematic/intuitive*	1974
Meredith		*focus/scan*	1981
Messick		*analytic/non-analytic conceptualising*	1976
Miller	Personality typology: cognitive, affective, conative	*analyst/holist – emotional stability/instability – objective-subjective*	1991
Myers-Briggs	**Myers-Briggs Type Indicator (MBTI)**	***perceiving/judging – sensing/intuition – thinking/feeling – extraversion/introversion***	**1962**
Paivio	Individual Difference Questionnaire (IDQ)	*imagery (dual coding)*	1971
Pask		*serialist/holist*	1976
Pettigrew	Scale of cognitive style	*category width (broad/narrow)*	1958
Pintrich, Smith, Garcia and McCeachie	Motivated Strategies for Learning Questionnaire	*goal orientation (intrinsic/extrinsic) – expectancy – anxiety – cognitive strategies (rehearsal, selection, organisation, elaboration, metacognition, surface processing, critical thinking, original thinking) – resource management*	1991
Reinert	Edmonds Learning Style Identification Exercise (ELSIE)	*types of perception: visual – verbal – aural – emotional*	1976
Renzulli-Smith	Learning Style Inventory	*teaching styles and learning contexts*	1978
Rezler-Rezmovic	Learning Preference Inventory	*abstract/concrete – individual/interpersonal – teacher structure/student structure*	1981
Richardson	Verbaliser Visualiser Questionnaire (after Paivio)	*verbaliser/visualiser*	1977
Riding	**Cognitive Styles Analysis (CSA)**	***holist/analytic – verbaliser/imager***	**1991**
Schmeck *et al.*	Inventory of Learning Processes	*deep processing – shallow processing – elaborative processing – serial processing – holistic processing*	1977
Sheehan	Shortened Betts Inventory	*imagery*	1967
Sternberg	**Thinking Styles**	***functions – forms – levels – scopes – meanings***	**1998**
Tamir-Cohen	Cognitive Preference Inventory	*modes – recall principles – questioning applications*	1980
Torrance	Style of Learning and Thinking	*creative thinking*	1990
Vermunt	**Inventory of Learning Styles (ILS)**	***meaning-directed – application-directed – reproduction-directed – undirected***	**1996**
Walters	Psychological Inventory of Criminal Thinking Styles	*confusion – defensiveness – mollification – cut-off – entitlement – power orientation – sentimentality – superoptimism – cognitive indolence – discontinuity*	1995

Author(s	Measure	Key terms/descriptors	Date introduced
Weinstein, Zimmerman and Palmer	Learning and Study Strategies Inventory	*cognitive processing – motivation – metacognitive regulation*	1988
Whetton and Cameron	Cognitive Style Questionnaire (CSQ) [based on McKenney and Keen]	*gathering: perceptive/receptive evaluating: systematic/intuitive responding: active/reflective*	1984
Wierstra			
Witkin	Group Embedded Figures Test (GEFT)	*field dependence/independence*	1962
Zimmerman and Martinez-Pons	Self-Regulated Learning Interview Schedule (SRLIS)	*14 strategies*	1986

List of search terms used in the literature review

Key terms

Learning style/s
Cognitive style/s
Conative style/s
Thinking style/s
Learning preference/s, strategy/ies, orientation/s

Key terms were linked with the following for
refined searches:

reliability
validity
attainment
impact
scores
instructional design
match
attributions
personality
gender
social class/socio-economic status
culture
decision making

adult applications
lifelong learning
learning cycle
field independence
brain/hemispheric dominance.

In addition, searches were made for references
to key instruments, as defined by this report.

Appendix 3

Glossary of terms

a priori
based on hypothesis or theory rather than experiment

accommodation
adapting actions to respond to new stimuli
(in Piaget's theory)

affective
characterised by emotion

alloic
other-oriented (in Apter's reversal theory)

analysis of variance
a statistical method for testing for significant
differences between groups of data, which may be
'explained' by one or more variables

analytic
focusing on the parts of a whole or on underlying
basic principles

alpha (coefficient)
a measure of internal consistency, to be interpreted
as an average correlation coefficient, showing how well
a set of test items 'hangs together'

assimilation
absorbing new information and fitting it into existing
knowledge (in Piaget's theory)

autic
self-oriented (in Apter's reversal theory)

catalytic validity
the extent to which those involved in research become
motivated to understand and transform the situations
in which they operate

cerebral dominance
an outdated theory, claiming that one half of the
brain controls or takes precedence over the other

cognitive
concerned with the psychological processes
of perception, memory, thinking and learning

conative/conation
refers to effort, endeavour and the will to achieve

concurrent validity
support for the meaning of a construct or the value
of a test, based on correlational evidence from another
set of measurements taken at the same time

construct
abstract or general idea inferred from specific instances

construct validity
how far test scores can be interpreted as measuring
only what they are intended to measure

convergent thinking
thinking directed at finding a single correct solution
to a well-structured problem

correlation
a measure indicating how far two variables are
totally unconnected (zero correlation), or are negatively
(e.g.–0.5) or positively related, as determined by
underlying or outside influences

curvilinear
in a curved line, expressing a non-linear relationship
between variables

deductive
reasoning from a general statement or definition
to a particular instance

defence mechanism
self-protective reaction to avoid distress or anxiety
(in Freudian theory)

diagnosis
identifying the nature or causation of a problem

dialectic
involving a contradiction of ideas which acts as
the determining factor in their interaction

dichotomous
dividing into two sharply distinguished parts
or classifications

disposition
habit of mind, mood or attitude

discriminant analysis
a statistical method for assigning new cases to groups
on the basis of characteristics shared by the members
of existing groups

divergent thinking
exploratory thinking, seeking different possible ways
of coping with ill-structured problems

dyad
pair

ecological validity
the quality of being well grounded in the reality
of a particular context

effect size
a measure of difference or gain in average scores,
whereby effect sizes of less than 0.2 are usually
considered trivial; between 0.2 to 0.5 small; between
0.5 and 0.8 moderate; and when 0.8 or more, large

electroencephalographic (EEG)
using a technique whereby electric currents generated
by the brain are recorded through sets of electrodes
glued to the scalp.

epistemology
the philosophical study of theories of knowledge

external validity
a form of concurrent validity, in which a particular set of test scores is correlated with scores from another instrument which is supposed to measure the same construct

extraversion
the inclination to be involved with social and practical realities rather than with thoughts and feelings

extrinsic motivation
the desire to do something in order to obtain an external reward

face validity
support for an assessment tool based on common-sense judgement that the test items appear to measure what they are claimed to measure

factor
an underlying dimension or influence

factor analysis
a statistical technique which identifies underlying dimensions in a set of measures by finding groups of items which vary between individuals in similar ways

factorial validity
a form of construct validity in which the proposed constructs emerge as recognisable factors when datasets of item responses are factor analysed

field dependence
responding to structures in a holistic fashion

field independence
being able to see parts of a structure distinctly and objectively

formative assessment
evaluation carried out in the course of an activity in such a way that the information obtained is used to improve learning and/or instruction

g (general intelligence)
an general cognitive ability factor which, in addition to specific abilities and skills, contributes to performance on a wide range of tasks

global
not interested in detail: holistic

haptic
perceiving through physical contact

heritability
the degree to which something is inherited, expressed as a percentage

heuristic
rule-of-thumb strategy intended to increase the chances of solving a problem

holistic
perceiving a whole object or focusing on the organic nature of a system

homeostatically
so as to maintain a state of equilibrium

inductive
reasoning from particular facts to a general conclusion

internal consistency (reliability)
the degree to which the items in a test measure the same thing, measured by the average correlation between each item and the other items

intrinsic motivation
the desire to do something for the sake of the experience alone

introversion
the inclination to shrink from social contact and to be preoccupied with internal thoughts and feelings

inventory
detailed checklist

ipsative scoring
scoring an instrument with forced-choice items, resulting in scores which are not comparable across individuals, artificially created negative correlations and the invalidation of factor analysis

item analysis
a process for identifying good items in a scale, usually those which have at least a moderate positive correlation with the scale as a whole

kinaesthetic
perceiving through an awareness of body movements

levelling
tending to rapidly assimilate and oversimplify one's perceptions (in Holzman and Klein's theory)

Likert scale
a scale in which the user can express a degree of agreement and/or disagreement

limbic system
a group of interconnected mid-brain structures found in all mammals

loading
in factor analysis, a correlation coefficient between an item and a factor

meta-analysis
the process of synthesising a range of experimental results into a single estimate of effect size

metacognition
awareness and conscious use of the psychological processes involved in perception, memory, thinking and learning

metaphysical
dealing with highly abstract ideas about being and
knowing which are not derived from the material world

neuroticism
state of, or tendency towards, nervous disorder

orthogonal
at right angles; meaning, in factor analysis,
independent or uncorrelated

parameter
a factor that defines a system and determines
(or limits) its performance

paratelic
activity-oriented and intrinsically motivated
(in Apter's reversal theory)

Pearson r
a measure of correlation, indicating the extent
to which two measures co-vary (with 1.00 indicating
a perfect correlation)

pedagogy
theoretical and procedural knowledge about teaching

percentile
a point on a scale below which a given percentage
of a population will score

perception
interpreting and understanding information received
through the senses

phenomenology
the study of human experience, based on
the assumption that there is no reality other
than human consciousness

predictive validity
the extent to which a set of scores predicts an expected
outcome or criterion

prosocial
acting in support of others or to meet their expectations
of good behaviour

psychometric
concerned with psychological measurement

psychoticism
a tendency towards a state of mind in which contact
with reality is lost or is highly distorted

quadrature
construction of a square with the same area as that
of another figure

reliability
the coherence (internal consistency) of a set
of test items, or the stability (test–retest) of a set
of test scores over time

self-regulation
the process of setting goals for oneself and then
monitoring and evaluating progress

serialist
step-by-step: sequential (in Pask's theory)

sharpening
tending to separate new perceptions and respond
accurately to complexity (in Holzman and Klein's theory)

split-brain research
studies of psychological function in patients who have
had the largest bundle of fibres linking the two halves
of the brain severed, in order to control or limit the
effects of epileptic seizures

summative assessment
evaluation of performance carried out at the end
of a piece of work

tactile
perceiving through the sense of touch

taxonomy
a principled classification of the elements of a domain

telic
goal-oriented and externally motivated
(in Apter's reversal theory)

test–retest reliability
the stability of test scores as indicated by retesting the
same group and calculating a correlation coefficient
using the two sets of scores

trait
a stable personal quality, inherited or acquired

validity
the quality of being well grounded in reality

variance
variability of scores in relation to their average (mean)
value in relation

How to contact the LSRC

The LSRC welcomes continuing
interaction with researchers and
research users. Please contact us with
your questions, ideas and information.

Feedback should be sent to:

Sally Faraday
Research Manager
Learning and Skills Development Agency
Regent Arcade House
19–25 Argyll Street
London W1F 7LS

Tel 020 7297 9098
Fax 020 7297 9190
sfaraday@LSDA.org.uk